THOMPSON'S HIGHWAY

OTHER BOOKS BY ALAN TWIGG

Understanding Belize: A Historical Guide
(Harbour, 2006)

Aboriginality: The Literary Origins of British Columbia, Vol. 2
(Ronsdale Press, 2005)

101 Top Historical Sites of Cuba
(Beach Holme, 2004)

First Invaders: The Literary Origins of British Columbia, Vol. 1
(Ronsdale Press, 2004)

Intensive Care: A Memoir
(Anvil Press, 2002)

Cuba: A Concise History for Travelers
(Bluefield Books, 2000; Penguin Books, 2002; Harbour, 2005)

Twigg's Directory of 1001 BC Writers
(Crown Publications, 1992)

Strong Voices: Conversations with 50 Canadian Writers
(Harbour, 1988)

Vander Zalm, From Immigrant to Premier
(Harbour, 1986)

Vancouver and Its Writers
(Harbour, 1986)

Hubert Evans: The First Ninety-Three Years
(Harbour, 1985)

For Openers: Conversations with 24 Canadian Writers
(Harbour, 1981)

THOMPSON'S HIGHWAY

British Columbia's Fur Trade, 1800–1850
The Literary Origins of British Columbia

ALAN TWIGG

RONSDALE

RONSDALE PRESS
3350 West 21st Avenue
Vancouver, B.C., Canada V6S 1G7
www.ronsdalepress.com

Typesetting: Get To The Point Graphics, in New Baskerville 11 pt on 14.1
Cover Design: David Lester & Alan Twigg
Paper: Ancient Forest Friendly Rolland "Enviro" – 100% post-consumer
        waste, totally chlorine-free and acid-free

Ronsdale Press wishes to thank the following for their support of its publishing
program: the Canada Council for the Arts, the Government of Canada through the
Book Publishing Industry Development Program (BPIDP), and the Province of British
Columbia through the Book Publishing Tax Credit program and the British Columbia
Arts Council.

Library and Archives Canada Cataloguing in Publication

Twigg, Alan, 1952-
Thompson's highway : British Columbia's fur trade, 1800-1850 : the literary
origins of British Columbia / Alan Twigg.

Includes bibliographical references.

ISBN-13: 978-1-55380-039-2
ISBN-10: 1-55380-039-7

1. Fur trade–British Columbia–History–19th century–Sources. 2. British
Columbia–History–Sources. I. Title. II. Title: Literary origins of British Columbia.

FC3821.3.T84 2006   971.1'01   C2006-903220-3

At Ronsdale Press we are committed to protecting the environment. To this end we
are working with Markets Initiative (www.oldgrowthfree.com) and printers to phase
out our use of paper produced from ancient forests. This book is one step towards
that goal.

Printed in Canada by AGMV Marquis

About the cover: for information on the images of Alexander Mackenzie, Narcissa
Whitman and Chief Sepayss, see pages 39, 195 and 91 respectively. For information on
the Hudson's Bay Company emblem, see page 9.

CONTENTS

PREFACE

The title of this third volume devoted to those who have written about British Columbia refers to David Thompson because he discovered what Alexander Mackenzie and Simon Fraser had failed to find—the main "highway" for commerce that linked both sides of the continent—and because Thompson was the most accomplished writer among his peers.

Thompson also provided reliable maps for nearly half of the North American continent, he erected the first trading post on the Columbia River system in 1807, and he persevered in wintry conditions to prove the Columbia could serve as a practical route from the Rocky Mountains to the Pacific Ocean in 1811.

"Thus he inaugurated the trade route over the mountains to be used for the next half-century," wrote Victor Hopwood, "first by the North West Company and then by the Hudson's Bay Company. The Athabasca Pass route to the Pacific was as near as men ever came before the twentieth century to finding the historical will-of-the-wisp, a practical Northwest Passage."

"He was an agent of revolutionary change in the region," concluded Jack Nisbet in his 1994 book *Sources of the River*, "its history turns on the moment of his arrival."

With the exception of Narcissa Whitman, all entries in *Thompson's Highway* concern men who set foot in British Columbia. Many relied on Thompson's pathfinding through the Rockies to reach the Pacific.

Information on the literary men chiefly associated with Astoria near the mouth of the Columbia River (Donald Mackenzie, Peter Corney, Ross Cox and Washington Irving), as well as North

West Company boss William McGillivray, politicians William Gladstone and James FitzGerald, Russian scientist George Heinrich Von Langsdorff and Alexander Mackenzie's cousin, Roderic, can be found at www.abcbookworld.com. Of these men, only Ross Cox reached British Columbia.

Information on early nineteenth-century missionaries Gabriel Franchère, Modeste Demers, Francis Norbert Blanchet and Pierre-Jean De Smet will be provided in a subsequent volume.

I am grateful to David Lester for designing the contents and to Ronald Hatch for serving as an enthusiastic publisher. I wish also to acknowledge the assistance of Victor Hopwood, Bruce Lamb, Catherine Whitehead, the Hudson's Bay Company Archives in Winnipeg and the Vancouver Maritime Museum. History is like exploring, in which one map leads to the next; I am indebted to all the historians whose books are listed in the bibliography.

The fur trade is well-known as it relates to eastern Canada and the Great Plains. It is a different story west of the Rocky Mountains. The "fort and furs" period of British Columbia's history tends to be overshadowed by famous explorers of the maritime fur trade (1774–1800) and the onset of colonialism after 1850, highlighted by James Douglas and the gold rush. Anyone hoping to understand how British Columbia arose as a political construct will nonetheless find this formerly obscure half-century no less fascinating or fundamental.

I hope an engaging panorama has been provided for those Canadians who have the urge to go exploring backwards. *Thompson's Highway* is a follow-up to *First Invaders*, a volume that highlighted the literature and history of the Pacific Northwest prior to 1800, but it is not necessary to have read *First Invaders* in order to enjoy this book.

—*A.T.*

ABOUT THE COVER: BRITISH COLUMBIA'S OLDEST FLAG

First raised at the founding of Fort Vancouver on the Columbia River in 1825, this flag was taken north by James Douglas to fly above newly founded Fort Victoria on Vancouver Island in 1849. The tattered Hudson's Bay Company emblem was later donated to Clark County in Washington State by a Canadian when Fort Vancouver was being redeveloped for tourism purposes.

James Delgado of the Vancouver Maritime Museum briefly brought the flag back to British Columbia to be incorporated into a Hudson's Bay Company exhibit at the Vancouver Maritime Museum in 1995. Previously stored folded in a cardboard box, the five-foot by eight-foot emblem was rolled in acid-free wrappings and returned to the Clark County Historical Museum—where it presently remains.

Dating from 1671, the motto of the Hudson's Bay Company, *Pro Pellem Cutem*, is a sly variation of the Devil's "skin for skin" remark about Job and mankind when God and Satan were discussing how Job might be tempted into sin. As it was common practice in the seventeenth century for English mottoes to have double meanings, the investors in the new English company were possibly implying, with cheeky humour, that they would need the patience of Job to make money.

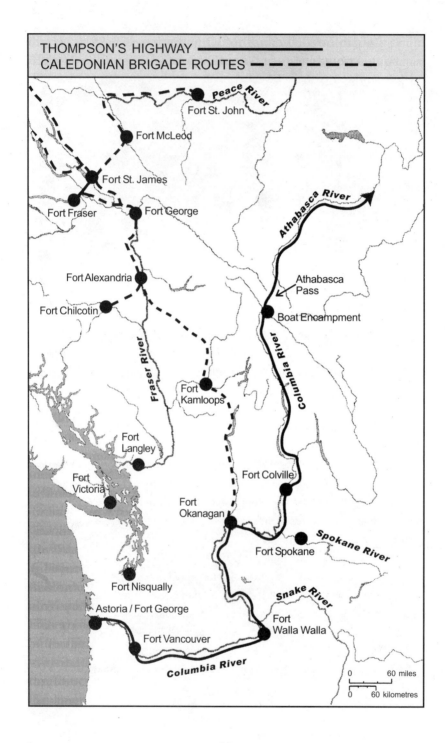

THOMPSON'S HIGHWAY
CALEDONIAN BRIGADE ROUTES

Peace River
Fort St. John
Fort McLeod
Fort St. James
Fort Fraser
Fort George
Athabasca River
Fort Alexandria
Athabasca Pass
Fort Chilcotin
Boat Encampment
Fraser River
Columbia River
Fort Kamloops
Fort Langley
Fort Victoria
Fort Colville
Fort Okanagan
Fort Spokane
Spokane River
Fort Nisqually
Snake River
Astoria / Fort George
Fort Walla Walla
Fort Vancouver
Columbia River

0   60 miles
0   60 kilometres

I
FORTS & FURS

"The Columbia is the line of communication from the Pacific Ocean, pointed out by nature. . . . By opening this intercourse between the Atlantic and Pacific Oceans, and forming regular establishments through the interior, and at both extremes . . . the entire command of the fur trade of North America might be obtained."

—ALEXANDER MACKENZIE AT THE CONCLUSION OF HIS
1801 MEMOIR, VOYAGES FROM MONTREAL

SCOTTISH COLUMBIA

U ntil a feckless English lawyer named Richard Blanshard arrived in Fort Victoria symbolically to represent British colonial government in 1850, the dominant European mentality west of the Rockies during the first half of the nineteenth century remained fortress and commercial.

Petticoats and Bibles would come later, after guns, booze and disease. This was not an era for heroes, or heroines. Pragmatism was the main rule of law. But if Hollywood North ever wanted to make a blockbuster movie about the fur trade west of the Rockies from 1800 to 1850, that motion picture would not be lacking in violence, sex and political intrigue.

Opening credits would introduce six main characters. In order of appearance, they would be Alexander Mackenzie, Simon Fraser, David Thompson (explorers for the upstart North West Company) & George Simpson, John McLoughlin and James Douglas (administrators of the Hudson's Bay Company). Bagpipes would be heard as the title appeared in bold tartan letters: Scottish Columbia.

In terms of size and appearance, Anthony Hopkins would be perfect as the "Little Emperor" George Simpson, the Hudson's Bay Company (HBC) governor who kept personality profiles on his workers like a nineteenth-century J. Edgar Hoover.

Sensitive changeling Johnny Depp would have to grow his hair for a bowl-cut to play David Thompson, the gifted and long-suffering orphan who ended up pawning his surveyor's equipment to feed his family.

With his Scottish accent, Sean Connery would need only a long, white beard to duplicate the magisterial "father of Oregon," John McLoughlin, mentor to James Douglas, the "father of British

Columbia."

Itinerant artist Paul Kane, undercover agent Henry Warre and botanist David Douglas would generate plum cameos as heartthrobs in their twenties.

Unfortunately the only plunging neckline would arise from the bosom of a Portsmouth barmaid named Miss Jane Barnes, "the flaxen-haired, blue-eyed daughter of Albion," who sailed around the Horn to become the first white woman on the mainland above California.

Francophones would be well represented by voyageurs such as Jules Maurice Quesnel who survived Simon Fraser's vainglorious escapades in the Fraser Canyon. While the American-born Fraser enviously schemed to match the achievements of Alexander Mackenzie, Quesnel could sit by the campfire and utter his one immortal line under his breath, "There is nothing to be had but misery and boredom."

First Nations characters would get short shrift because fur traders' journals offer scant reportage of Aboriginals as individuals. Chief Kwah, the Carrier leader who captured and intended to kill young HBC trader James Douglas—because Douglas had allowed his men to beat an untried Aboriginal murder suspect to death—could be an exception. This gruesome beating could flash through Douglas' mind as he kneels to receive his knighthood for his noble service to the empire.

Newcomers had to learn to co-exist with Aboriginals or starve. Whereas David Thompson, James Douglas and John McLoughlin all remained faithful to their mixed-blood wives—Charlotte, Amelia and Margaret (who bore more than 25 children between them)—Simon Fraser and Alexander Mackenzie did not.

After he was knighted and he tried unsuccessfully to gain ascendancy in the North West Company (NWC), Alexander Mackenzie left behind his mixed-blood offspring and retired to baronial ease in Scotland, marrying his fourteen-year-old cousin at age fifty.

Subtitles would be required; otherwise the audience would be mystified by the weird mixture of Gaelic, French, English, Cree,

Latin and the trading dialect of Chinook, usually rendered with thick Scottish accents.

With the noteworthy exceptions of David Thompson and American-born Simon Fraser, it was largely Highlanders and Orkneymen who unwittingly laid the foundations for Canada's western-most province prior to 1850. The clan-oriented Scots prevailed west of the Rockies by mapping the region, discouraging American incursions north of the 49th parallel, generating an export economy, publishing their journals and achieving mutually advantageous relations with the clan-oriented First Nations.

WHY THE SCOTS?

Scots prevailed in British Columbia prior to 1850 in part because of poverty in the Highlands, English arrogance and the Scottish Enlightenment (1740–1800), a period of intellectual ferment that gave rise to thinkers such as David Hume, Adam Smith and James Hutton. (Hume was the moral philosopher who wrote *A Treatise on Human Nature*; Smith was the economist who wrote *The Wealth of Nations*; and Hutton was the geologist who wrote *A Theory of the Earth*.)

Such men—including Robbie Burns—were the flowering of a unique public educational system envisioned by religious philosopher John Knox (1515–1572). To allow everyone to read Scripture themselves, Knox wanted to introduce schooling into every parish. Classes for the great unwashed were not free, but parents could pay for education with goods in kind. Teachers' salaries were paid from local taxes. Hence, Robbie Burns, born in his mother's kitchen as the son of an impoverished tenant farmer, was able to boast, "Though I cost the schoolmaster some thrashings, I made an excellent English scholar."

Scotland introduced a second level of "grammar school" (basically Latin and grammar) and a third college level or "high school." As the foundation for Canada's educational system, Scotland's radically inclusive system encouraged unusually gifted students to attend Scotland's venerable universities: St. Andrews (founded 1411), Glasgow (1451), King's College, Old Aberdeen (1495), Edinburgh (1583) and Marischal College (1593).

By the time the Scottish Enlightenment reached its zenith around 1800, it was said a man could stand in Market Square in Edinburgh and shake hands with fifty men of genius in an hour. Even remote Highlanders gained access to books and education, thanks in part to the Society in Scotland for Propagating Christian Knowledge (SSPCK).

Scottish universities reputedly produced ten thousand medical doctors between 1750 and 1850, whereas Oxford and Cambridge produced five hundred. Only Jews, it has been suggested, developed an equal respect for scholarship.

"We look to Scotland," wrote Voltaire, "for all our ideas of civilization."

This social progress to the north of England made London uneasy. In the aftermath of the Battle of Culloden, victorious England, aided by complicit Scottish lairds, enacted a series of draconian measures known as the Proscriptions and the Clearances. Bagpipes were banned, estates confiscated, etc.

Once again, Scots were victims of England's "chains and slavery," but this time England's legislated oppression bordered on genocide when Scotland's crippled economy was exacerbated by famines and an unprecedented population explosion.

These developments explain why literate but poor Scots—such as Alexander Mackenzie and Robert Campbell—were eager to test their survival skills in the hinterlands of Canada. The New World could not be much worse.

Scotland's loss was the Hudson's Bay Company's gain. So-called

oatmeal savages were willing to work for relatively
low wages and they were
able to endure the priva-
tions that arose from hor-
rendous Canadian win-
ters.

HBC ships bound for
Canada made their final
stops, prior to their Atlan-
tic crossing, at the Orkney
Islands or the Hebrides.
There the Honourable
Company established re-
cruiting stations at
Stromness (Orkney Is-
lands) and Stornoway / Steòrnabhagh (Outer Hebrides).

The derogatory term oatmeal savage arose from Samuel Johnson's innumerable jibes at the Scots, as well as his famous dictionary in which he cheekily defined the word oatmeal: "A grain, which in England, is generally given to horses, but in Scotland supports the people." As a rejoinder, Johnson's Scottish-born biographer James Boswell replied: "Which is why England is known for its horses, and Scotland for its men."

In his letter of advice to doomed Arctic explorer Lt. John Franklin in 1819, Alexander Mackenzie wrote: "Amongst the Crew there should be two of the HB Company's old Servants, Natives if possible of the Orkneys."

No part of Scotland was more than 50 miles from seawater, so most Scots were good sailor material. Frugal by nature and ne-cessity, Scots also made ideal clerks. Not only could they add and subtract, they would be able to paddle loaded canoes from Que-bec to British Columbia and back again. In the first five years of the nineteenth century, at least six thousand Scots left Scotland for North America.

One obvious result of this migration from starvation was the creation of a province within eastern Canada to be named Nova Scotia, where Gaelic is still sometimes heard. A lesser-known re-sult was the formation of a network of forts and trading stations west of the Rocky Mountains, from San Francisco to Alaska. Most were constructed prior to 1850. About one-third of those forts were built in the interior of present-day British Columbia, in a zone generally called New Caledonia (meaning New Scotland).

NEW CALEDONIA

"The Situation of our New Caledonia Friends in regard to the good things of this Life is anything but enviable." —GEORGE SIMPSON

"... this vile country" —JOHN TOD, AT MCLEOD LAKE

"... land of privation & misery" —ARCHIBALD MCDONALD

Known as the Siberia of the fur trade, New Caledonia was a largely unmapped region from the Cariboo/Chilcotin to the Yukon and beyond. "This district extends from 51° 30' north lat. to about 56°," wrote Joseph McGillivray, mixed blood son of North West Company boss William McGillivary. "Its extreme western boundary is 124° 10'. Its principal trading post is called Alexandria, after the celebrated traveller Sir Alexander Mackenzie."

Traders who were unfortunate enough to be stranded in New Caledonia referred to themselves as exiles. The dozens of lonely, literate and frequently desperate souls who built and managed commercial outposts on the Western Slope were the embodiment of fortitude in Canada, especially in New Caledonia.

The disadvantages of being posted to New Caledonia were noted by James R. Gibson in *The Lifeline of the Oregon Country* as extreme isolation, monotonous diet, debilitating diseases, wearisome labour and violent death from accident or murder.

While it is statistically impossible to gauge whether one of those debilitating diseases, "Chinook love fever," was more widespread in New Caledonia than elsewhere, some traders suggested that was the case.

If the salmon runs were late or negligible—as was the case in 1811, 1820, 1823 and 1828—life inside a palisade was prison-like.

There was also a higher prevalence of alcoholism and black flies than along the coast.

When George Simpson visited McLeod Lake, he noted John Tod and his two employees were starving, "having had nothing to eat for several Weeks but Berries." Their "countenances were so pale and emaciated that it was with difficulty I recognized them."

John Work bemoaned the "eternal Solitude" and the "Starvation & Solitude in N.C." Frank Ermatinger resented the "misery of Damned Dried Salmon," which was said initially to have the effect of a strong laxative.

It did not help that misfits and convicts were sometimes sent to New Caledonia as a form of punishment. Chief Factor Connolly pleaded, "We have outdoor Rogues enough to guard against without having any among ourselves."

John Tod recalled in his memoirs: "New Caledonia was then looked on in the light of another Botany Bay [a penal colony], Australia, the men in dread of being sent there."

As early as 1806, the North West Company saw fit to supply more generous provisions for anyone sent to New Caledonia. In 1827, Governor Simpson was obliged to pay higher wages to New Caledonians. "The spirit of discontent," according to Chief Factor Connolly in 1824, "was such that not one of the men whose times were expired could be prevailed upon to renew their contracts."

Whereas maritime fur traders could sometimes exercise an option of wintering in the Sandwich Islands (Hawaii), inland fur traders had no recourse but to suffer fearful nights, empty bellies and sub-zero temperatures. Nonetheless, clannish Scots somehow managed to coexist with clannish Aboriginals, almost peacefully, without the written rule of law, in the remote area described by missionary Modeste Demers as "a sterile country with a vigorous climate."

The men who were sent to New Caledonia were primarily motivated by self-advancement—not sea-to-sea-to-sea nationalism—but their feats of endurance and exploration, their stick-with-itness and frontier diplomacy, their adaptability and sufferings, and their journals, are no less remarkable for it.

The name New Caledonia was chosen by Simon Fraser because its unforgiving terrain reminded him of his mother's descriptions of Scotland. George Simpson often referred to the area as Western Caledonia.

When it came time for Queen Victoria to name her new colony west of the Rocky Mountains in 1858, she gave Fraser's term serious consideration. New Caledonia

A young Queen Victoria near the time she named British Columbia

probably would have endured on maps to this day were it not for the fact that New Caledonia already existed—twice.

Back in the early seventeeth century, King James VI of Scotland (aka James I of England, he of the famous Bible version) was convinced by fast-talker William Alexander, Earl of Stirling, to match the creation of a New France and a New England with his own New Scotland.

Ignoring French claims to Acadia, King James granted much of the present-day Atlantic Provinces and Gaspé Peninsula to the Earl of Stirling. In a 1624 pamphlet entitled *An Encouragement to Colonies*, Stirling divided his Nova Scotia into two provinces, Alexandria and (New) Caledonia.

The other New Caledonia was also created by the son of a Scotsman. In 1774, Captain James Cook illogically decided that an island situated between Australia and Fiji in the South Pacific should bear the name New Caledonia.

So Queen Victoria rejected New Caledonia III. Instead, to designate her empire's holdings above the 49th parallel, she combined her favourite adjective British with the name already given to the main trading area to the south.

The Columbia District derived its name from the river that served as the main thoroughfare for trade. That river, in turn, had received its name from the American sea captain Robert Gray, in reference to his own ship, *Columbia Rediviva.*

Hence the origins of the name British Columbia are as much American as they are British.

COMMERCE, SEX & VIOLENCE

Scots and French-Canadians in the Pacific fur trade after 1800 were mainly employed by the North West Company, the Hudson's Bay Company and the much smaller Pacific Fur Company (PFC).

Cynics have long suggested the initials HBC stand for "Here Before Christ" because the self-regulated HBC received its fur trading charter from King Charles II in 1670. Although shareholders known as partners had operated as the North West Company since the 1770s, the North West Company was not formally incorporated until 1799, at which time the NWC had approximately 115 posts employing approximately one thousand men.

HBC employees were encouraged to take "country wives" to solidify trading relations, whereas formalized fidelity tended to be discouraged by the Nor'Westers.

Headquartered in Montreal, the upstart North West Company allowed for more private initiative, whereas the HBC tended to be penny-pinching and bureaucratic.

Competition between the highly structured HBC and the flexible NWC could be fierce, even "suicidal" according to some historians. With more incentives for promotion, the NWC traders soon explored

NWC's Simon McTavish

The short-lived Pacific Fur Company, an offshoot of the American Fur Company, was controlled by a German butcher's son, John Jacob Astor. He became America's first millionaire and died aboard the Titanic.

beyond the realm of their HBC rivals, gaining precedence in areas west of Saskatchewan.

Nepotism reigned in both companies. Englishmen controlled the HBC from London whereas the NWC was more complex but definitely clannish. The NWC's Montreal agents, headed by Simon McTavish, met each summer with their "wintering" trading partners (*hivernants*) at the NWC's Lake Superior headquarters, first at Grand Portage, and later at Fort William, to discuss management and to get very, very drunk.

In 1811, with the blessings of Thomas Jefferson, John Jacob Astor's Pacific Fur Company established Astoria as the first permanently occupied American fort west of the Rockies.

Located at the mouth of the Columbia River, Astoria was absorbed by the North West Company in 1813. Even after the advent of steam-powered ships such as the *Beaver*, the company that controlled the Columbia River effectively controlled the overall fur trade.

The North West Company, in turn, was merged into the Hudson's Bay Company in 1821. The Hudson's Bay Company monolith, according to Hamar Foster, in *BC Studies*, ultimately stood for almost everything Americans had been taught to dislike: "It was British, monopolistic, undemocratic, authoritarian and owned by absentees."

Considering the organizational clout and longevity of the Hudson's Bay Company, it is easy to assume Aboriginals were easily manipulated and exploited—but the opposite was true, especially west of the Rockies where Aboriginals were particularly difficult to pacify and drove unusually hard bargains. Already sophisticated traders among themselves, Aboriginals on the Western Slope effectively haggled by citing the competing prices offered by American vessels and Russian forts to the north.

As well, the newcomers' reliance on Aboriginals for food, furs and females placed them at a profound disadvantage. Despite their advanced weaponry, the corporate invaders were pitiable in their isolation. Most NWC and HBC traders would have starved without the fishing and hunting skills of their Aboriginal and Métis associates.

Keen to trade and to serve as middlemen, Aboriginals moved entire villages in order to make their camps near the new stockades, the superstores of yesteryear. Although liquor was certainly one major incentive to relocate, Aboriginals were not duped into trading. Journal entries reveal they were quite capable of outwitting the white man and they could always steal from him.

It was common for an Aboriginal to present a land otter pelt, claiming it was a sea otter pelt. "When a skin is rejected as being deficient in size, or defective in quality," George Simpson wrote, "it is immediately, according to circumstances, enlarged, or coloured, or pressed to order, and then is submitted, as a virgin article, to the buyer's criticism by a different customer."

As much as it has become *de rigueur* in some quarters to revise B.C. history into a paradigm of exploitation, there is much evidence to suggest that intercourse of all kinds between fur traders and Aboriginals tended to be voluntary, even cordial.

"Certainly the Indians involved in the trade became dependent on the company for European goods," historian Robin Fisher has noted, "but no more than the company was dependent on the Indians for furs."

Aboriginals shared their food and knowledge mostly by choice, not by coercion, and with their superior knowledge of the wilderness, their mobility and their vastly superior numbers, they did not feel unduly threatened by white men until the second half of the nineteenth century, when settlers began to arrive.

"The trapline was pitted against the plough," historian Barry Gough has noted, "and in the end it was settlement that gained the day."

Settlement gained the day with much help from disease. The notorious Whitman Massacre in Washington State occurred only in response to the influx of white immigrants who brought with them, in the words of trader Peter Skene Ogden in 1848, "their pleasant travelling companions the Measles, Dysentry and Typhus Fever." Prior to 1850, some equilibrium had evolved between most Aboriginals and fur traders, motivated by self-interest on both sides.

With the noteworthy exception of John McLoughlin, who repeatedly provided humanitarian assistance, HBC employees mostly discouraged white settlement as detrimental to commerce. Whereas land-hungry white settlers would be relatively unconcerned about the welfare of their Aboriginal neighbours, HBC traders commenced an extensive program of smallpox vaccinations for Aboriginals in the 1830s.

Land-based fur traders, in the words of Robin Fisher, "had a considerable investment and interest in keeping much of the Indian way of life intact."

The journals of Scotsmen frequently decry the often base treatment of Aboriginals by American and Russian traders. George Simpson abhorred the slave trade practised by the Native peoples and forbade his employees from engaging in it, even though he knew his rivals in the Pacific Northwest were profiting by it.

"We are traders," McLoughlin declared in 1843, "and apart from more exalted motives, all traders are desirous of gain. Is it not self-evident we will manage our business with more economy by being on good terms with the Indians than if at variance?"

The common notion that fur traders acquired their "country wives" exclusively for sexual gratification also requires some reconsideration. From Alexander Mackenzie onwards, traders who passed through the Rockies understood that Aboriginal and Métis women were necessary companions to combat loneliness, to break down language barriers and to secure diplomatic relations, to say nothing of their crucial ability to make footwear suitable for completing any long journey.

Stranded in 1786, Alexander Mackenzie wrote: "I have no one

at the fort that can make raquettes [snowshoes]; I do not know what to do without those articles. See what it is to have no wives."

Whether it was a formalized marriage or a Highland fling, "Traffic in the Fair Sex," as Malcolm Ross called it, was certainly widely practised, but such transactions were undertaken to secure, in the words of Hearne, "the strongest ties of friendship" as much as they were libidinous indulgences.

Aware that commercial harmony depended to some extent on domestic harmony, the Council of the Northern Department of the Hudson's Bay Company passed an ordinance in 1824 that directed its men to ensure country wives received adequate financial recompense if they became separated.

Among the traders west of the Rockies who remained married to their country wives and provided for their needs in their wills were James Douglas, John McLoughlin, David Thompson, John Tod, Archibald McDonald, Daniel Harmon, Alexander Ross, Peter Skene Ogden and William McNeill.

Other Nor'Westers who took their country wives with them to live in eastern Canada included William Morrison, James Hughes, Alexander Fraser and William Connolly.

While country wives and their offspring were sometimes abandoned as inconvenient, or arrangements were made for them to be transferred to other partners, it is incorrect to assume *all* country wives were accorded the status of chattel.

If traders' journals are reliable indicators—and they are not entirely to be trusted, given that self-censorship was widespread—many of the cross-cultural unions were harmonious. Evidently there was no shortage of Aboriginal women who preferred the relative comfort of teacups and fiddle music in a fort to a difficult nomadic life on the land.

Ultimately the acceptability of country wives waned as more British women made their way to Canada and the West Coast. This acceptability factor was influenced by the marriage of George Simpson, a prodigious philanderer, to his eighteen-year-old English cousin in 1830.

By 1840, the mulatto James Douglas, son of a Creole mother

and a Scottish father, wryly summarized: "There is a strange revolution in the manners of the country; Indian wives were at one time the vogue, the half breed supplanted these, and now we have the lovely tender exotic from its parent bed, to pine and languish in the desert."

The path of true love and fur trading never did run smooth, but for the most part connubial alliances paved the way for commerce. "The history of the land-based fur trade west of the Rockies is remarkable," Robin Fisher has suggested, "for the absence of mass attacks on forts."

This helpful comment overlooks the attack on Fort McLoughlin in 1833, John Tod's interruption of an attack force bound for his Thompson River Post in 1846 and two sieges (one at Kootenai House; another at Fort Victoria).

In addition, several major slaughters occurred:

- In 1794, Chief Cumshewa and the Haida massacred all but one crew member of the American schooner *Resolution*.
- In 1803, Aboriginals massacred all but two crew members of the *Boston,* north of Friendly Cove.
- In 1806, Aboriginals massacred the crew of the *Atahualpa* at Millbanke Sound.
- In 1811, Aboriginals massacred all but one crew member of the *Tonquin* in Clayoquot Sound.
- In 1823, Beaver Indians murdered the occupants of St. John's, a small post at Beatton River mouth.
- In 1852, Chilkat warriors ransacked Fort Selkirk.

Violence was common west of the Rockies, but rarely unprovoked.

Crew members of the *Boston* were massacred in response to previous killings by Euro-American traders who had earlier visited Nootka Sound, and also to avenge a great insult to Maquinna's pride. Similarly the 23 crewmen and the captain of John Jacob Astor's flagship *Tonquin* were killed only after Captain Thorn persistently behaved in an arrogant and foolhardy manner, insulting the local chief in front of his people. The chronically combative trader Samuel Black received his deadly comeuppance in Kamloops after a dispute over a woman, and two fur traders were also murdered in their beds at Fort George due to their alleged sexual trespasses.

History written by whites has tended to overlook or diminish acts of barbarism or cruelty perpetrated by the invaders. Any such reportage in journals is perfunctory, at best, but it is known that Aboriginals who absconded with women presumed to belong to fur traders sometimes had their ears cut off.

At Fort Vancouver, after one Chinook dressed himself as a woman and visited the ships anchored nearby, repeatedly offering himself to the sailors, this transvestite was brought to the infirmary of Dr. Meredith Gairdner who obliged the ship's crew by castrating him.

Generally there was a code of silence when it came to murderous acts committed by whites. During and after his brief tenure at Fort Vancouver, Reverend Herbert Beaver broke that code by reporting barbarous acts in the Columbia District, likely in reference to the Snake River expeditions led by Peter Skene Ogden, rampages that were sanctioned by the HBC.

Beaver wrote: "the same party killed one Indian, wounded another, supposed mortally, and threw a child into a fire, in consequence of a quarrel respecting a knife, which was afterwards found upon one of themselves. And during the year before, they put four Indians to death for stealing their horses, which might be pleaded as some excuse for the brutality, but that they afterwards killed ten or twelve more in cold blood, and set fire to their village. The Indians lived in such constant dread of this party, that they were unable to descend into the plains from their fastnesses in the mountains, to procure their usual modes of subsistence. Do not these things imperatively demand inquiry and interference?"

Peter Skene Ogden reputedly volunteered to eradicate all Aboriginal males from the Snake country. But NWC and HBC fur traders, at least in theory, were advised not to respond to so-called

Hubert Howe Bancroft

hostiles with sweeping retribution. It was simply not in their best interest to do so.

"In all our intercourse with the natives," James Douglas stated, "we have invariably acted on the principle that it is inexpedient and unjust to hold *tribes* responsible for the acts of *individuals.*"

Nevertheless, trials and executions of Aboriginals tended to be brisk affairs. San Francisco-based historian Hubert Howe Bancroft once shrewdly noted: "We have seen the forms of justice, or rather justice without form, as administered by the factors and traders of the fur company. And we must confess it, that although far-reaching and strong enough, justice hitherto has been barely respectable, appearing oftener in elk-skin than in ermine, and quite frequently with gaunt belly and tattered habiliments."

James Douglas' hasty retribution against a suspected murderer in 1828 stirred so much resentment among the Carrier people of Chief Kwah that Douglas had to be transferred out of New Caledonia, along with his new wife, for his own safety.

To maintain trading networks stretching all the way back to Hudson Bay and Montreal, fur traders west of the Rockies had to be unusually cagey and resolute characters, little given to sentiment, feisty when challenged, ready to compromise if necessary, frequently of a literary bent, physically strong and able to endure long bouts of isolation.

Small wonder the motto of the North West Company was boiled down to one word—Perseverance.

ASTORIA & VICTORIA

The political connections between British Columbia and the Oregon Territory are little-appreciated in the twenty-first century, but these zones were incubated as twins—New Caledonia and the Columbia District—in the early nineteenth century.

Astoria, the first permanent fort at the mouth of the Columbia River, built in 1811, was the precursor to the first major European settlement in present-day British Columbia, Fort Victoria, established in 1843.

Canada might have retained political control of the area north of the Columbia River but for the vainglorious posturing of a British sea captain who arrived *after* representatives of the North West Company had coercively influenced employees of the Pacific Fur Company to sell Fort Astoria in 1813, by threatening the Astorians with the imminent arrival of a British warship.

When Captain William Black arrived in the *Racoon* and made a formal fuss of raising the British flag—as if a military victory had been won—he changed the name of Astoria to Fort George and noted in his journal that he had conquered Astoria.

Soon afterwards, when Britain and the United States signed the Treaty of Ghent in 1814 to terminate the War of 1812, both countries agreed to relinquish control of any territories seized by either country during the war. The Americans consequently argued that Astoria must be restored to the U.S. because the captain of the *Racoon* had claimed a military triumph in 1813. Plenty of journals kept by Astorians and Nor'Westers had recorded Black's ceremonial acts of hubris.

Little concerned with maintaining a tiny trading post on the other side of the world, Great Britain forfeited control of tiny Fort George—even though it had been, in reality, a privately

owned fort purchased by another privately owned company—
and paperwork was accordingly signed in October of 1818 by
British and American commissioners aboard the British ship *Blossom* at Fort George.

The American ship *Ontario* had entered the Columbia River
two months earlier and claimed land on both its banks for the
U.S. An American flag was raised and the *Blossom*'s guns saluted
the formal exchange of ownership of the Astoria site—the first
step in the protracted process of securing control of the Oregon
Territories.

A period of formalized "co-occupation" ensued. Still cognizant that the Columbia was the main highway for trade, the Hudson's Bay Company moved its headquarters upriver to Fort Vancouver under the management of John McLoughlin in 1825.

McLoughlin and his assistant James Douglas would both prove
themselves to be creatures of expediency and commerce, not
statesmen, who rose to political prominence more by circumstance than design. Their values and their educations were primarily Scottish and commercial.

Fort Vancouver remained the commercial hub for the fur trade
west of the Rocky Mountains until the HBC cautiously retreated
to build Fort Victoria in 1843.

*British colonial authority formally arrived on Vancouver Island seven years after
James Douglas selected the site for Fort Victoria (as shown).*

Scottish-born fur traders and their sons (as shown above) raised families with Aboriginal wives in British Columbia throughout the nineteenth century.

II
PEOPLE

"It was withal a cutthroat business."
—BARRY M. GOUGH, HISTORIAN

*"To suggest that the Hudson's Bay Company
was anything but a good corporate citizen borders on heresy
(unless you are Native, in which case it is gospel.)"*
—KENNETH S. COATES, HISTORIAN

*"British Columbia became British rather than American
or Russian largely because of the work of a small number
of fur-traders and of the capitalists they represented."*
—JOHN S. GALBRAITH, HISTORIAN

[SIX LEADING MEN]

ALEXANDER MACKENZIE

"If we cut out all the noble-explorer crap, Mackenzie wanted to make a large profit so he could go back to Great Britain and live like a gentleman. Sort of like Conrad Black."
—BRIAN FAWCETT, SOCIAL CRITIC & NOVELIST

"This northern Sinbad" —BARRY GOUGH, HISTORIAN

The explorations of Alexander Mackenzie, sometimes referred to as "the hero who failed," culminated with his overland trek to the mouth of the Bella Coola River on the British Columbia coast in 1793. Although Mackenzie didn't discover a viable fur trading route to the Pacific Ocean as he had envisioned, his twin forays to the Arctic and Pacific Oceans from Lake Athabasca were the fulcrum point for radical change west of the Rocky Mountains.

The publication of Alexander Mackenzie's *Voyages from Montreal* in 1801, including an uncredited history of the fur trade by his bookish cousin Roderic Mackenzie, marked the onset of overland fur trading in British Columbia coincidental with the decline of the maritime-based sea otter trade.

Born at Luskentyre House, Stornoway, on Isle of Lewis in the Outer Hebrides of Scotland, in 1762, Alexander Mackenzie had a relatively privileged upbringing at nearby Melbost, a farm near the sea that was granted to his father in return for his loyalty as a military leader within the venerable Mackenzie clan. Alexander Mackenzie's father and grandfather had been military adjuncts to the ruling laird, but as Scottish landlords began to demand rents in lieu of loyalty, the Mackenzies, although well-educated, quickly became downwardly mobile and desperate.

In 1774, twelve-year-old Alexander Mackenzie sailed for New York from Stornaway with two aunts in the *Peace & Plenty*. Likely speaking both English and Gaelic, he was blessed with innate self-confidence and what biographer Roy Daniells described as "the self-reliance of the Lewismen," combined with traditional Scottish caution and foresight, along with "the Stornowegian instinct for trade." Strong, haughty, secretive, prone to depression, widely read and quarrelsome, he was a born leader.

After Mackenzie's widowed father Kenneth Mackenzie had also immigrated to America, either slightly before or after his son, both Kenneth Mackenzie and his brother John Mackenzie recommenced their military careers by enlisting as lieutenants in the King's Royal Regiment of New York, keen to fight for the British in the American Revolutionary War. On May 7, 1780, Kenneth Mackenzie died at Carleton Island, near Kingston, on Lake Ontario, probably of scurvy.

After several years in the Mohawk Valley of New York, Alexander Mackenzie was brought to live with aunts in the relative safety of Montreal, where he briefly attended school. Soon after his arrival in Montreal, Alexander Mackenzie entered the employ of a nascent fur trading company in 1779. Started by Gregory McLeod, and named Finlay, McLeod and Company, it operated within a very loose consortium that would eventually become widely known as the North West Company.

As a young man, Mackenzie impressed his superiors and was sent to trade in Detroit, where he was offered a partnership in the redefined company called Gregory, McLeod and Company. Initially this company chose to compete against the emerging Nor'Westers, but increasingly deadly competition between traders induced Gregory, McLeod and Company to be subsumed, with the fortunate result that Mackenzie became a partner within the much larger North West Company.

At the annual general meeting of the NWC partners at Grand Portage in 1785, Alexander Mackenzie was placed in charge of the Churchill River, also known as the English River, in the Île-à-la-Crosse area of northwestern Saskatchewan. There it has been assumed he took his first country wife, an Aboriginal or Métis known as the Catt, who died in 1804, having given Mackenzie at least one child.

In the company of volatile Peter Pond, a pioneer geographer and a suspected double murderer, Mackenzie was sent to the Athabasca River area, northwest of Lake Superior, in 1787. There he first heard about a great river that might take him to the salt waters of the Pacific, a body of water that would be referred to by his Aboriginal informants as "the stinking lake."

Alexander Mackenzie's memoir Voyages from Montreal *contained a history of the Canadian fur trade now generally attributed to his long-suffering cousin Roderic Mackenzie.*

Motivated by the widely travelled Pond, who insisted, with his own maps, that the Pacific Ocean was reachable overland from Lake Athabasca, Mackenzie recalled: "I not only contemplated the practicality of penetrating across the continent of America, but was confident in the qualifications, as I was animated by the desire, to undertake the perilous enterprise."

In 1778, Peter Pond had crossed the Methy Portage and built Pond's Fur Trading Post on the Lower Athabasca River. Some forty miles from Lake Athabasca, it became the first fort in the Arctic Drainage System and Alberta's first white settlement. Relying on hearsay, Pond had concocted a map that showed the Pacific Ocean was only 150 miles further west from the Chipewyan tribe.

With Pond's departure in 1788, Mackenzie found himself in sole command of the Athabasca district and determined to test the merits of Pond's geography. Mackenzie was much heartened by the arrival of his cousin Roderic Mackenzie who agreed to oversee Athabascan operations during Alexander's absence. Previously sworn to secrecy about his cousin's plans, Roderic Mackenzie helped relocate Pond's House to Old Fort Point on the south shore of Lake Athabasca, renaming it Fort Chipewyan. He also amassed a renowned library that would contain 2,000 books.

Departing from Fort Chipewyan in June of 1789, seeking that stinking lake, Alexander Mackenzie completed a 102-day journey to the Arctic Ocean and back, inadvertently becoming the first European to reach the mouth of the Mackenzie River. He would later ruefully conclude, "Mr. Pond's Assertion was nothing but conjecture."

In 1792, Alexander Mackenzie wintered at the junction of the Peace and Smoke Rivers, and resumed his quest to find a path across the continent in 1793, this time with nine men, one dog and one canoe. Once again having procured the essential help of Aboriginal guides, Mackenzie travelled up the Peace River, across the Rocky Mountains, part way down the Fraser River and eventually traversed one of several Chilcotin "grease trails" (paths enabling inland tribes to trade for oolachan oil) to the ocean.

Upon his arrival near the mouth of the Bella Coola River, on North Bentinck Arm, Mackenzie was unable immediately to record his presence on the Pacific. The Bella Bella were less than hospitable, having recently been fired upon by whites in a very large boat. Mackenzie recorded in his journal the names of two significant white men repeatedly referred to by the Bella Bella as "Macubah" and "Benzins." One of the survey boats from Captain George Vancouver's *Discovery* expedition had been in Dean Channel six

In his journal, Mackenzie wrote, "I mixed up some vermilion in melted grease, and inscribed, in large characters, on the South-East face of the rock on which we had slept last night, this brief memorial—Alexander Mackenzie, from Canada, by land, the twenty-second of July, one thousand seven hundred and ninety-three." Today it is difficult to imagine anyone ever slept atop this rock monument, located near the head of Elcho Harbour, into which the Historic Sites and Monuments Board of Canada had inscribed a similar message in 1926.

weeks previously so it is often presumed these were references to Captain Vancouver ["Macubah"] and the botanist Archibald Menzies ["Benzins"], although there's no record of Menzies being a member of a shore party at this time.

Mackenzie's party paddled by canoe to Dean Channel where he mixed grease and vermilion paint to leave his famous message on a rock in Elcho Harbour.

Mackenzie returned to Montreal in 1794 where he became embroiled in fur trading politics and a personal dispute with Simon McTavish, chief founder of the North West Company. McTavish's brother John alleged in a letter of 1803, printed in the *Beaver* in 1947, that Mackenzie was particularly piqued because Simon McTavish would not allow Mackenzie's name to be added to the formal name of the firm McTavish, Frobisher and Company.

Having extensively investigated this dispute (unrecorded in Mackenzie's own memoirs), the even-handed historian W. Stewart Wallace has concluded Mackenzie was not only relatively well-treated by McTavish, he was "...shown especial consideration. On the reorganization of the North West Company in 1795, he was not only given six shares in the Company, but he was also made a partner of the firm of McTavish, Frobisher and Company, and was appointed, with William McGillivray (the nephew of Simon McTavish), one of the 'agents' or representatives of McTavish, Frobisher and Company to meet the wintering partners each summer at Grand Portage."

Nevertheless, after attending the general meeting of NWC stakeholders at Grand Portage in 1799, during which "a very violent discussion" ensued about Mackenzie's demands for higher status, Mackenzie remained resolute and quit the North West Company. He went to England in 1799 where he met extensively with John Fraser, a London partner of Simon McTavish, who examined Mackenzie's complaints and concluded: "McKenzie's abrupt departure from Mont. proceeds, I believe, entirely from a fit of ill-humour, without any fix'd plan or knowing himself what he would be at." John Fraser reassured Simon Fraser in 1800 that

Mackenzie "has I'm convinc'd no schemes of business in view, and does not think of interfering with you."

John Fraser was mistaken. To oppose McTavish and the NWC, Mackenzie helped form a fledgling consortium, the New North West Company, soon generally known as the XY Company. Founded in 1800, this enterprise likely gained its nickname because its traders marked their trade bales with the initials X and Y. Mackenzie's enmity even extended to his stalwart supporter and cousin Roderic, who became an NWC partner in his place.

In London, where he came to regret his imprudent schism with Simon McTavish, Mackenzie published his two major journals in 1801, edited by William Combe, a professional writer who had reworked the fur trading memoirs of John Meares and William Colnett. The extent to which Mackenzie relied on Combe to modify and improve his memoir cannot be known. T.H. McDonald's version of Mackenzie's journals, entitled *Exploring the Northwest Territory*, contains a transcription of the only remaining manuscript that partially served as the original for *Voyages from Montreal*. According to historian W. Kaye Lamb, "The journal of the second expedition exists only in the version edited by William Combe in the published accounts of Mackenzie's voyages."

At the behest of Napoleon, a translated version of Mackenzie's bestseller *Voyages from Montreal* appeared in Paris in 1802, along with versions from Hamburg and Edinburgh (based on the French version). A Russian edition appeared in 1808.

U.S. President Thomas Jefferson read *Voyages from Montreal* in 1802 and initiated the Lewis and Clark expedition. Headed by Captain Meriwether Lewis, a former secretary to the President of the United States, and Captain William Clark, this well-provisioned Corps of Discovery expedition used David Thompson's map of the Upper Missouri and reached the Pacific Coast in 1804, 12 years after Alexander Mackenzie had accomplished the cross-continental feat. Many Americans believe Lewis and Clark were the first "white men" to reach the Pacific Ocean by travelling overland.

Prince Edward and Alexander Mackenzie frequently dined at the Beaver Club in Montreal, where Mackenzie gained his reputation as a heavy drinker and ardent party-goer. Mackenzie's friendship in Canada with Prince Edward, Duke of Kent, the king's son, likely had much to do with his prompt elevation to knighthood.

Just as *Voyages to Montreal* stirred Jefferson to recognize the need to combat the spread of the Canadian fur traders in the Pacific Northwest, Mackenzie's description of the Red River valley served as the catalyst for Lord Selkirk's ambitious emigration schemes for that region. Selkirk, too, would become one of Mackenzie's enemies.

Dedicated to King George III, Mackenzie's journal effectively portrayed his heroism and gained him the title of Knight Bachelor in early February of 1802.

Upon his return to Canada in 1802, the lionization of Mackenzie prompted the XY Company, or New Northwest Company, to alter its name to Sir Alexander Mackenzie & Company. Although Mackenzie's new company had extensive working capital and a network that stretched to the Athabasca region, he lost some of his corporate-minded zeal for revenge when his nemesis, Simon McTavish, died unexpectedly on July 6, 1804.

Four months later, Mackenzie and Simon McTavish's NWC replacement, William McGillvray, negotiated a merger of their companies under the banner of the NWC. The union of these companies generously accorded Mackenzie's company one quarter of the joint concern with one provision: that Sir Alexander Mackenzie would be henceforth "excluded from any interference" in the Canadian fur-trade.

Two years later Mackenzie helped formulate the Michilimackinac Fur Company, an enterprise designed to compete against John Jacob Astor's expansion of the fur trade in the United States. Having distanced himself from his cousin, Mackenzie now found himself working in opposition to Alexander

MacKay, his hand-picked lieutenant who had bravely accompanied him on his journey to the Pacific.

After MacKay and four other Nor'Westers joined Astor in 1804, MacKay became the first person to reach the West Coast of North America by travelling both overland and by sea, arriving at the mouth of the Columbia River on Astor's ship the *Tonquin* on March 22, 1811. Alexander MacKay was murdered aboard the *Tonquin* by Aboriginals at Clayoquot Sound.

Mackenzie, who left Canada for the last time in 1808, continued to accumulate wealth and aggravate his opponents and partners. Or as biographer Barry Gough wrote: "Tight-fistedness and secrecy were enduring characteristics of Mackenzie."

There are few reliable portraits of Alexander Mackenzie or the individuals who travelled with him in the early 1800s. Painted one hundred years after Mackenzie reached the Pacific Ocean, this 1893 portrait of Mackenzie by B.C. artist Ren Emile Quentin (1860–1914) has been criticized as "clumsy" and "dreadful" by Patricia Roy and John Herd Thompson, editors of British Columbia: Land of Promises. It was intended to mimic Nathaniel Dance's portrait of Captain Cook. The best and most famous Mackenzie portrait, by the king's painter-in-ordinary, Sir Thomas Lawrence, was commissioned by Mackenzie for sixty guineas in 1802. It is reproduced on the cover.

In 1812, at age fifty, Alexander Mackenzie married his beautiful fourteen-year-old cousin Geddes Margaret Mackenzie. She was the twin daughter of a wealthy, Scottish-born Londoner who had died in 1809, leaving the ample estate of Avoch in the Black Isle, Ross and Cromarty. Already extremely well-off from his shares in the fur trade that were monitored for him by Roderic, Alexander Mackenzie purchased the remainder of the Avoch estate that his young bride had not inherited.

Mackenzie and his wife divided their time between London in the winter and Avoch in the summer. Their first daughter Margaret Geddes was born in 1816 followed by two sons, Alexander George in 1818 and George in 1819. As for his Métis offspring in Canada, one son, Andrew, became a fur trader, but Daniel Harmon reported "he departed this life" at Fort Vermillion in 1809.

In 1799, Alexander Mackenzie discreetly sent fifty pounds to Roderic to provide for a "Mrs. Mackenzie" of Trois Rivières, adding, "This sum I mean to continue to her annually while Kitty remains single." Possibly Kitty was a daughter from his marriage to the Catt. While attending the unveiling of the Mackenzie Monument at Bella Coola in 1927, Provincial Archivist John Hosie met a young man in the area who claimed to be a descendant of the explorer.

On March, 12, 1820, having been to Edinburgh for medical advice about his deteriorating health (likely Bright's disease), Alexander Mackenzie died in a wayside inn, near Dunkeld, during his return journey to Avoch.

Alexander Mackenzie's achievements as an explorer have been widely touted in schoolbooks, but his role as commercial visionary remains under-appreciated.

In his Afterword to *Voyages from Montreal*, Mackenzie, the chronic dissembler, argued ironically that greater profits could be obtained if competing fur trading companies worked together, extending export markets to China and the East Indies. This global perspective echoed a trans-Pacific vision first articulated by the late-eighteenth-century geographer Alexander Dalrymple and the American world traveller John Ledyard, who had sailed to Nootka Sound with Captain Cook.

In conjunction with his plan to amalgamate fur companies, Mackenzie unsuccessfully requested a license for The Fishery and Fur Company. As articulated in a blueprint entitled *Preliminaries to the Establishment of a Permanent British Fishery and Trade in Furs Etc. on the Continent and West Coast of North America,* he hoped to oversee the establishment of a Sea Otter House at 55° north latitude and he advised the British to establish a military base at Nootka Sound, supported by a modest military presence at the mouth of the Columbia River.

John Woodworth (above) and Halle Flygare helped commemorate the controversial Alexander Mackenzie Heritage Trail from Blackwater River near Prince George to Bella Coola and published a guidebook for hikers.

Mackenzie imagined nothing less than combining, under one corporate umbrella, "the fishing in both seas, and the markets of the four quarters of the globe. Such would be the field for commercial enterprise, and incalculable would be the produce of it." The North West Company partially responded to Mackenzie's prescience by erecting posts in New Caledonia, and by mapping the Fraser and Columbia River systems. His corporate vision for the "Columbian enterprise" was partially realized with the union of the Nor'Westers and the Hudson's Bay Company in 1821. Whereas the Nor'Westers had been exclusively concerned with furs, the HBC, under George Simpson, managed to develop the NWC's string of money-losing outposts west of the Rockies into a profitable network, chiefly by his diversification of exports—as Mackenzie had insisted.

In two books, Prince George-born Brian Fawcett has written persuasively about Mackenzie, alleging he was a corporate overachiever driven by profit motives, not an altruistic explorer. Similarly, the antiquarian bookseller R.D. Hilton Smith noted, "His achievements were great, but his record of them has no inner glow." But despite deficiencies of Alexander Mackenzie's character, his unintentional influence on Canadian history was great. After he reached the Pacific Ocean by an overland route, it was only a matter of time before commercial forces resolved the remaining mysteries of geography west of the Rocky Mountains and European-style governments were installed by remote authorities.

The northern town of Mackenzie was named for Alexander Mackenzie in 1966 and there are many other names in Canada, such as the Mackenzie Highway and Mackenzie Valley, that pay tribute to his journeys.

To mark and commemorate Mackenzie's overland route to the Pacific, a 279-mile heritage trail from Blackwater River near Prince George to Bella Coola was formally established in 1987 but Aboriginals in the Chilcotin have steadily opposed the affixation of Mackenzie's name to the centuries-old Nuxalk-Carrier grease trail, arguing it is a route that Alexander Mackenzie neither devised nor discovered.

SIMON FRASER

"I have never seen anything to equal this country, for I cannot find words to describe our situation at times. . . . We had to pass where no human should venture." —SIMON FRASER, IN THE FRASER CANYON, 1808

Simon Fraser was born to Roman Catholic parents on the eve of the American Revolution on May 20, 1776, in the hamlet of Mapleton, Hoosick Township, Vermont. His mother Isabel Fraser (neé Grant) was from Duldreggan, Scotland; his father Simon Fraser, Sr., was from Culbokie, Scotland.

Embarking from Fort William on the west coast of Scotland, the Frasers had emigrated on the *Pearl* in 1773, along with 425 clansmen from the Highlands. Relatively well-off, Simon Fraser,

Sr., was able to purchase a quarter section of land and raise extensive livestock, but he soon became embroiled in territorial squabbles over jurisdiction between New York and Vermont. The bitter turmoil was essentially religious: most Scottish immigrants were Roman Catholics and the Vermont secessionists were mostly Anglican.

Having had New York title to almost 25 hectares of his best cropland declared void in Vermont, Fraser, Sr., sided with Britain when civil strife erupted into the American Revolutionary War. He and his eldest son William enlisted in the Queen's Loyal Rangers commanded by Colonel John Peters. Wounded and captured on the battlefield during the Battle of Bennington in 1777, a decisive battle during which the United Empire Loyalists were defeated by the upstart Americans, Fraser, Sr., was placed in a crowded Albany jail where he died amid sordid conditions in 1779.

Stripped of her property rights, in poor health, with her household looted by her neighbours, and her collection of Gaelic books destroyed, Isabella Grant and her children were banished by the rebel colonies shortly after her husband's death. At age fifty, when the Americans emerged victorious against the British forces, she and her seven remaining children fled to Canada, settling near Cornwall, Ontario.

Fortunately for Simon Fraser, the North West Company under Simon McTavish was managed with Highland clannishness. An age-old alliance between the McTavishes and the Frasers had continued overseas from Scotland. Simon Fraser was able to attain an introductory position as a sixteen-year-old clerk in 1792 with the assistance of his uncle Captain John Fraser, a judge of the Court of Common Pleas in Montreal. This uncle had been prominent in the Fraser's Highlanders regiment in Quebec and later became a member of the Legislative Council.

Sent to the Athabasca region in 1793, Fraser quickly rose through the ranks and was appointed one of the company's youngest partners in 1801. Although Fraser was a forceful character, it helped a great deal to have relatives in high places.

BRUCE LAMB PHOTO FROM OUTPOSTS & BUSHPLANES (HANCOCK HOUSE)

The Fort McLeod trading post founded by Simon Fraser remained operational until the early 1960s, manned by well-respected old-timer Justin McIntyre (wearing suspenders).

By 1805, having risen to the rank of shareholder, Simon Fraser was given the task of expanding operations west of the Rockies and exploring the river presumed to be the Columbia.

While heading the first European-led exploratory expedition into the Peace River area, Fraser built four trading posts, most notably Fort McLeod at McLeod Lake, an encampment that has endured as the oldest permanent European settlement west of the Rocky Mountains.

Fraser also founded Fort George (now known as Prince George), Rocky Mountain Portage House (the beginnings of Hudson's Hope), Fort St. James on Stuart Lake and Fort Fraser on Fraser Lake.

For the winter of 1806–1807, Fraser remained at Fort St. James where he took a country wife, abandoning her in the spring. Describing the rough territory west of the Rocky Mountains and north of the 49th parallel as a "land of brown heath and shaggy wood," Fraser named this inland area New Caledonia—even though he had never seen Scotland.

Determined to find a waterway to ship furs from New Caledonia to the Pacific Ocean, the thirty-two-year-old explorer began his expedition down the Fraser River from Stuart Lake on May 22, 1808, with four canoes and approximately twenty NWC employees.

The expedition included clerks John Stuart, aged twenty-two, and Jules-Maurice Quesnel, aged twenty-nine, and two Aboriginal guides. The other men recorded in Fraser's diary were French Canadians: La Chappelle, Baptiste, D'Alaire, La Certe, Jean Baptiste, Boucher, Gagnier Bourbonnais and La Garde.

Spring was not the best season to have chosen for the trip; on June 2, Fraser noted a rise of eight feet in one day. His men increasingly had to portage their canoes to avoid dangerous areas. Aboriginals and John Stuart advised him to renounce the river route in favour of horses, but Fraser was keenly aware of the necessity to develop waterways for trade.

"Going to the sea by an indirect way was not the object of the undertaking," he wrote. "I therefore would not deviate."

In addition to opening a viable shipping route for the fur trade, Fraser was eager to rival the accomplishments of Sir Alexander Mackenzie and produce an equally popular journal. He would later recall for his readers, "It was a desperate undertaking!"

Upon reaching Camosin (Lytton), where a much clearer river flowed into the muddy waters of his river, Fraser decided to name the other greenish river after NWC share-holder David Thompson, presuming incorrectly that Thompson was exploring its headwaters.

Fraser's party could not ride their canoes through the harrowing rapids of the Fraser Canyon. They cached their canoes near

Simon Fraser led by Aboriginal guides across the Fraser Canyon, in a painting by John Innes

Aboriginal and Métis assistants and guides have tended to be under-acknowledged in journals, and their place in history is rarely appreciated. There are no reliable portraits of the individuals who travelled with Alexander Mackenzie and Simon Fraser in the early 1800s. As well, voyageurs and First Nations guides were seldom portrayed as individuals in the many fanciful works of art that depict the era. A lone exception was generated eleven years later by the Lewis and Clark expedition sent to counteract Mackenzie's trek to the Pacific. After the Mandan chief Sheheke (or Shé-he-ke, meaning Coyote) had provided integral assistance to Lewis and Clark at Fort Mandan in the winter of 1804–1805, he was brought to Washington, D.C., where he was given a medal. Known to Lewis and Clark as "Big White," Sheheke remained in the eastern United States for a year, during which time an exacting portrait of him was made, with the aid of physionotrace, by Charles Balthazar Julen Fevret de Saint Mémin. Born about 1765, Sheheke, was also known to the fur trader Alexander Henry (the Younger) as "Le Gros Blanc." He was killed during a fight with the Sioux.

Lytton and travelled by land to the lower end of the canyon. In his journal, Fraser described their Indiana Jones-like progress with precarious rope ladders. In the deadliest sections, Aboriginals carried their ninety-pound shoulder packs of supplies.

After circumventing Hell's Gate, dugouts could once more be used. Near the present-day site of Yale, Fraser and his men absconded with one canoe after its owner refused to sell it.

The final stretch was equally dangerous and unpredictable. Initially, near the site of present-day Fort Langley, Fraser was able to acquire the temporary use of a large canoe in order to proceed to the mouth of the river, but overnight thefts of some possessions resulted in physical confrontations. Fraser had to use his considerable wits to convince the chief to allow his expedition to proceed.

Opposite the site of present-day New Westminster, Kwantlens forewarned Fraser of fearsome people at the mouth of the river, the Musqueam, whereupon his Aboriginal escorts refused to accompany him further.

For the first time, Fraser was unable to honour the protocol of sending an emissary in advance to apprise the Musqueam of his pending arrival.

Upon reaching the Gulf of Georgia on July 2, forty days after he began, Simon Fraser calculated his latitude was 49° north. He knew the mouth of the Columbia was located at latitude 46°20', so it was obvious he had not found the mouth of the Columbia, as hoped.

Just as Alexander Mackenzie was not able to tarry long when he reached waters of the Pacific Ocean, Fraser was met with hostility by the Musqueam band and barely escaped with his life. "The warriors made their appearance from every direction, howling like so many wolves, and brandishing their war clubs."

A frantic struggle to retain control of their canoe ensued, forcing Fraser to retreat up the river, pursued by both Musqueams and Kwantlens, only to be forced to return the canoe to its owners, who also became hostile. "It was then," Simon Fraser wrote, "that our situation might really be considered as critical. [We were] placed upon a small sandy island, few in number without canoes, without provisions, and surrounded by upwards of 700 barbarians. However, our resolution did not forsake us."

Half-starved, exhausted, and sleep-deprived, Fraser's men threatened mutiny until he persuaded them all to take a vow of mutual allegiance. Fraser recorded in his diary that he would never have tackled the dangers of the canyon had he known the outcome of his journey.

Not only had Simon Fraser discovered the Fraser River was not the Columbia, his journal could serve as evidence that it was not navigable for fur trading purposes. But Fraser had duplicated the career of Alexander Mackenzie in one respect: each man had discovered his own River of Disappointment and those two rivers bear their names today. Thompson would soon designate "Fraser's River" on one of his maps.

It took Simon Fraser and his men 33 days to return upriver to Fort George. Along the way he overcame harassment from Aboriginals along the riverbanks and dissent within his own ranks for refusing to switch to an overland route.

Fraser subsequently served at posts on the Mackenzie and Athabasca Rivers. Placed in charge of the Red River Department

in 1811, he reputedly declined a knighthood because it might entail too much
expense to maintain.

By 1816, competition between the
Hudson's Bay Company and the North
West Company was so fierce that Aborigi-
nals were sometimes encouraged to kill
members of rival companies. On June 19,
Aboriginals killed twenty Red River set-
tlers in what came to be known as the
Seven Oaks Massacre.

The only known possible
profile of Simon Fraser

Since Simon Fraser had been present
at Seven Oaks, when Lord Selkirk took Fort William in retalia-
tion, Fraser and some of his fellow NWC owners were arrested as
accessories to murder and sent to Montreal for trial. They were
acquitted.

Having made a small fortune in the fur trade, Simon Fraser
left the North West Company after his trial and returned to his
family-owned land near Cornwall, Ontario, in 1818, where he
operated mills and a farm. On June 7, 1820, at age forty-four, he
married Catherine MacDonell of Matilda, Ontario. They had five
sons and three daughters.

Simon Fraser died on August 18, 1862, at the age of eighty-six.
His wife died the following day and they were buried in the same
grave at St. Andrews West cemetery in Ontario.

According to journalist Stephen Hume, who believes Simon
Fraser ought to be glorified as the founder of British Columbia,
there are at least 37 place names honouring Fraser in the province. Officially opened on September 9, 1965, the university atop
Burnaby Mountain in Burnaby is named Simon Fraser University
because the Fraser River is visible from its location.

The much-circulated profile of Simon Fraser by an unknown
artist cannot be authenticated as a genuine likeness, but it remains the only purported portrait of the man once described as
"that square, bushy-haired fellow with a face like a thundercloud."
A painting of Simon Fraser clinging to the cliff-face in Fraser

Canyon, by John Innes, as well as the heroic image of Fraser at the front of a canoe, leading the way through rapids, by C.W. Jefferys, are also well-known.

The relative lack of biographical details about Simon Fraser is complicated by the fact that University of Toronto librarian W. Stewart Wallace, in his book *The Pedlars and Other Papers on the Nor'Westers*, has identified four other Simon Frasers in the fur trade, and two of these were also partners in the North West Company.

Prominent in the Fraser's Highlanders, an older Simon "Bonhomme" Fraser was a cousin of Simon McTavish. He had a son, also named Simon Fraser, who became a NWC shareholder and died in London in 1796.

A third Simon Fraser of Ste. Anne's, born about 1760, was elected as a member of the Beaver Club in 1803 and remained active until 1816. The fifth and final Simon Fraser during the era of the North West Company was a clerk who was present at the NWC's annual meeting in 1821.

DAVID THOMPSON

"Thompson was indeed among the most literary of explorers."
—RICHARD GLOVER

". . . the ways of Providence are unknown to us." —DAVID THOMPSON

Born in London, England, on April 30, 1770, David Thompson was the son of parents with Welsh heritage, but he can't properly be described as a Welshman. "In David Thompson's letters and manuscripts," says Victor Hopwood, a leading authority on Thompson's writing, "I found nothing about Wales or the Welsh, nothing to indicate he ever thought of himself as Welsh."

David Thompson's father was buried in a pauper's grave before David Thompson turned three. At age seven he was accepted into London's Grey Coat School, a charity institution near Westminster Abbey for both boys and girls of "piety and virtue." There he excelled at spelling, penmanship, mathematics, navigation and literature. Books such as *Robinson Crusoe, Gulliver's Travels* and *Tales of the Arabian Nights* kindled his spirit for adventure.

In 1784, at age fourteen, Thompson gained a position with the Hudson's Bay Company as an indentured apprentice after his school paid the Honourable Company five pounds to accept him. Having been given a Hadley's quadrant and a copy of Robertson's two-volume *Elements of Navigation* as graduation gifts, Thompson sailed on the HBC ship *Prince Rupert*, stopped at Stromness on the Orkney Islands as the last port of call, and arrived in Rupert's Land for his seven-year apprenticeship.

He arrived in the New World, at Fort Churchill on Hudson Bay, on September 1, 1784, and was at first disappointed by his limited responsibilities. At Fort Churchill, as well as at York Factory, 150 miles to the south, Thompson discovered, ". . . neither writing or reading was required. And my only business was to amuse myself, in winter growling at the cold and in the open season, shooting Gulls, Ducks, Plover and Curlews, and quarrelling with Musketoes [mosquitoes] and Sand Flies."

During this period, he copied some of Samuel Hearne's journals of exploration and took advantage of Joseph Colen's impressive library at York Factory, containing 1400 volumes. He also bought his own copies of Milton's *Paradise Lost* and Samuel Johnson's *Rambler*.

Transferred to forts on the Saskatchewan River, Thompson was introduced to the birchbark canoe in 1786 and passed the winter of 1787 with Peigan Indians, learning their language and customs. He later observed: "Writers on the Indians always compare them with themselves, who are all white men of education. This is not fair. Their noted stoic apathy is more assumed than real. In public, the Indian wishes it to appear that nothing affects him. But in private, he feels and expresses himself sensitive to every-

Alice Saltiel-Marshall painted this commissioned portrait of how David Thompson might have appeared at age thirty-seven when he first crossed Howse Pass in 1807. The period style is based on the portrait of Alexander Mackenzie by Sir Thomas Lawrence.

thing that happens to him or his family. On becoming acquainted with the Indians I found almost every character in civilized society can be traced to them—from the gravity of a judge to a merry jester, from open-hearted generosity to the avaricious miser."

When Thompson broke his leg in an accident two days before Christmas in 1788, the injury turned out to be fortuitous. Months later, as an invalid, he was sent on a sleigh to Cumberland House where he was able to further his aptitude for surveying and astronomy by studying with the cartographer and "practical astronomer" Philip Turnor. Using a sextant, a compass, thermometers, watches and a *Nautical Almanac*, Thompson was able to survey most of northern Manitoba and Saskatchewan for his employers between 1792 and 1796. Although he was rewarded with pay increases and promoted, Thompson felt his employers did not fully grasp his potential.

Feeling under-employed by the HBC, Thompson accepted an offer to work for the rival North West Company in 1797. In the aftermath of the Treaty of Paris in 1783, the NWC needed someone to tell them whether their existing forts lay within the boundaries of Canada or the United States. Having been promised map paper and a new set of drawing instruments, Thompson, at age twenty-eight, proceeded to travel more than four thousand miles in his first year with the NWC, mapping the locations of their various posts.

In 1797, Thompson discovered the source of the Mississippi River was Turtle Lake and predicted the Anglo-Saxon population of North America would eventually "far exceed the Egyptians in all the arts of civilized life." Usually accompanied by voyageurs, he roamed from the Missouri and Mississippi Rivers to Sault Ste. Marie and back to Grand Portage. Early in 1798 he first met "Mountain Indians" who piqued his interest in the largely unexplored territories of the Rocky Mountains.

While on the prairies, David Thompson met his mixed-blood wife of 57 years, fourteen-year-old Charlotte Small, daughter of the Irish-born trader Patrick Small. Charlotte's father had retired from the North West Company and returned to live in Great Britain when she was five. The couple was married in the country fashion (*au facon du nord* or *au facon du pays*) on June 10, 1799, at Île-à-la-Crosse (in present-day Saskatchewan) and had the first of their 13 children at Rocky Mountain House, a cluster of cabins in the foothills of Alberta, on the North Saskatchewan River near the Clearwater River, in 1801. Ten of their children would survive into adulthood.

While stationed at Rocky Mountain House in the winter of 1800, Thompson made his first contacts with Kootenai Aboriginals who had ventured east of the Rockies to trade, despite their fears of the hostile Peigans. "I cannot help admiring the Spirit of these brave, undaunted, but poor Kootenaes," he recalled. Aware the Peigans were notorious horse thieves who wished to retain their superiority as middle-men between the Kootenaes and the white traders, Thompson befriended the mild-mannered Kootenais and gained their trust in spite of animosities from the Peigans.

Taking along his wife, their three children and ten packhorses that bore 300 pounds of pemmican, Thompson reached the Columbia River near Golden, B.C., via Howse Pass, located southwest of Rocky Mountain House, in 1807. (According to Victor Hopwood, Howse Pass was not named by Thompson on his 1814 map in honour of North West Company trader Jasper Hawes, who manned a supply depot at Brûlé Lake, on the Athabasca River, built in 1813. Nor was it named by Thompson for his rival Hudson's Bay Company trader, Joseph Howse, who followed Thompson over the pass and took one of the first Hudson's Bay parties onto the Pacific Slope in 1810.)

At Howse Pass, Thompson reportedly let one of his horses to destroy two kegs of alcohol. "I had made it a law unto myself," he recalled, "that no alcohol should pass the Mountains in my company. . . . I wrote my partners what I had done; and that I should do the same to every keg of alcohol. And for the next six years that I had charge of the fur trade on the West side of the Mountains, no further attempts were made to introduce spirituous liquors."

Whereas the Hudson Bay Company tended to distribute raw

gin tinctured with molasses, calling it "English brandy," the Nor'Westers mostly traded with diluted raw alcohol called "licker." Frank Rasky claims in *The Taming of the Canadian West* that "where [Simon] Fraser patronized the Indians, Thompson loved them. He was the only Nor'Wester trader who refused to debauch them with rum." This statement is an exaggeration given that Thompson frequently dispensed alcohol to Aboriginals, in keeping with corporate policies, prior to 1807.

During Thompson's inaugural excursion into present-day British Columbia, one of his voyageurs, Beaulieu ("a clever active man"), took ill in May after their party was forced to butcher one of their dogs for food. The dog had been speared by a porcupine and the unfortunate Beaulieu, having eaten heartily, had ingested a porcupine quill. When Beaulieu took ill, Thompson found the end of the black quill had punctured Beaulieu between his ribs. Thompson recalled: "enlarging the place with a lancet, and applying a pair of pincers, I drew it out; and the pain ceased."

By June 22, Thompson saw the mighty Columbia River and prayed to God that he would one day see where it reached the ocean. That summer Thompson and Beaulieu established Kootenai House at Lake Windermere and the following winter they endured a three-week siege by a 40-man Peigan war party. Before he left the Kootenay region, Thompson named Windermere Lake as Kootenae Lake, and he named the north-flowing river as Kootenai River, not realizing it was the Columbia. He also named a mountain range after Admiral Horatio Nelson who had died two years earlier at the Battle of Trafalgar.

In the spring of 1808, while exploring the Kootenay and Moyie Rivers, Thompson became aware the Columbia River he sought was only approximately fifty miles to the west, but the poor condition of his men and horses prevented him reaching it. Only the reliable advice of his guide Ugly Head enabled Thompson to reunite with Charlotte and his children, thereafter returning to Rocky Mountain House in late June.

By 1809, John Jacob Astor was openly planning to build a fort for the Pacific Fur Company at the mouth of the Columbia. In return for offering the NWC a one-third interest in his Pacific enterprise, Astor proposed to William McGillivray that he grant him a half-share in their Great Lakes enterprise.

McGillivray gave his tentative assent to the deal during a visit to New York in early 1810 but stalled the American by saying any such contract would have to be confirmed by his wintering partners during their annual Fort William gathering. These directors of the NWC were not able to accept Astor's offer until July of 1810 by which time McGillivray and his colleagues in Montreal had conceived a preventative measure.

The NWC sent an urgent message to David Thompson to hasten to the mouth of the Columbia River in advance of Astor's settlement party who were intending to round the Horn in a ship called the *Tonquin*.

A Columbia brigade of four canoes, dispatched by Thompson along the Saskatchewan River in early September, reached Rocky Mountain House by late September. While Thompson was hunting for fresh provisions, his main Columbia-bound contingent was forewarned by a Peigan chief named Black Bear to proceed through Howse Pass at their peril. According to Black Bear, the Peigans were setting up a blockade to prevent the voyageurs from having further contact with the so-called Flat Heads (Kootenai). The voyageurs watched and waited, then opted to return to Rocky Mountain House.

Aware that the hostility of Blackfeet tribes could not be taken lightly, Thompson respected his men's decision. Rather than resort to violence or attempt to bribe the Peigans, he would attempt a detour on an untried route to the north, near the headwaters of the Athabasca River.

While Alexander Henry successfully diverted the attention of the Peigans with copious amounts of rum, Thompson's Columbia brigade was re-commenced with a long and arduous traverse between the Saskatchewan and Athabasca Rivers. Meanwhile news reached Rocky Mountain House that Hudson's Bay Company traders had been similarly stymied by Peigans near Canal Flats.

Attempting to cross the Rocky Mountains in December and

DAVID THOMPSON

A Gray Coat boy from London
At fourteen came over the sea
To a lonely post on Hudson Bay
To serve the H.B.C.
A seeker of knowledge,
   a dreamer of dreams
And a doer of deeds was he.

'Twas but a step from the
   factor's door
And the wilderness was there,
Rivers stretching a thousand miles,
Lakes for his thoroughfare,
And forests fresh from
   the hand of God,
Waiting his will to dare.

Where did they lead,
   these waterways?
Where did they end, those plains?
And what is the joy of the wilderness
Only its lover attains?
Ask little Whitethroat, Killoolet,
Who sings through the soft
   gray rains.

Wherever they led,
   wherever they end,
This lad must find and know.

With pole and paddle and
   slender birch,
On snowshoes over the snow,
With saddle and pack and pony track,
'Twas his dream and delight to go.

He followed the song the rivers sang
Over their pebbly bars;
By spruce and larch he tallied
   his march;
The moons were his calendars;
And well he could reckon and
   read his path
By the faithful shining stars.

Up he followed the azure thread
Of the winding branch for guide,
By rapid and reach and shingly beach,
Then over the great divide,
Then he saw a river broad and strong
Swing past in a silver tide.

Down through a maze of Canyon walls
He watched the mighty stream
Sweep on in conquering plenitude
With arrowy flight and gleam,
And knew that he had found at last
The river of his dream.

[Invermere, B.C., August, 1922]

Selected by the Canadian Authors Association to serve in the honorary position of Poet Laureate of Canada, Bliss Carman attended ceremonies on Lake Windermere in British Columbia to mark the erection of the David Thompson Memorial Fort on Canterbury Point in 1922. The pageant included Kootenay Aboriginals and someone dressed as David Thompson in period costume. Bliss Carman subsequently wrote the above poem about David Thompson finding "the river of his dream" with its "arrowy flight and gleam."

January, using an unknown route, soon took its toll on morale. Even Thompson privately confided in a letter written on December 21, "I am getting tired of such constant hard journeys; for the last 20 months I have spent only barely two months under the shelter of a hut, all the rest has been in my tent, and there is little likelihood the next 12 months will be much otherwise."

By the end of the year, Thompson's party, guided by an Iroquois named Thomas, was reduced to twelve men, four horses and eight dogs. Trudging on snowshoes through uncharted territory, enduring temperatures that dipped to 26°-below-zero, Thompson managed to discover Athabasca Pass, the main route westward for British traders thereafter, but his horses could not accompany them in the deep snow.

Reaching the crest of the pass, Thompson sent one of his voyageurs and the guide Thomas back with messages for William Henry, his NWC partner. Dogs and men floundered and faltered. "The courage of part of my men," wrote Thompson, ". . . is sinking fast. . . . When Men arrive in a strange Country, fear gathers on them from every Object."

After his party descended a 2,000-foot-glacier, three disheartened voyageurs essentially deserted, taking with them a companion who was snow-blind. Thompson and his two remaining able-bodied men, Vallade and L'Amoureux, built a twelve-by-twelve foot hut at a place to be called Boat Encampment.

After his men Pareil and Coté returned with a Cree hunter and an additional voyageur, Thompson set his mind to improvising a 25-foot canoe to be built from cedar trees, binding the planks with pine roots. It took him much of the month of March to succeed.

After some harrowing paddling and a series of portages, Thompson was able to descend the turbulent Kootenay River, buy horses at Kettle Falls, acquire four Aboriginal paddlers and a new canoe, and begin his descent of the Columbia.

Stopping to befriend the Shahaptin Indians in eastern Washington, Thompson was embarrassed to witness a ceremonial dance in which the women were naked. However, unlike most traders, he was not repelled by their different ways of living.

"The women would pass for handsome," he wrote, "if better-dressed. But they were all as cleanly as people can be without the use of soap—an article not half so much valued in civilized life as it ought to be. What would become of the beau and belle without it? Take soap from the boasted cleanliness of the civilized man, and he will not be as cleanly as the savage, who never knows its use."

Prior to reaching the mouth of the Columbia River, Thompson raised a Union Jack on July 9, 1811, and affixed a piece of paper on which he claimed the territory for Britain. "The N.W. Company of Merchants from Canada do hereby intend to erect a factory in this place for the commerce of the country around," he wrote.

But he was too late. On July 15, Thompson discovered John Jacob Astor's hired crew of former Nor'Westers had already reached the mouth of the Columbia River in March and built four log cabins at the river's mouth. This was to be Astoria, located not far from where Lewis & Clark had built their temporary Fort Clatsop some six years earlier. It would be augmented by the arrival on February 15, 1812, of an overland expedition of Astorians led by Wilson Price Hunt, having travelled for nineteen-and-a-half months from Montreal.

David Thompson's arrival was witnessed and recorded by both Alexander Ross and Gabriel Franchère. The latter noted: "Mr. Thompson had kept a regular journal and had traveled, it seemed to me, more like a geographer than a fur trader." Franchère was correct. With his sextant always at hand, David Thompson, along with eight Iroquois and voyageurs, and an interpreter, descended most of the Columbia River and proved it was a navigable route through the Rocky Mountains to the Pacific.

"The trail by which Thompson crossed the Rockies at this time," Victor G. Hopwood has noted, "later became the historic trail of the Columbia fur trade, from Jasper House on the Athabasca River to Boat Encampment at the Big Bend of the Columbia River. Its adoption first by the North West Company and later by the

Hudson's Bay Company was a tacit admission of the rightness of Thompson's earlier contention that a new trail should be found to replace the Howse Pass route across the mountains."

Thompson and his men were duly feted by the Astorians who understood he had opened the way for a thriving new fur trade on the Pacific Slope.

Thompson's alleged "failure" to reach the mouth of the Columbia River prior to the Astorians has been criticized by some Anglophiles as cowardice in the face of hostilities from Peigans who were restricting his access to Howse Pass. Helen and George Akrigg, in particular, have dubbed Thompson the "Hamlet" of the fur trade because he was not always as decisive in his movements as he might have been.

Such retrospective charges absurdly fail to appreciate that David Thompson, among all the fur traders, was the only person who was taking in everything as he went—humanity, geography, natural science and astronomy. Unlike Alexander Mackenzie and Simon Fraser, whose motivations were strictly commercial, Thompson was *not* ruthless. Often laden with furs, Thompson was thoroughly curious and concerned with maintaining civil relations with all he met. He recorded birds and weather and topography and foreign words and events in the heavens, evidently in search of knowledge as much as fame. "To ascertain the height of the Rocky Mountains above the level of the Ocean," he wrote, "had long occupied my attention."

It is difficult to imagine another fur trader observing, "No dove is more meek than the white grouse. I have often taken them from under the net, and provoked them all I could without injuring them, but all was submissive meekness, rough beings as we were, sometimes of an evening we could not help enquiring why such an angelic bird should be doomed to be the suffering prey of every carnivorous animal, the ways of Providence are unknown to us."

As a transcriber of Aboriginal myths, Thompson has been admired by the likes of poet A.J.M. Smith for his "almost Homeric freshness of vision." Rather than impose his own prejudices onto others, he made compromises with the First Nations he encountered. Bullying was not his way. His business enterprises in Ontario would later fail because he was reluctant to be aggressive in demanding monies owed to him.

Thompson grasped how the coming of the white man was drastically altering the natural order in the North American wilderness, eliminating the beaver and other animals, and degrading Aboriginal societies. Intensely self-aware, Thompson also explored his own philosophical nature by maintaining his journal writing until he reached age eighty—for twenty-two years in the West and another thirty-eight years in eastern Canada.

Upon moving his family to eastern Canada in 1812, David Thompson solemnized his marriage to Charlotte as soon as possible.

While serving as an ensign in the Sedentary Militia during the war of 1812–1814, Thompson set about making one great map that showed all of the Northwest Territory of Canada. More than ten feet long, it would take Thompson more than two years to produce, locating 78 NWC trading posts and encompassing the approximately one-and-a-half million square miles David Thompson had travelled. Thompson's unprecedented map was presented to his former employers and it hung for many years in the dining hall of the NWC headquarters at Fort William on Lake Superior. It remained in use into the next century. This map was published by the NWC in a pamphlet that became the primary source for subsequent maps.

In 1814, Thompson improved upon his first map. A copy of this version was sold by one of his sons to the Upper Canada government. It subsequently served as the basic map of Western Canada for much of the nineteenth century. This second map, in Thompson's own words, "embraces the region lying between 45 and 60 degrees North latitude and 84 and 124 West longitude comprising the surveys and discoveries of 20 years, namely the discovery and survey of the Oregon Territory to the Pacific Ocean, the survey of the Athabasca Lake, Slave River and Lake from which flows Mackenzie's River to the Arctic Sea by Mr. Phillip Turner

C.W. Jefferys' illustration of David Thompson using the sextant

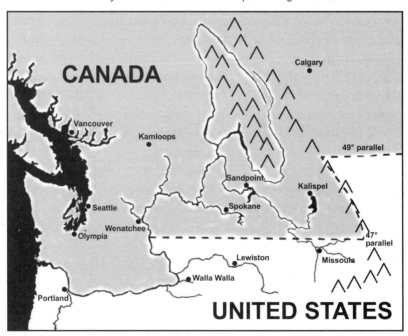

Map of David Thompson's proposed border

the route of Sir Alexander Mackenzie in 1792 down part of Frasers River together with the survey . . . by the late John Stewart of the North West Company."

Thompson continued to refine his cartography, sending improved versions of his maps to Britain in 1826 and 1843. These became the property of the British Museum and the Public Records Office in London. It is seldom noted that David Thompson also drew the map that appeared in Alexander Mackenzie's *Voyages from Montreal*, published in 1801, a work that incorporated Thompson's extensive cartography work up to 1800. Mackenzie rarely, if ever, accorded any credit to others.

David Thompson was never properly recognized or well-paid for his labours. "His employers permitted London cartographers, like the firm of Arrowsmith, to publish his discoveries," wrote Richard Glover in *BC Studies*, "—an act which Professor Hopwood describes as 'pirating.' This term is hardly correct, for Thompson's maps were the property of the employers who had paid him to make them. The result was nevertheless unfortunate. It caused the world that used Thompson's splendid maps to be denied almost all knowledge of their author."

Following the Treaty of Ghent, Thompson worked for at least ten years (1816–1826) as the British surveyor and astronomer for an international boundary commission that defined the border between Canada and the United States from the St. Lawrence River island of St. Regis to Lake of the Woods, near what is now the Ontario-Manitoba border. He spent his summers mostly in the field and his winters at Williamstown, preparing his maps. When the American-appointed surveyor resigned halfway through this project, he was not replaced. Such was Thompson's trustworthiness and competence that his work was accepted as correct by both sides.

His work for the Boundary Commission included the difficult task of finding the most north-westerly point of the Lake of the Woods. This work was undertaken after it was discovered a 1755 map by John Mitchell map had erroneously depicted the most northerly reaches of the Mississippi River. Thompson had already made more than a dozen trips through Lake of the Woods, but the exacting process of ensuring Rat Portage (modern-day Kenora, Ontario) lay within Canadian territory took him several more years to complete. This difficult accomplishment has been documented by historian and cartography expert David Malahar who has located some of the cairns that were placed by Thompson around the north-westerly shores of the lake.

When David and Charlotte Thompson purchased their farm and house at Williamstown, Glengarry County, in 1815, they already had five surviving children. Six more were born in the house that was previously occupied by Reverend John Bethune, who had introduced Presbyterianism to Upper Canada. The first of these six, Elizabeth, was born on April 25, 1817; the last of these, Eliza, was born on March 4, 1829.

Family life was hard. The bankruptcy of McGillivray, Thain and Company, which owed Thompson 400 pounds, combined with Thompson's tendency to forgive the debts of others, placed him in a precarious financial situation.

Thompson rented out eight properties, from small lots to 36-hectare farms, but he was unable to meet his own mortgage payments when his tenants were unable to pay their rents in the early 1830s. He also tried operating a general store, a tavern and potash production facilities.

David Thompson was forced to work for twenty years as a private surveyor in Glengarry County, Ontario. His varied assignments in the Muskoka Lakes area, the Eastern Townships near Sherbrooke, along the shores of Lake St. Peter south of Montreal, and along the St. Lawrence River, were extensive but his earnings were slight. His eyesight severely worsened. Thompson was forced to leave Williamstown, bankrupt, with his family, at age sixty-five.

Despite his 28 years in the fur trade, Thompson was eventually forced to sell his sextant and other instruments to buy food for his family. He even pawned his overcoat. After borrowing two shillings and sixpence from a friend, he wrote his final journal entry: "Thank God for this relief."

David Thompson died poverty-stricken on February 10, 1857, in Longueuil, Quebec. Charlotte Thompson died three months later.

A son-in-law purchased a burial plot on Mount Royal for David and Charlotte Thompson but the site in Section C, Lot 507, remained unmarked until geographer Joseph B. Tyrrell erected a modest monument there in 1927. He also arranged for Thompson's succinct epitaph on the tombstone: "The greatest practical land geographer that the world has produced."

David Thompson, the orphaned apprentice from Grey Coat School, mapped the main travel routes for approximately 1,200,000 square miles of Canada and 500,000 square miles in the United States, travelling more than 80,000 miles by foot, canoe and horse.

He also traced the Columbia River to its source, established the first Columbia River trading post, surveyed the headwaters of the Mississippi and pioneered the use of Athabasca Pass—to name only a few of his achievements prior to 1813.

Despite such accomplishments, David Thompson's name is lesser known than that of his contemporaries, Simon Fraser and Alexander Mackenzie.

David and Charlotte Thompson's home in Williamstown, Ontario, renamed the Bethune-Thompson House, has been preserved as a heritage site, and some of his instruments have been recovered by the Ontario Archives. The Royal Ontario Museum contains one of the two gigantic maps Thompson made for the North West Company to locate accurately the major drainages on both sides of North America north of the forty-fifth parallel. David Thompson Highway #11 connects Red Deer to Rocky Mountain House National Historic Site, but Thompson, Manitoba, is *not* named in Thompson's honour. (Instead it is named for INCO chairman John F. Thompson.) Rocky Mountain House has a David Thompson sextant.

The man who earned the nickname "Koo-koo-sint" (meaning "the man who looks at the stars" in the language of Nez Percé Indians) never saw the Thompson River, the longest tributary of the Fraser River, named after him in 1808 by Simon Fraser.

Following the closure of short-lived David Thompson University-College in Nelson, British Columbia, in 1984, the David Thompson Cultural Society continues to organize social and cultural presentations for the Nelson community.

In 2005, a David Thompson exhibit at Spokane's Northwest Museum of Art and Culture opened to present Thompson's journals, maps, and mountain sketches, along with field sketches by artists Paul Kane and Henry James Warre.

With the advent of the David Thompson 2007 Bicentennial initiatives to commemorate Thompson's arrival in British Columbia, there is growing agreement that Thompson's cartography, his endurance, his consistent respect for Aboriginal peoples, his pathfinding, his versatility in at least six languages and his prodigious literary legacy qualify him as the most under-celebrated hero in Canadian history.

No other fur trader spent more time outside forts rather than in them. No other person in the Canadian fur trade was more faithful, diligent and articulate.

David Thompson not only opened the route for commerce that would connect both sides of the North American continent, pioneering the use of the Columbia River for trade, his cross-continental astronomy and cartography became the basis for depicting the geography of Canada and much of the United States for a half-century.

In the words of Katherine Gordon, in her study of land surveying in British Columbia, *Made to Measure*, "Thompson laboured over detailed measurements of the lengths of rivers and the heights of mountains he observed, contributing astoundingly accurate information to the burgeoning material available to British cartographers. Unable to use the heavy and bulky marine chronometers available to Vancouver and his ocean-going counterparts, Thompson resorted to the use of a basic watch combined with astronomical observations to determine longitude. His methods were reliable: he painstakingly and repeatedly observed lunar eclipses of Jupiter's moons, then compared the time difference between observations at his location and at Greenwich. If Jupiter for some reason wasn't visible, Thompson measured the angle of the moon against two fixed astronomical bodies instead.

"Thompson's greatest asset was his diligence in recording thousands of observations over the years in his journals, then following them up by physically surveying the ground between his fixed points to fill in the details."

Thompson's fame might have been secured if he had been able to edit and publish his 39 journals in his lifetime. Joseph Tyrrell purchased Thompson's unfinished manuscript and his journals, then provided an edited version of Thompson's explorations and accomplishments in *David Thompson's Narrative of his Explorations in Western America, 1784–1812,* first published in Toronto in 1916.

It is difficult to celebrate Thompson without a portrait. In his 1850 travel book entitled *The Shoe and Canoe,* British army surgeon and geologist John Jeremiah Bigsby published the following description of Thompson arising from an 1823 canoe trip for the Boundary Commission.

"His figure was short and compact, and his black hair was worn long all round, and cut square, as if by one stroke of the sheers, just above the eyebrows. His complexion was of the gardener's ruddy brown, while the expression of his deeply furrowed features was friendly and intelligent, but his shortened nose gave him an odd look. His speech betrayed the Welshman, although he left his native hills when very young. I afterwards traveled much with him. He was a very powerful mind and had a singular faculty of picture making."

Bigsby's description of Thompson, as well as pictures of Thompson's 30-year-old grandson, have served as references for a new, imaginary portrait by Alice Saltiel-Marshall of Canmore, Alberta, to coincide with David Thompson Bicentennial celebrations organized from Invermere, B.C. It is an attempt to portray how Thompson might have looked in 1807 when he first crossed Howse Pass, on the Alberta/British Columbia border, and made contact with the Columbia River. Howse Pass has since been touted as a possible highway route to shorten the driving time between Vancouver and Edmonton.

GEORGE SIMPSON

"My orders are not to be disputed." —GEORGE SIMPSON, 1820

"He surely could say of the Hudson's Bay Company, as Augustus Caesar said of Rome, that he found it brick and left it marble."
—F.W. HOWAY, 1939

Known as the Little Emperor, George Simpson was governor-in-chief of the Hudson's Bay Company, the most powerful organization of its time in Canada, overseeing an area larger than western Europe. Described by his subordinate John Tod as "that crafty fox," Simpson played a major role in the evolution of British Columbia. It was Simpson's decision to combine the fur trading domains of New Caledonia (interior B.C.) and Columbia (Columbia River and lower West Coast) that led to the establishment of a string of new forts within present-day B.C., starting with Fort Langley (1827).

"The trade of this side of the mountains [the Rockies]," he wrote, "if properly managed I make bold to say can not only be made to rival, but to yield double the profit that any other part of North America does for the Amount of Capital employed therein but in order to turn it to the best advantage New Caledonia must be included and the Coasting trade must be carried on in conjunction with the inland business."

Previously the nineteenth-century forts and trading posts west of the Rockies included Fort McLeod (1805), Fort Nelson (1805), Fort Fraser (1806), Fort St. James (Stuart Lake Fort, Fort New

Caledonia, 1806), Fort George (1807), Kootenae House (1807), Fort Astoria (1811) and Fort Thompson (Shewaps Fort, 1812).

New forts and posts that arose under Simpson's jurisdiction prior to 1850 would include Fort Alexandria (1821, not to be confused with Fort Alexander in present-day Manitoba), Fort Babine (1822), Fort Vancouver (1825), Fort Connolly (1827), Fort Chilcotin (1829), Fort Halkett (1829; 1832), Fort Simpson (aka Fort Nass, 1831), Fort McLoughlin (1833), Fort Essington (1835), Dease Lake Post (1838), San Francisco (aka Yerba Buena, 1839), Honolulu (1839), Fort Stikine (1840), Fort Yaku (aka Fort Durham, 1840), Fort Victoria (aka Fort Camosun, 1843), Fort Youcoun (1847), Fort Yale (1848) and Fort Hope (1848).

Simpson also decided that the Hudson's Bay Company ought to compete with the Americans and Russians in the maritime fur trade, resulting in the arrival of the first steam-powered ship on the West Coast, the *Beaver*.

In 1670, King Charles II had afforded control of much of British North America to the London-based Hudson's Bay Company for the purpose of harvesting furs. Faced with increased rivalry from the mainly Scottish traders of the Montreal-based North West Company, the Hudson's Bay Company was reconstituted in 1821 to include the NWC upstarts and to retain its monopoly position. This amalgamation had been under consideration since 1816. With amalgamation, the HBC/NWC essentialy gained control of all fur trading from Labrador to Oregon, and from the Red River to the Yukon. At this time, there were so few "settlers" in Western Canada that the HBC would continue to carry all letters for any persons free of charge until 1845.

At age twenty-three, George Simpson arrived in Canada in 1820 as a London-trained bookkeeper. His potential had been recognized by one of the HBC directors, Andrew Colville, who, as historian George Woodcock put it, "was related to him on the wrong side of the blanket." Simpson had been born out of wedlock at Dingwall in Ross-shire, Scotland, in either 1792 (according to the National Dictionary of Biography) or else in 1787, the date supplied on his tombstone in Montreal. Either way, it is known that Simpson was raised by relatives, not his parents. His subsequent attitudes towards women were possibly affected by his less than secure upbringing.

As a novice, Simpson spent his first winter at Norway House on Lake Winnipeg. At the time, the HBC's governor for North America, William Williams, was operating under considerable duress because the Nor'Westers had warrants for his arrest. The HBC needed another man "on the ground" in case Williams was apprehended. In 1820, Williams

George Simpson's profile from his Narrative of a Journey Round the World During the Years 1841–1842

sent his new deputy, George Simpson, westward with a brigade of voyageurs to get acquainted with the operations and possibly relieve some tensions with the North West Company. According to historian Douglas McKay, Simpson was sent to the Athabasca District, "the very storm centre of the fur trade battle and the last stronghold of the enemy [Nor'Westers]."

Upon amalgamation in 1821, Simpson took charge of the Northern Department, an area that included much of Western Canada and parts of the United States, and took measures to reassure disgruntled Nor'Westers that they were welcomed by their former rivals in the HBC. According to John Tod's eyewitness report of Simpson's diplomacy, "Their previously stiffened features began to relax a little; they gradually but slowly mingled together, and a few of the better disposed, throwing themselves unreservedly in the midst of the opposite party, mutually shook each other by the hand."

To further limit acrimony from his former enemies, Simpson afforded control of the New Caledonia, Columbia, Athabasca and Mackenzie River trading districts to Nor'Westers, placing Nor'Westers in charge of eighteen out of 25 fur-trade districts in all. Simpson then proceeded to rationalize the operations that he felt were mismanaged, reducing the company's staff by more than 50 percent by 1825, and also reducing wages. In his campaign for frugality he was aided by Archibald McDonald, a fellow trader he had met during his stint in the Athabasca District the previous year. After McDonald arrived at the mouth of the Columbia River in 1821, the two men corresponded extensively. McDonald completed a report in 1822 that was critical of the wastefulness and self-indulgence that had prevailed in four NWC posts in the Columbia District—Fort George (Astoria), Spokane House, Fort Walla Walla and Thompson River (Forts Okanagan and Kamloops).

When Simpson went west to survey the situation for himself in 1824–1825, he was critical of everything he saw west of the Rockies. ". . . if my information is correct," he wrote, "the Columbia Department from the day of its origin to the present hour has been neglected, shamefully mismanaged and a scene of the most wasteful extravagance and the most unfortunate dissension. It is high time the system should be changed and I think there is an ample field for reform and amendment."

George Simpson meant business—and little else. Upon visiting Fort George in 1824, he wrote, "Extravagance has been the order of the day." For the sake of efficiency, not morality, he tried to reverse the HBC custom of supplying liquor to Indians. "His password was economy," wrote historian F.W. Howay. "Economy in the use of food; economy in supplies; economy in Indian credits; economy in wages and in every expenditure."

Simpson was present at the ceremonial christening of Fort Vancouver on the Columbia River on March 19, 1825. Simpson travelled extensively, preferably with a Scottish piper and a flag flying from the stern of his specially made, over-sized canoe whenever he approached a trading post. He was a demanding judge of his personnel, maintaining a private "Character Book" in which he kept track of his opinions. The entry for Chief Trader Alexander McLeod, for example, described him as "a most overbearing Tyrannical fellow." He is said to be "arrogant; does not confine himself to plain matter of fact, annoys everyone near him with details of his own exploits; 'I did this,' 'I did that' and 'I did the other thing' continually in his mouth, but it unfortunately happens that he rarely does anything well."

Ending their visits to forts in New Caledonia in 1828, Simpson's party learned first-hand that the Fraser River could not serve as a viable trade route to enable Fort Langley to serve as the HBC's principal depot on the Pacific. "I should consider the passage down, to be certain Death, in nine attempts out of ten," he wrote. After a week at Fort Langley, Simpson and his large party encountered hostile Aboriginals in the Puget Sound area in the aftermath of bloody reprisals conducted by Chief Trader A.R. McLeod whose HBC contingent had killed more than twenty Aboriginals in the Clallum country.

Simpson addressed the problems of coastal transport and shipping by writing his superiors in London in 1832 to request a steam vessel. "We have no idea what the cost of such a Vessel might be," he concluded, "but should not consider her too expensive at about 6,000 pounds." The idea to acquire such a vessel was first supplied by John McLoughlin who later opposed his own opinion on the grounds that "we ought not to open a new Channel of expense." The Company decided in Simpson's favour on this issue on March 5, 1834.

The 109-ton *Beaver*, under Captain David Home, left Gravesend, England, under sails with the *Columbia*, under Captain William Darby, on August 27, 1835. Both ships anchored at Fort Vancouver on April 10, 1836. After it was outfitted with its own cargo of engines and paddlewheels in Fort Vancouver, the 101-foot-long *Beaver* dramatically improved communications on the West Coast with its 70-horsepower engines and a maximum speed of nine and three-quarters miles an hour. This ship greatly diminished the HBC's reliance on forts. Although it was not the first steam-powered ship in the Pacific Ocean, as is often presumed, it was the first to operate in the North Pacific.

Simpson was based at the HBC's Canadian headquarters at Lachine Rapids, near Montreal, as of 1833. In 1839, Simpson, the bean-counter, was made Governor-in-Chief of all Hudson's Bay Territories, not just the northern department, and he would retain that position as "the Little Emperor" until 1860.

He went on a trans-global expedition, via Siberia, in 1841–1842, and published a two-volume journal of his adventures. One volume of his travel memoir concerns his journey across Canada on horseback and by canoe, and includes visits to California; the other mostly concerns Hawaii and Simpson's journey across Siberia. A map traces his path. In her book *The Canadian Rockies: Early Travels and Explorations*, Esther Fraser has dubbed Simpson "Banff's First Tourist" even though he was travelling for business reasons. Simpson's entourage frequently covered 40 to 50 miles per day. He arrived at Fort Vancouver on August 25, 1841.

During this expedition, Simpson became the "grandfather" of British Columbia by recommending the creation of Fort Victoria. While travelling with James Douglas to Sitka, Alaska, for talks with the Russians, the two men discussed the possibilities of replacing Fort Vancouver on the Columbia with an alternate HBC trading headquarters somewhere to the north.

"The Southern end of Vancouver's Island forming the Northern side of the Straits of De Fuca," Simpson wrote, "appears to be the best situation for such an establishment. . . . I had not an opportunity for landing on the southern end of the Island, but from the distant view we had of it in passing between Puget's Sound and the Gulf of Georgia and the report of C.F. McLoughlin and others who have been there, we have every reason to believe there will be no difficulty in finding an eligible situation in that quarter for the establishment in question."

George Simpson was knighted in 1841. As Sir George Simpson, he was necessarily involved in the machinations during the 1840s to acquire Vancouver Island as a proprietory responsibility for the Hudson's Bay Company, but he could be less than enthusias-

Re-enactment of George Simpson entering Fort St. James, 1924

tic about the potential long term benefits. He was not supportive of colonization because he foresaw that it might impede business. "I think the capabilities of the Island are greatly overrated by Messrs Gladstone, Hume, & others who have been so severe on the Colonial Office for putting Vancouver Island under the Company's direction," he wrote to James Douglas in 1850.

Much concerned with decorum and maintaining appearances as "an exemplary bachelor," as he once put it, George Simpson maintained and discarded his mostly mixed blood mistresses with apparent ease. Prior to his marriage to his eighteen-year-old cousin Frances in London in 1830, he had fathered at least five children by four different women, including one relationship in England prior to joining the HBC. Jennifer S.H. Brown has outlined Simpson's profligate and condescending relations with Aboriginal and mixed-blood women in *Strangers in Blood*.

First there was Betsey Sinclair, daughter of Hudson's Bay factor William Sinclair and his Aboriginal wife Margaret (Nahoway) Norton, who gave birth to Simpson's child (a daughter) in 1822. In correspondence he referred to his connubial companion as "my article" and "my Japan helpmate." Simpson saw fit to discard her in 1822. He wrote to J.G. McTavish: "if you dispose of the Lady it will be satisfactory as she is an unnecessary & expensive appendage, I see no fun in keeping a Woman without enjoying her charms which my present rambling Life does not enable me to do: but if she is unmarketable I have no wish that she should be a general accommodation shop to all the young bucks at the Factory."

Later that same month, Simpson wrote to McTavish again: "White Fish seems to be favourable to procreation and had I a good pimp in my suite I might have been inclined to deposit a little of my Spawn but have become . . . vastly tenacious of my reputation." Next Simpson had two sons by Margaret Taylor, another Factor's daughter, while maintaining a liaison with another woman at his Lachine headquarters, with whom he likely also had a child. Upon marrying his cousin, Simpson made arrangements for another man to marry Taylor, as he had done in the case of Betsey Sinclair.

Simpson's attachments and detachments were not remarkable given his powerful position, but his directives to his employees on sexual matters were frequently contradictory or hypocritical. While he recommended that his inland employees "form connections with the principal families immediately on their arrival," he was quick to condemn men who took such relationships seriously, especially if such arrangements proved costly or interfered with business.

Simpson wrote, "We must really put a stop to the practise of Gentlemen bringing their Women & Children from the East to the West side of the Mountain, it is attended with much expense and inconvenience on the Voyage, business itself must give way to domestick considerations, the Gentlemen become drones and are not disposible. In short the evil is more serious than I am well able to describe."

Evidently Simpson was bereft of any appreciation for family. It was fine for men to dally with "copper-coloured mates" for pleasure, but business and pleasure must be kept separate. In 1831, he described how one trader named Robertson, after a decade

Governor George Simpson (in top hat)

of marriage to a country wife named Theresa Chalifoux, sought to introduce her to polite society at Red River: "Robertson brought his bit of Brown with him to the Settlement this Spring in hopes that she would pick up a few English manners before visiting the civilised world; but it would not do—I told him distinctly the thing was impossible, which mortified him exceedingly. . . . He takes his departure I understand tomorrow, mortified and chagrined beyond description." Racism was part of the times, but Simpson could be cruel, wielding power to emasculate or belittle others. Arrogant, cold and harsh, he retained his imperial and thrifty ways until his death in 1860.

Although it is tempting to view Simpson as an inflexible tyrant, one of British Columbia's pre-eminent historians, W. Kaye Lamb, cautioned in *BC Studies* in 1945: "It is often assumed that, so far as the fur trade was concerned, Simpson was something in the nature of a supreme being, whereas in actual fact he worked within limits and in accordance with policies that were determined in surprising detail in London. . . . The far-flung trading system that he perfected in the 'golden age' of the fur trade never became a sacred thing that he was unwilling to modify when changing conditions made this desirable. On the contrary, he was ever on the watch to see that the Company changed with the times. Thus in our own region he encouraged farming, fishing, lumbering, and mining as well as fur-trading, and if circumstances had permitted he was prepared to experiment with whaling."

Historian Theodore J. Karamanksi offers this summary: "Above all, Simpson was a man of continental vision."

JOHN MCLOUGHLIN

". . . that anomolous Mammoth McLoughlin" —EMPLOYEE JOHN TOD

Prior to James Douglas, the shrewdest and most powerful administrator in the Pacific Northwest was his mentor John McLoughlin, the white-haired "Father of Oregon" who passed along George Simpson's instructions (to Douglas) to establish Fort Victoria, having visited Vancouver Island himself in 1839. According to W.K. Lamb, "Legend has tended to exaggerate McLoughlin's stature, and to make him an incredible paragon of all virtues. . . . The man himself was less perfect but more interesting—cursed with passions and a stubbornness that made him a difficult and eventually an impossible subordinate; but blessed with a broad humanity, more than a little foresight, and a constructive mind." George Simpson initially described McLoughlin as "very zealous in the discharge of his public duties and a man of strict honor and integrity."

John McLoughlin was born near Rivière du Loup, Quebec, on October 19, 1784, to a poor Roman Catholic father and a well-born Protestant mother. Baptized as a Roman Catholic, he was raised as an Anglican and began his formal studies of medicine at age fourteen with Dr. Sir James Fisher. Upon receiving his medical license on April 30, 1803, he reputedly fled Quebec after a scuffle with a British Army officer. Having joined the North West Company, McLoughlin mainly served at Fort William, where he took an Aboriginal wife who bore him five children. Made a NWC partner in 1814, McLoughlin rose to prominence as one of the preliminary negotiators of the merger between the Nor'Westers and the Hudson's Bay Company.

McLoughlin's hair turned white in the aftermath of the murder of Robert Semple, governor of the Red River colony. Unwilling to see Aboriginals unfairly accused of the murder, McLoughlin had intervened to represent the Nor'Westers only to find himself accused of the crime. While McLoughlin was being taken across Lake Superior, the canoe capsized and several men drowned before he could be taken to trial and acquitted of all blame on October 30, 1818.

McLoughlin was appointed Chief Factor of the Hudson's Bay Company in the Columbia District in 1824, with Peter Skene Ogden to assist him. In 1825, under his direction, Fort Vancouver was built on the Columbia River's north bank, at Belle Vue Point, to supplant Fort George, formerly called Fort Astoria, as the HBC's new headquarters on the West Coast. McLoughlin remained as Chief Factor for the HBC when the Districts of New Caledonia (interior B.C.) and Columbia were united in 1826.

Tireless, responsible and humane, McLouglin adopted a relatively liberal policy of cooperation with Aboriginals, sometimes doctoring their infirmities, and became known as White-Headed Eagle. He also gained a reputation for helping hungry and exhausted overland American settlers, offering humanitarian assistance against the wishes of his British employers.

Fond of dancing and reading, McLoughlin established a library at the fort and enjoyed entertaining guests such as the Scottish botanist David Douglas, after whom the Douglas fir is named. McLoughlin initially read church services himself, prior to the arrival of the sanctimonious Rev. Herbert Beaver, with whom he quarrelled violently. McLoughlin later opened the first school west of the Rockies in 1832, with John Ball as the first teacher.

Whereas his protégé James Douglas remained a lifelong friend and admirer, the non-deferential McLoughlin began to have serious differences with Governor George Simpson, who began to worry that McLoughlin might defect and form a rival fur trading faction. By 1832, Simpson privately cited McLoughlin's "ungovernable violent temper and turbulent disposition" and presumed that McLoughlin "would be a Radical in any Country under any Government and under any circumstances." The more Simpson began to be suspicious of McLoughlin's republican sympathies, the more McLoughlin and Simpson began to disagree on company matters. Whereas McLoughlin favoured a series of trading posts for commerce, Simpson preferred an ongoing reliance on visiting ships such as the *Beaver*. Whereas McLoughlin wanted to encourage immigrants, Simpson did not.

The greatest schism between McLoughlin and Simpson arose from the tragic death of McLoughlin's second son, John Jr. Born in 1812 and sent to Montreal for schooling in 1821, McLoughlin's son lived with his great-uncle Simon Fraser in Montreal but failed to thrive. Sent to learn medicine in France with his uncle David McLoughlin, John Jr., continued to cause problems wherever he went.

Despite lacking credentials, he was granted a position as an HBC physician and dispatched to Fort Vancouver, then sent in 1840 to provide token medical services at Fort Stikine. There he gained a reputation as a volatile drunkard. At age twenty-nine, on April 20, 1842, he was shot and killed by one of his own men.

Whereas McLoughlin was convinced his namesake was murdered, Governor Simpson undertook a cursory investigation and

Although John McLoughlin, the "father of Oregon," has been criticized by pro-British historians for being overly generous to settlers, his open-mindedness deeply impressed the migrants. "Dr. McLoughlin was a perfect gentleman," recalled Daniel Waldo from Virginia. "All the Hudson's Bay men were. You will find very few men such as the old Doctor. I saw him trust an immense number of men there. He never asked them if they could ever pay or not. He gave them all the goods they wanted. We had his boats for 9 days. I wanted to pay him but he would not have a cent. I told him we had damaged the boats. He said they would 'soon mend that, soon mend that.' He was a magnificent old fellow; there are very few men better than he. We could hardly have lived if it had not been for the Hudson's Bay Co."

concluded McLoughlin's mixed-blood son was partially blame-worthy.

Animosities between McLoughlin and Simpson ensued, lead-ing to McLoughlin's eventual resignation, after he received an officious letter from Simpson that read, in part: "From all I can collect, the whole conduct & management of Mr. McLoughlin [Jr.] were exceedingly bad, and his violence when under the in-fluence of alcohol, which was very frequently the case, amount-ing to insanity. . . . The occurrence having taken place within Russian Territory, no legal steps against the parties can be taken by me; but my belief is, that any Tribunal by which the case could be tried, would find a verdict of 'Justifiable Homicide'. . . . The business of the post seems to have been very badly managed. . . . The accots [accounts], I fear, are in a very irregular state."

John McLoughlin proceeded to undertake his own thorough investigation of his elder son's death. He soon realized Simpson's judgement was superficial and simplistic, made hastily to avoid complicating his own dealings with Russian Governor Etolin at Sitka. By gathering first-hand statements, and also some vital in-telligence gleaned by James Douglas from an Iroquois named Kanaquassé who had been at Fort Stikine at the time of the death, McLoughlin was able to learn that his son had not overly taken to drink, as was alleged by Simpson's informants. Instead, his son had rightly tried to prevent his unruly staff from absconding with Company wares and trading them for sexual favours outside the fort.

Forbidden to bring Aboriginal women into the fort, and also forbidden from leaving the fort to meet their mistresses after nightfall, the men at Fort Stikine had drawn up a compact to murder their commander. John McLoughlin, Sr., became espe-cially critical of Simpson's earlier decision to remove his son's main assistant and fellow clerk Roderick Finlayson to Fort Simpson, thereby leaving his son without a forceful ally to re-strain the ne'er-do-wells who had been exiled to Fort Stikine. An audit of Fort Stikine's books further revealed that his son's book-keeping had only a discrepancy of eleven pounds. Records of his liquor consumption showed only a moderate intake, as confirmed by his country wife.

The murderers at Fort Stikine had collectively lied to Simpson. These findings were sent to Governor Pelly and the Hudson's Bay Company Committee in London. In 1843, Pelly responded: "From this evidence it appears that the murder of Mr. John McLoughlin was the result of a preconcerted plot, and that there was no just foundation for the charges of drunkenness and of excessive severity in punishing the men under his command, which were brought against him after his death." But the murderers of John McLoughlin, Jr., were never brought to trial.

Pro-British historians have alleged that John McLoughlin, Sr., essentially "sold out" Canada by helping American settlers and taking American citizenship, but likely he was responding as much to the cynicism of Hudson's Bay Company management as he was drawn to republicanism.

With the arrival of Catholic clergy, McLoughlin reverted to Catholicism in the 1840s and invited Roman Catholic missionary F.N. Blanchet to solemnize his marriage on November 19, 1842. Until his death, McLoughlin remained loyal to his second wife Marguerite, or Margaret, the mixed-blood daughter of former Nor'Wester Jean Etienne Wadin. The Scottish traders were closely knit: McLoughlin met Marguerite in 1812, the year after her husband Alexander McKay was slain aboard the *Tonquin*. McLoughlin willingly served as a father figure to her son from that previous marriage, Thomas McKay, who himself had three wives.

Family life in the hinterlands was difficult at the best of times. While on the West Coast, McLoughlin attempted to play an active role in the unhappy lives of his mixed-blood children from Fort William. McLoughlin's eldest daughter Maria Elizabeth (b. 1814) was raised by McLoughlin's sister, an Ursuline nun. After she married and her husband died, Maria received support payments from her father until his death. A second daughter, Eloisa, born at Fort William in 1817, was reputedly his favourite. She came west to join her father and married the fort's Chief Clerk,

William Glen Rae, who later committed suicide. After her second husband also died, Eloisa and her children lived with her father, then remarried in 1850.

Partially raised at Fort Vancouver, McLoughlin's son David, born at Fort William in 1821, was sent to Paris to live with his uncle. McLoughlin, Sr., persuaded him to forego a military post in Calcutta in order to learn the fur trade at Fort Vancouver. Unimpressed with life at the fort, David McLoughlin resigned from the Hudson's Bay Company in 1849, married a Kootenay Indian named Annie Grizzly, daughter of a chief, and lived for most of the time on 160 acres near the Idaho-Canadian border, squandering his sizeable inheritance before his death in 1903.

Dispirited by his disagreements with Simpson, McLoughlin chose to retire from HBC administration in 1846. In 1847, he was accorded the Knighthood of St. Gregory, bestowed by Pope Gregory. He went to Oregon City where he ran the HBC's mill and store and was elected mayor in 1851, winning 44 of 66 votes. Known for his philanthropy, he donated large amounts of property for public projects. Although McLoughlin became an American citizen, the U.S. government expropriated a substantial share of his holdings, treating him as if he were a foreigner. Nonetheless, McLoughlin died of old age, wealthy and respected, on September 3, 1857. Nobody has ever resolved the mystery, revealed in his accounts, as to why John McLoughlin was sending quarterly payments of between ten to 50 pounds, from 1838 until he died, to an unknown woman named Catherine O'Gorman.

If McLoughlin was the Father of Oregon, he was the Grandfather of British Columbia, but little is left to mark his name. Located at McLoughlin Bay on Campbell Island in Millbanke Sound, Fort McLoughlin was founded on May 23, 1833. Physician and fur trader William Fraser Tolmie worked there from 1833 to 1836. The fort was abandoned and burned to the ground in 1843. The Hudson's Bay Company built a store at McLoughlin Bay as a replacement with the advent of the steamers *Beaver* and *Otter*. This store gradually gave rise to the coastal community now called Bella Bella.

JAMES DOUGLAS

"Never break your word to an Indian, even if it is a promise to give him a licking." —JAMES DOUGLAS (ADVICE GIVEN TO SETTLER ANDREW MUIR)

"The best form of government, if attainable, [is] that of a wise and good despotism." —JAMES DOUGLAS (JOURNAL ENTRY)

A practical autocrat who married the boss's daughter—his father-in-law was Chief Factor William Connolly—James Douglas became widely regarded as the founding father of British Columbia. Born in Demerara, British Guiana (now Guyana) in 1803, Douglas was the illegitimate son of Glasgow merchant John Douglas who had business interests in Demerara. His mother was a Creole remembered as Miss Martha Ritchie, from either British Guiana or Barbados. He once wrote that he had been born on June 5, but his tombstone in Ross Bay Cemetery gives the date as August 15.

It is conceivable that James Douglas' lifelong distaste for "the abominable traffic in slaves" arose partially in response to his own mixed family background. By 1829, he was well aware that Americans were buying slaves at Cape Flattery and the Strait of Juan de Fuca, transporting them to Haida territory, and trading them for between thirty and fifty beaver pelts per person.

"This detestable traffic and the evils it gives rise to," he wrote, "are subjects of deep regret to us, but we know of no remedy within our power, or we would use it were it only for the sake of our own interest."

Although Douglas recognized that slaves had long been "the principal circulating medium on this Coast," he refused to allow Hudson's Bay Company traders to procure furs by offering hu-

mans for sale or barter, unlike many Russian and American traders, and he disdained the tradition of slavery along the Pacific
Coast.

After James Douglas' father married in Scotland in 1809 and
started a second family, James and his brother were brought to
Scotland to be educated. James attended school at Lanark, Scotland, where he gained a solid training in French, enabling him
to enter the fur trade in the service of the North West Company
at age sixteen in 1819. That year he sailed to Montreal in the brig
Matthews and spent his first winter in Canada, on the shore of
Lake Superior at Fort William, as a second-class clerk.

Known for having a violent streak for much of his trading career, Douglas fought a duel, without any fatalities, in 1821.

After the merger of the North West Company with the Hudson's Bay Company in 1821, Douglas was stationed at Île-à-la-
Crosse on the Churchill River in northern Saskatchewan. He was
briefly sent to Fort Vermilion in the Peace River region in the
summer of 1825 before he was transferred to Fort St. James on
Stuart Lake in central British Columbia. Here, in New Caledonia, he met and married Amelia Connolly, the sixteen-year-old
mixed blood daughter of Chief Factor William Connolly and his
Cree wife Miyo Nipiy, in 1828.

The Cree heritage of James Douglas' wife would prove to be a
sensitive matter for Douglas, who once advised his youngest
daughter Martha not to mention the origins of her compilation
of 14 Cowichan and six Cree stories. "I have no objection to your
telling the old stories. . . ." Douglas wrote to her, "but pray do not
tell the world they are Mamma's."

The most controversial incident in Douglas's fur trading career occurred in the year he took a wife. Back in 1823 two Aboriginals had allegedly murdered two white fur traders at Fort
George (now Prince George). Considering themselves insulted
by their victims, the pair of Indians had cut off the heads of the
two white men and they had escaped capture for five years.

One fugitive was killed at the hands of another tribe, but the
other surfaced in the Stuart Lake District in the summer of 1828

when James Douglas was temporarily in charge at Fort St. James during his father-in-law's absence. Douglas took several men with him and apprehended the alleged criminal in a nearby Carrier village. There was not a rudimentary trial or hearing. In the words of fur trader John McLean, the Hudson's Bay Company contingent "executed justice on the murderer," essentially by beating the man to death.

Douglas later recalled the incident for one of his daughters in a letter. "It was a desperate adventure," he wrote, "which nothing but a high sense of duty could have induced me to undertake." An eye for an eye, a tooth for a tooth.

Douglas' Hammurabi-like retribution earned him the enmity of the local Carrier Indian Chief Kwah (or Quah), who attacked Fort St. James and overpowered Douglas, binding him hand and foot. According to some reports, his quick-thinking wife Amelia came to his rescue, providing all manner of articles from the fort for his ransom. Another interpretation is that Douglas, threatened with a dagger until he relented, simply agreed to his captor's terms and his wife hastily provided the necessary ransom of clothes and other trade goods.

Later Douglas and two men were accosted en route to Fraser Lake, and once more threatened with death, until Douglas' unflinching attitude reportedly convinced his Indian captors to let him go.

To avoid further confrontations, Chief Factor Connolly transferred Douglas and his daughter to Fort Vancouver on January 30, 1830. Connolly recommended his son-in-law to McLoughlin by saying, "wherever he may be placed he cannot fail of being essentially useful."

Governor George Simpson agreed with this estimation. In 1832, the Little Emperor made the following assessment of Douglas in his confidential "Book of Servants' Characters":

"A Scotch West Indian; About 33 Years of Age, has been 13 years in the Service. — A stout powerful active man of good conduct and respectable abilities: — tolerably well Educated, expresses himself clearly on paper, understands our Counting House

Chief Kwah's daughter Koezl (above). His son Taya succeeded him as chief.

business and is an excellent Trader. — Well qualified for any Service requiring bodily exertion, firmness of mind and the exercise of Sound judgement, but furiously violent when roused. — Has every reason to look forward to early promotion and is a likely man to fill a place at our Council board in course of time. — Stationed in the Columbia Department."

At Fort Vancouver, James Douglas became the protégé of John McLoughlin and his marriage to Amelia Connolly was solemnized with an Anglican ceremony performed by newly arrived Reverend Beaver.

Douglas was elevated to Chief Trader in 1835 and he rose to the position of Chief Factor in 1839. Already Douglas was aware of the antipathy between the fur trade and colonization. In 1838 he wrote: "The interests of the Colony and Fur Trade will never harmonize, the former can flourish only through the protection of equal laws, the influence of free trade, the accession of respectable inhabitants; in short by establishing a new order of things, while the Fur Trade must suffer by each innovation."

In 1840, James Douglas travelled to California on behalf of the Hudson's Bay Company to establish commercial relations with the Spanish authorities, having conducted similar diplomatic liaisons with Russian Governor Kopreanoff in Alaska earlier that same year. Douglas was much impressed by the Salinas and Santa Clara Valleys, pronouncing California to be "a country in many respects unrivalled by any other part of the globe." Although he did not publish any memoirs and he is seldom perceived as an author, Douglas kept a journal that was later published as *A Voyage from the Columbia to California in 1840*.

In 1842, on the strength of recommendations made by Captain McNeill of the *Beaver* in 1837, Douglas was sent by McLoughlin to conduct preliminary investigations for the site of a new fort near the southern end of Vancouver Island. In 1843, Douglas anchored off Clover Point near the present-day Beacon Hill Park and selected the site for Camosack (Camosun), later renamed Fort Victoria, near the site of Victoria's inner harbour. "The place itself appears a perfect 'Eden' in the midst of the

VPL #13478

Amelia Douglas (seated) and family

dreary wilderness of the Northwest coast. . . . One might be pardoned for supposing it had dropped from the clouds into its present position," Douglas wrote. Having rejected Sooke and Esquimalt as possible building sites, Douglas oversaw some of the initial construction of the new fort that was completed without a single nail the following year.

James Douglas' attitude to the "natural barbarity" of the Aboriginals he encountered on Vancouver Island in 1843 was expressed in a letter to James Hargrave that year: "What a contemptible thing is the untutored reason of man, I sometimes think that the fools who madly deny the ennobling influence of religion, might learn humility and be cured of their idle fancies, by a few months residence among these desperate savages."

In 1846, James Douglas succeeded John McLoughlin in command of the Hudson's Bay Company territory west of the Rocky Mountains. "His affection for John McLoughlin, to whom he largely owed his climb up the ladder of success," historian Derek Pethick observed, "would seem to have diminished as soon as McLoughlin could be of no further use to him, and he recorded his death in terms which in the circumstances seem callous."

In 1849, the same year that the British Government ceded Vancouver Island to the HBC for an annual rent of seven shillings, Fort Victoria became the western headquarters for the HBC, replacing Fort Vancouver. Douglas resided for the remainder of his life in Victoria, except for one tour of Europe.

On October 30, 1851, while chief HBC factor, Douglas became governor of Vancouver Island, succeeding Richard Blanshard, an alcoholic, who Douglas had stymied with relative ease since his arrival in 1850. The historian Hubert Bancroft succinctly summarized the neophyte Blanshard's predicament by saying, "Though backed by the greatest nation on earth, he was more helpless than the seventh wife of a savage."

But the newcomer Blanshard, trained in the law, was no fool. He was, as he noted, mostly victimized by "the whole tendency of the system pursued by the Hudson's Bay Company, being to exclude free Settlers, and reserve the Island either as an enlarged Post of their own, or a desert."

To the consternation of Imperial authorities such as Sir Edward Bulwer Lytton, who served as Secretary of State for the Colonies, Douglas set up his own Supreme Court in 1853, without lawful authority to do so. He also had few qualms about appointing his newly arrived brother-in-law from Demerara, British Guiana, as the first presiding judge of the Court of Appeal.

Yet for all his high-handed tendencies, Douglas chose to follow Bulwer Lytton's advice to pursue a middle course between the rigid authoritarianism that had resulted in the so-called "Eureka Stockade" incident in Victoria, Australia, in 1854, and the lawlessness that had characterized the California gold rush. Certainly, recent historians have accorded Douglas a great deal of credit for essentially following this middle course.

Unable to serve two masters, Douglas resigned his position as the head of the HBC in 1858 in order to serve solely as the governor of the new colony of British Columbia on the mainland. With remarkable acumen, Douglas managed to retain control in both the mainland and Vancouver Island territories after the discovery of gold on the Fraser River. He did so by supporting the law enforcement measures taken by Police Chief Chartres Brew and Judge Matthew Begbie, building roads (including the Cariboo Trail), importing loyal blacks from San Francisco, concocting treaties with Aboriginals and overseeing the development of both New Westminster and Fort Langley.

Swift to respond to the influx of unruly gold miners, Douglas issued a proclamation on May 8, 1858, that presumptuously claimed administrative powers that were well beyond his legal rights to assert.

Violence from Aboriginals, especially any assault or murder of settlers, was countered with swift and substantial militarism. Nonetheless, between 1850 and 1854, when Douglas was the Chief Factor of the Hudson's Bay Company at Fort Victoria, then second Governor of the Colony of Vancouver Island, he had had the foresight to generate 14 treaties or land agreements with Aboriginals on Vancouver Island. Known as the Douglas Treaties, these provisions allocated approximately three percent of Vancouver Island to the indigenous inhabitants.

With the exception of the federal government's Treaty 8 in 1899, which included the northeastern section of British Columbia (and now includes eight B.C. Indian bands), no other treaties were successfully negotiated after James Douglas' tenure until Premier Glen Clark and Chief Joe Gosnell signed the Nisga'a Agreement in 1998, ratified as law in 2000.

Douglas' bitter adversary and main critic was Amor de Cosmos, a populist who correctly viewed Douglas as elitist and inflexible. Although Douglas was mostly aloof and stern in public office, he had a rich private life with his wife and their daughters, one of whom married young Dr. John Helmcken. Douglas resigned his governorship in 1864, toured Europe and was knighted in 1866. This was frequently the reward for administrators who had not rocked the boat of Empire in far-flung colonies.

Without being either charitable or condescending, it is easy to suggest Douglas developed the mindset of a would-be Roman general and never lost it. In a letter to George Simpson in 1845, James Douglas observed, "When the Legions were recalled from

ALAN TWIGG PHOTO

James Douglas' tombstone (above) in Victoria's James Bay Cemetery. The stern paternalist Douglas admitted in a letter to Henry Labouchere, Secretary of State for the Colonies, in 1845, that he possessed "a very slender knowledge of legislation."

Britain, and other remote possessions, the Roman Empire fell rapidly into decay; with a territory nearly as extensive, our dominion would suffer from the same course; there is danger in receding; strength, power and safety are to be found only in a bold advance."

Sir James Douglas returned to live as a wealthy man in Victoria until his death in 1877. "There was something grand and majestic about Douglas," his son-in-law John Sebastian Helmcken observed. But there was also something base and hostile about him, too. Derek Pethick, an admirer of Douglas, once concluded he was "a judicious blend of the Christian and the Machiavellian." He combined the anti-democratic, corporate tradition of George Simpson with the benevolent, paternalistic tradition of John McLoughlin, the two most influential figures in his life.

[ARTISTS & SCIENTISTS]

PAUL KANE

Often considered the founding father of Canadian art, Paul Kane was the first professional Canadian artist skillfully to depict the Pacific Northwest. Among his subjects was Chief Sepayss, aka Chief of the Waters, who was father or grandfather of Chilliwack Chief William Sepass (aka K'HHalserten, meaning "Golden Snake") of Skowkale, near Sardis in the Fraser Valley. William Sepass, it might be noted, became the earliest-born (but not the first) Aboriginal author of British Columbia.

Nearly one hundred of Kane's sketches have survived from his three months spent on and around the southern tip of Vancouver Island. In 1847, Kane painted Fort Victoria and individual Aboriginals from different tribes who were visiting that fort. As the result of his unprecedented work along the Western Slope, Paul Kane became the first Canadian painter to have a best-selling book. *Wanderings of an Artist,* published in 1859, was soon translated into French, Danish and German.

On February 25, 2002, one of Paul Kane's paintings—a portrait of Jon Leffroy—sold for $4.6 million, the highest price ever paid for a Canadian work of art at auction.

Born in Mallow, County Cork, Ireland, in 1810, Paul Kane (Keane) immigrated to Little York (now Toronto) in Upper Canada in 1819 with his Lancashire-born father Michael, a former artilleryman, who became a "wine and spirit" merchant. Kane received some painting lessons from Thomas Drury, an art teacher at Upper Canada College, then began work as a sign painter. This was followed by a stint as a decorative painter of furniture in a factory. After painting portraits in Detroit, Michigan and Mobile, Alabama, as an itinerant artist for five years, he saved enough money to sail from New Orleans in 1841 to Marseilles. For three years he studied and painted copies of masterpieces in Rome, Florence, Venice and London. In 1843, in London, Kane met George Catlin who was exhibiting his paintings of the American West. Inspired by Catlin's boldly non-European outlook, Kane resolved to undertake similar work in the Canadian West, sailing from Liverpool to Mobile, Alabama.

Kane returned to Toronto, at age thirty-five, in 1845. Penniless but determined, the red-bearded Kane made an initial painting foray to the Great Lakes, but he did not proceed past Sault Ste. Marie. He returned to Montreal where he wisely sought permission for further travel from the "Little Emperor," George Simpson, who met him in March of 1846.

Self-portrait by Paul Kane, circa 1847

Simpson granted permission for Kane to travel freely as a guest in Hudson's Bay Company transports and he commissioned 12 paintings of buffalo hunts, feasts, conjuring

92

Paintings by Paul Kane. *"The next tribe lying north of these on the continent are called by the voyageurs "Babines," or Big-lips, from the fact of the females having their under lips enlarged by the insertion of a piece of wood. A small, slender piece of bone is inserted through the underlip of the infant, from below upwards, and is gradually enlarged, until a flat piece of wood three inches long, and an inch and a half wide, has caused the lip to protrude to a frightful extent, the protrusion increasing with age. Great importance is attached to the size of the lip, as it constitutes the standard of female beauty; it also marks the difference between native free women and their slaves. When the stick is removed on any occasion the lip drops down to the chin, presenting one of the most disgusting spectacles imaginable."* —Paul Kane

matches, dances "or any other pieces of savage life you may consider to be most attractive or interesting."

The following spring, Kane joined a westward brigade from Fort William, taking part in a buffalo hunt, and staying at Hudson's Bay Company trading posts. In November of 1846 he crossed the Athabasca Pass and proceeded down the Columbia River to Fort Vancouver in January. He then travelled north and stayed at Fort Victoria intermittently between April 8 and June 9, 1847. At Fort Victoria he was able to make portraits of noteworthy Aboriginals who visited Fort Victoria from more northerly regions of the coast and he recorded his observations of their lives in the various encampments.

"One morning while I was sketching, I saw upon the rocks the dead body of a young woman, thrown out to the vultures and crows, whom I had seen a few days previously walking about in perfect health. Mr. Finlayson, the gentleman in charge of Fort

Victoria, accompanied me to the lodge she belonged to, where we found an Indian woman, her mistress, who made light of her death, and was doubtless the cause of it. She told us that a slave had no right to burial, and became perfectly furious when Mr. Finlayson told her that the slave was far better than herself. 'I,' she exclaimed, 'the daughter of a chief, no better than a dead slave!' and bridling up with all the dignity she could assume, she stalked out, and next morning she had up her lodge and was gone. I was also told by an eye-witness, of a chief, who having erected a colossal idol of wood, sacrificed five slaves to it, barbarously murdering them at its base, and asking in a boasting manner who amongst them could afford to kill so many slaves."

While at Fort Victoria, Kane hired Aboriginals to take him and his interpreter across Haro Strait ("canal De Aro") to a village described as Cawa Chin (Cowichan). Before proceeding to Whitby's Island and Puget Sound, he observed the following:

"About 10 o'clock at night I strolled into the village, and on hearing a great noise in one of the lodges I entered it, and found an old woman supporting one of the handsomest Indian girls I had ever seen. She was in a state of nudity. Cross-legged and naked, in the middle of the room sat the medicine man, with a wooden dish of water before him; twelve or fifteen other men were sitting round the lodge. The object in view was to cure the girl of a disease affecting her side. As soon as my presence was noticed a space was cleared for me to sit down. The officiating medicine-man appeared in a state of profuse perspiration from the exertions he had used, and soon took his seat among the rest as if quite exhausted; a younger medicine-man then took his place in front of the bowl, and close beside the patient. Throwing off his blanket he commenced singing and gesticulating in the most violent manner, whilst the others kept time by beating with little sticks on hollow wooden bowls and drums, singing continually. After exercising himself in this manner for about half an hour, until the perspiration ran down his body, he darted suddenly upon the young woman, catching hold of her side with his teeth and shaking her for a few minutes, while the patient seemed to

"Those [Aboriginals] at the mouth of the Columbia, and for a hundred miles up it, as well as those at Puget's Sound, and the Straits of De Fuca, and at the southern part of Vancouver's Island, have their heads flattened down in their infancy. . . . The Chinooks and Cowlitz Indians carry the custom of flattening the head to a greater extent than any other of the Flathead tribes. The process is as follows: — The Indian mothers all carry their infants strapped to a piece of board covered with moss or loose fibres of cedar bark, and in order to flatten the head they place a pad on the infant's forehead, on the top of which is laid a piece of smooth bark, bound on by a leathern band passing through holes on the board on either side, and kept tightly pressed across the front of the head, — a sort of pillow of grass or cedar fibres being placed under the back of the neck to support it. This process commences with the birth of the infant, and is continued for a period of from eight to twelve months, by which time the head has lost its natural shape, and acquired that of a wedge; the front of the skull flat and higher at the crown, giving it a most unnatural appearance. . . . This unnatural operation does not, however, seem to injure the health, the mortality amongst the Flathead children not being perceptibly greater than amongst other Indian tribes; nor does it seem to injure their intellect." —Paul Kane suffer great agony. He then relinquished his hold, and cried out he had got it, at the same time holding his hands to his mouth; after which he plunged them in the water and pretended to hold down with great difficulty the disease which he had extracted, lest it might spring out and return to its victim.

"At length, having obtained the mastery over it, he turned round to me in an exulting manner, and held something up between the finger and thumb of each hand, which had the appearance of a piece of cartilage, whereupon one of the Indians sharpened his knife, and divided it in two, leaving one end in each hand. One of the pieces he threw into the water, and the other into the fire, accompanying the action with a diabolical noise, which none but the medicine-man can make. After which he got up perfectly satisfied with himself, although the poor patient seemed to me anything but relieved by the violent treatment she had undergone."

Having concluded his sketches, Kane left Fort Victoria for Fort Vancouver on June 10, 1847. He returned to Toronto in October and spent six years completing approximately 100 oil paintings based on his travels. Kane grew blind and embittered by lack of recognition. He died in Toronto on February 20, 1871.

HENRY JAMES WARRE

"The scenery was grand in the extreme; similar in form to the Alps of Switzerland." —SIR HENRY JAMES WARRE

The first artist's impressions of the Canadian Rockies were made by Lt. Henry James Warre while travelling as a British undercover agent in 1845, accompanied by Lieutenant Mervin Vavasour of the Royal Engineers. Warre's ostensibly amateur drawings and paintings were undertaken as military reconnaisance in case the Anglo-American territorial dispute over the Oregon Territory degenerated into war.

Disguised as two gentlemen seeking "the pleasure of field sports and scientific pursuit," Warre and Vavasour left Montreal in May of 1845 to examine transportation networks, British defences and American military capabilities between Montreal and the Oregon Territory, taking the HBC route from Fort Garry on the Red River to the Rockies, then taking the White Man Pass (named for Father Pierre-Jean De Smet) to Kootenai Lake, reaching their coastal destination of Fort Vancouver on August 25, 1845.

After half of their 60 horses died en route, Warre, an English army officer, concluded: "Our passage over the magnificent range of the lofty mountains was not accomplished without much difficulty and a fearful sacrifice of the noble animals that aided us in the transport. We left Edmonton with sixty horses; on our arrival at Fort Colvile, on the Columbia River, we had only twenty-seven, and several of these so exhausted they could not have continued many more days. The steepness of the mountain passes, the want of proper nourishment, the fearful falls that some of the animals sustained, rolling in some instances many hundred feet into the foaming torrent beneath, combined to cause this great loss. . . . The idea of transporting troops . . . with their stores, etc., through such an extent of uncultivated country and over such impractable [sic] mountains would appear to us quite infeasible."

What he was suggesting was that it would be impractical to dispatch British forces from eastern Canada to travel overland to the Pacific Ocean.

At Fort Vancouver, Warre and Vavasour played to the hilt their roles as monied gentlemen, purchasing beaver hats of the highest quality, frock coats, cloth vests, tweed trousers, nail brushes, hair brushes, fancy handkerchiefs, shirts, tobacco, pipes, wines, whiskeys and a quantity of extract of roses.

At Fort Vancouver, Warre also had the pleasure of witnessing the first theatrical production in Oregon when the crew of H.M.S. *Modeste* performed two plays, *Mayor of Garratti* and *The Deuce is in Him*, before an assembled audience on its deck of 300 people.

Warre noted the "Ladies" in the plays were particularly charm-
ing: "The sailor boys made rather large Women & had (as was
remarked by a nice little girl of Mr. Douglas) 'very red necks.'
Some of the ladies (nearly all of whom are half-breeds) wondered
that they were not before aware that 'any Women lived on
board'—So that the deception was perfect."

British interest in controlling the Pacific Northwest was complicated by the presence of American settlers north of the Columbia River led there by Michel Troutman Simmons, a wagon
train colonel, and George Washington Bush, a black pioneer, as
well as French-Canadian farmers along the Willamette River.

By 1843, a provisional American government for the Oregon
Territory had been improvised at Champoeg on the Willamette
River (in Oregon). The vote to establish regional government
was 53 in favour, 50 against.

Warre and Vavasour noted the increasing influx of Americans
to the West Coast, as well as the relatively weak defensive fortifications of the Hudson's Bay Company forts. "Till the year 1842–
43, not more than thirty American families were resident in the
country," Warre wrote. "In 1843 an emigration of about one thousand persons with a large number of wagons, horses, cattle, etc.,
arrived on the Willamette having traversed the vast desert sec-

*Oregonians created an independent settlement at Champoeg, much to the alarm of the
roaming British spies, Henry James Warre and Mervin Vavasour.*

tion of the country between the Missouri, the Rocky Mountains and the Columbia. . . .

"The American immigrants have as yet confined themselves principally to the valley of the Willamette which has by far the richest soil and finest land in the whole country. The cultivable part of it, however, cannot be said to extend more than sixty to eighty miles in length, and fifteen or twenty miles in breadth. Nearly all the Prairie land is now taken up, and the Immigrants are too indolent to clear the woods. They are consequently forming new settlements on the banks of the Columbia at the mouth of the same river and on the beautiful but not very rich plains to the north, in the neighborhood of Nisqually and Puget's Sound."

From the mouth of the Columbia River, Warre and Vavasour travelled up to Puget Sound and onto Vancouver Island. As he provided pencil sketches of Fort Victoria in September of 1845, Warre correctly predicted "it will ere long eclipse Fort Vancouver and become the Head Quarters of the HBCo. West of the Rocky Mountains." While assessing meagre American military capabilities, Warre made over eighty watercolour drawings, some of which portrayed subjects of military importance. He often placed small figures of Aboriginals in the foreground, so as not to convey the true purpose of his landscapes.

When the sovereignty dispute between Britain and the United States dissolved, Warre published *Sketches in North America and the Oregon Territory*, including a map and a narrative entitled Sketch of the Journey. It contains some of the earliest and best lithographed views of the Rockies and Pacific Northwest.

Warre's adventures had been prompted by a meeting at Number 10 Downing Street on April 3, 1845, with Sir George Simpson, governor of the Hudson's Bay Company, Sir Robert Peel, British prime minister, and the Earl of Aberdeen, Peel's foreign minister. The threesome had discussed the latest rhetorical salvo of the newly elected American President, James K. Polk, who, in his inaugural address, had declared the United States would claim the entire area west of the Rockies from Mexico to Russian America in Alaska. His bellicose campaign slogan, "54–

40 or Fight!" sufficiently rattled the British that George Simpson proposed sending four war ships, two of which would guard the entrances to Puget Sound and Juan de Fuca Strait.

Peel and Aberdeen were more inclined to interpret Polk's promises to the electorate as bluster. Peel had therefore decided that two undercover agents should be sent "to gain a general knowledge of the capabilities of the Oregon territory in a military point of view, in order that we may be enabled to act immediately and with effect in defense of our rights in that quarter, should those rights be infringed by any hostile aggression or encroachment on the part of the United States."

Warre and Vavasour returned to Montreal in July of 1846. By the time Warre's report from Montreal reached Prime Minister Robert Peel in London, Peel had already decided to yield the area between the Columbia and the 49th parallel to the Americans. Warre proceeded to have a distinguished military career and was knighted for his services.

It is worth mentioning a few additional facts about Warre's life. His early years were instrumental in developing his abilities. Born in 1819, at Cape of Good Hope, he enrolled at Royal Military Academy, Sandhurst, in 1832. Gaining his appointment as an Ensign in 1837, he spent six months in Paris, studying the paintings at the Louvre and learning French.

He rejoined the 54th Regiment of Foot in Canterbury in 1839 and sailed from Portsmouth, England, on H.M.S. *Pique* as an aide-de-camp to Sir Richard Downes Jackson, Commander-in-Chief of the Forces in British North America. He was promoted to lieutenant in 1841. After his West Coast adventures, Warre reached the rank of captain in 1847, and this was when he published his aforementioned *Sketches in North America and the Oregon Territory*.

After service in Ireland and the Ionian Islands, he married Georgiana-Emily Lukin in 1855. Promoted to lieutenant-colonel two months later, he departed for the Crimean War where he took command of the 57th Regiment upon the death of Colonel Shadforth. That same year Warre was named Companion of the Order of the Bath and he also published *Sketches in the Crimea*.

He was garrisoned in Malta in 1856 and promoted to Colonel in 1858. He led the 57th Regiment from Egypt to Bombay in 1859, the year he was appointed Brigadier-General. His military career continued with stints in India, New Zealand and Belfast, Northern Ireland.

Henry James Warre died in London on April 3, 1898.

Named in 1918, Mount Vavasour and Mount Warre are located in the Rocky Mountains, east of White Man Pass, through which both men crossed.

DAVID DOUGLAS

"Science has few friends among those who visit the coast of North-West America." —DAVID DOUGLAS

During the first two decades of European contact, at least three major voyages reached the Pacific Northwest with mandates for scientific discovery: Cook for the British, La Pérouse for the French and Malaspina for the Spanish. One might also add Captain Vancouver's surveying expedition, which included the botanist Archibald Menzies.

In the ensuing 50 years, as the fur trade expanded overland, only the name of David Douglas resonates as a significant scientist. Scotland's most famous explorer-botanist, after whom the Douglas fir is named, was the first European not involved in the fur trade to penetrate British Columbia's interior. Thereafter he steadfastly maintained that the border between the United States and Canada ought to be the Columbia River.

David Douglas introduced at least 254 plants to Britain and reputedly sent approximately seven thousand species to Kew Gardens and the Linneaus Society, comprising 13 percent of the then-known plant species in Europe—more than any other person in history. With John Scouler, he also made the first 40 collections of plants on the Galapágos Islands on January 10, 1825.

Born on June 25, 1799, in the village of Scone in Perthshire, Douglas was the son of a stonemason. As a boy he showed a keen interest in animals and nature, collecting birds and keeping pet owls. His favourite book was *Robinson Crusoe*. At age eleven he gained an apprentice position with William Beattie, in charge of the palace garden in Scone, once the ancient capital of Scotland. During his teens he received access to the library of Sir Robert Preston at Valleyfield, where he rose to the position of under-gardener.

An autodidact, Douglas never received any formal degree. As an employee at the Glasgow Botanical Garden, he became a protégé of Dr. William Jackson Hooker, Chair of Botany at Glasgow University, who took him on botanical trips and recommended his services to the Horticultural Society of London.

In 1823 the Society sent Douglas to collect specimens in Upper Canada and New York. Having proved himself capable in eastern Canada, Douglas was next sent from London in 1824, as arranged by Secretary of the Horticultural Society Joseph Sabine, on the annual Hudson's Bay Company supply ship *William and Ann* to describe and collect flora and fauna in the Columbia River region.

Hired by the Horticultural Society, Douglas was nonetheless obliged to operate under the aegis of the HBC to gather information on "the vegetable treasures of those widely extended and diversified countries" where the HBC was active. Douglas was accompanied by the Scottish botanist John Scouler who would concentrate his research on the coast; Douglas would investigate inland areas.

After an eight-and-a-half month voyage via Cape Horn, during which Douglas catalogued the California vulture and the California sheep, Douglas and Scouler arrived at Fort Vancouver early in 1825. Before he landed, the story goes, he noted three types of trees on shore—the hemlock, the balsam fir and one species that was new to him. Although Archibald Menzies had already gathered samples of this unknown specimen in 1792–1794, the popular name for the tall evergreen tree would become Douglas fir after his death, to honour Douglas (no relation to James Douglas). He initially described the Douglas fir as *Pinus taxifolia.*

"The wood may be found very useful for a variety of domestic purposes," he predicted, "the young slender ones [being] exceedingly well adapted for making ladders and scaffold poles, not being liable to cast; the larger timber for more important purposes."

David Douglas

Based at Fort Vancouver, Douglas befriended botany enthusiast Archibald McDonald and he reputedly travelled more than seven thousand miles in what is now British Columbia, Washington, Oregon and Idaho under the auspices of the Hudson's Bay Company. Douglas was initially distrusted and feared by some Indians for his strange habits, such as putting spectacles on his nose, tea-drinking and lighting his pipe by using sunlight and a magnifying glass, for which he gained the nickname *Olla-Diska,* Chinook jargon for fire. As his motives became better understood, he also garnered the nickname "Grass Man."

On his way back to England via Athabasca Pass and Hudson Bay, Douglas traversed eastern British Columbia from April 19 to May 2, 1827. At the outset of May he made the first recorded climb of any peak in the Canadian Rockies, on Mount Brown. While drastically over-estimating their heights, he prudently named Mount Brown after Robert Brown (1773–1858; first keeper of the botanical department of the British Museum) and nearby Mount Hooker after his mentor Hooker (who became director of Kew Gardens). Both mountains are within Jasper National Park.

Douglas gained notoriety and acclaim after his return voyage from Hudson Bay in the company of doomed Arctic explorer Sir

John Franklin. Aware of his shortcomings as a geographer, Douglas set to work learning how to calculate latitude and longitude. In addtion, he gained some knowledge of spherical trigonometry and logarithms, from Sabine, Secretary of the Royal Society.

Once more accompanied by his Scottish terrier, Douglas returned to California in 1830 better equipped and joined by a white man-servant. Douglas explored and collected in California for a year-and-a-half until he received word from the Governor of Alaska that he would be welcome to visit Alaska. It was Douglas' fervent wish to conduct botanical and astronomical research in New Caledonia, then proceed via Fort St. James and Sitka, Alaska, to Siberia for more scientific research.

"What a glorious prospect!" he wrote to Professor Hooker, with ". . . the work of the same individual on both Continents, with the same instruments, under similar circumstances and corresponding latitudes! . . . People tell me that Siberia is like a rat-trap, which there is no difficulty in entering, but from which it is not so easy to find egress. I mean at least to put this saying to the test. And I hope that those who know me know also that trifles will not stop me."

Douglas' foray into New Caledonia in 1833 would pose many dangers beyond "trifles." In fact, he would have to survive a tuberculosis epidemic that killed 24 Hudson's Bay Company men and thousands of Indians in the Columbia district. He was to encounter wild rapids and extreme temperatures. He also had to deal with the loss of much of his eyesight and the threat of a duel.

Douglas wintered at Fort Vancouver and departed with Edward Ermatinger for Fort Okanagan on March 20, 1833, planning to obtain fresh horses at Thompson's River Post (Fort Kamloops), proceed up the Bonaparte River to Horse Lake, and continue in a north-westerly direction to Williams Lake and the Fraser River, then onto Fort Alexandria. Boats and canoes would take him along the Fraser, Nechako and Stuart Rivers to reach Fort St. James, the largest post in New Caledonia.

On May 1, Ermatinger shot a partridge that Douglas skinned

and preserved, recognizing it as a new species and naming it Franklin's partridge after Sir John Franklin.

Upon his arrival at Fort Kamloops, Douglas insulted his brother Scot Samuel Black by giving the Fort Kamloops commander his honest and forthright opinion of his host's employer. "The Hudson's Bay Company," Douglas said, "is simply a mercenary corporation; there is not an officer in it with a soul above a beaver-skin." Given Douglas' expressed gratitude to his host John McLoughlin at Fort Vancouver, this statement perhaps says as much about Douglas as it does about the Hudson's Bay Company.

Black, who fancied himself a man of some learning, interested in both geology and geography, had a brother who was editor of the *London Morning Chronicle*. He was more sophisticated than his appearance might attest. Unaccustomed to any insubordination, Black challenged Douglas to a duel. Early the next morning, Black confronted his guest. "Mister Doooglas! Are ye ready?" But the intemperate flower-collector wisely declined combat.

Douglas enjoyed a much kinder reception from Chief Factor Peter Warren Dease when he reached Fort St. James on June 6, 1833, but he found himself stranded for lack of transportation or guides. Difficulties had arisen for Douglas within the Royal Horticultural Society that limited the willingness of the Hudson's Bay Company (which would undoubtedly be apprised of Douglas' opinion of the HBC by Black) to provide escort and provisions.

Since Aboriginals near the coast were notoriously hostile, fueled by liquor from American traders, and temperatures in New Caledonia could become severely cold, Douglas and his servant could not risk making the journey to the coast on their own. It was 500 miles to the mouth of the Nass River, at Fort Simpson, then another 300 miles north to Sitka, Alaska.

As with the aborted duel, discretion was the better part of valour. Douglas and his servant William Johnson (a HBC employee who would become the first resident of Portland, Oregon) descended the Stuart and Nechako Rivers in a birch-bark canoe to

Fort George, but soon after met with disaster nonetheless. Somewhere between present-day Prince George and Quesnel they overturned in the rapids. Douglas was swept downstream for more than an hour, losing his diary, his food and blankets, and his collection of 400 plant species.

Distraught, Douglas and Johnson somehow managed to return to Fort St. James and make a second, successful canoe trip to Fort Alexandria. (Not long thereafter, the Fort George clerk, George Linton, with his wife and three children and three others, would be drowned near much the same spot.)

By August, Douglas and his servant reached Fort Vancouver, much the worse for hunger and exposure, and troubled by fever. "This disastrous occurrence has much broken my strength and spirits," he wrote to Hooker.

Douglas was somewhat relieved by the recent appearance at Fort Vancouver of two "doctors" who were also aspiring botanists, Meredith Gairdner and William Fraser Tolmie. Gairdner succumbed to tuberculosis in 1836, but Tolmie, who had known Douglas in Scotland, would continue collecting plant samples in B.C.

While the glare of sunlight during his various travels took its toll on his vision, Douglas is sometimes credited with making the first discovery of gold in British Columbia. He supposedly found enough gold somewhere on the shore of Okanagan Lake to make a seal. Douglas has also been mentioned in terms of gold discoveries in California. Gold flakes were supposedly found in some plant samples he sent to England in 1831, but there is little verification. Douglas' collection of rocks from the Pacific Northwest was transferred to the British Museum, but these rocks have long since disappeared.

The eminent geologist George Dawson repeated a story that Douglas had also found a deposit of carbonate of lead, galena and copper on the eastern shore of Kootenay Lake, later the site of the Bluebell Mine. This outcrop of galena ore was located opposite Hot Springs or Ainsworth. Unfortunately there is no evidence that Douglas ever visited Kootenay Lake. It is possible one of his assistants did, or else he gleaned information from some Aboriginals who knew of a mountain near Kettle Falls they called Chicamen (metal) Mountain.

In December of 1833, Douglas and his trusty terrier Billy sailed for the balmier climate of Hawaii where he collected ferns and became the first European to make recorded ascents of two great volcanic peaks.

Tragedy struck on July 12, 1834, when, at age thirty-four, David Douglas was supposedly gored to death by a wild bull.

An unnamed editor of his journals, unpublished until 1914, provided some details about this supposedly accidental death in a bullock pit, but the circumstances lead to an easy assumption that he was murdered.

"The manner in which that melancholy event was said to have taken place seemed to us all about the Hudson's Bay Company so very improbable," wrote Archibald McDonald, "that we were unwilling to give the report implicit credence."

Of the many indigenous North American plants David Douglas introduced to cultivation abroad, the wild hyacinth (camassia quamish) was noteworthy as a foodstuff for Pacific Northwest Aboriginals. Edible bulbs of the large blue flowers provided starchy tubers that tasted "much like baked pears" but Douglas complained of the flatulence they produced.

The British Consul to the Sandwich Islands, Richard Charlton, reported the death to England in a letter dated August 6, 1834. Douglas, it was alleged, had retraced his steps and wandered from a path after being forewarned about the danger of three pits that were built to entrap wild cattle. Inside one pit there was a bullock that trampled Douglas to death, or else the bullock fell into the pit after Douglas was entrapped.

Both scenarios were equally improbable, given that Douglas and his dog had managed to survive approximately twelve thousand miles of travel in the wilderness. On the other hand, Douglas, notoriously short-sighted, once had to be rescued from a ravine in Oregon into which he had fallen.

It is known that Douglas was trekking overland to Byron's Bay (now called Hilo) in the company of a black man named John, a servant of a missionary who had been lent to Douglas, who could not keep pace with him. On the morning of his death, Douglas breakfasted at the hut of a bullock hunter named Ned Gurney, a fearsome ex-convict from the penal camps in Australia.

Testimony and rumours later surfaced that Douglas had shown Gurney and others his money. Douglas made arrangements with Gurney to leave the servant behind, and departed early in the morning. The servant John was never heard from or seen again.

Gurney disappeared from Hawaii in 1839. No money was found with Douglas' corpse. A minister who interred the body noticed cuts on Douglas' body that were not in keeping with injuries that might have been sustained from attacks by a bull. An enquiry was launched, but physicians concluded the bull was the most likely killer. Years later, informants surfaced who accused the notorious Ned Gurney of the murder.

The grave was left unmarked at the time, possibly because Douglas was not officially an employee of the Royal Horticultural Society in Hawaii. Douglas had resigned in response to Royal Horticultural Society wrangles that had ousted his major supporter from the Society.

It has been suggested that Douglas may have committed suicide because he was receiving credit from people he met in Hawaii under false assurances that he was still employed by the Society. As soon as lenders learned that they would not be reimbursed by the Society, Douglas' reputation would have been ruined and he would have been deeply in debt.

A white marble monument to mark his burial in the cemetery of the Kawaiahao Church ("the Westminster Abbey of Hawaii") was purchased by a world traveller and author named Reverend Julius L. Brenchley in 1855. An archivist in Honolulu named William F. Wilson published a pamphlet in 1919 entitled *David Douglas, Botanist at Hawaii.* A plaque to mark his place of death has been installed on Mauna Kea, and there is a large monument to David Douglas in Scone. As well, Mount Douglas in the Rocky Mountains bears his name.

Apart from his one known dalliance with a Chinook "princess" (it seems as if every second Aboriginal woman who had sex with a European in the 1800s was called a princess), Douglas was a loner, keen to make a name for himself, driven by a passion for collecting seeds instead of spreading them. But the definitive work on David Douglas has yet to be written. Allegations have been made that the heroic botanist was sometimes willing to take credit for the findings of others. His preference for *Robinson Crusoe* as a boy might well have led him to romanticize and inflate his own self-image as a man.

Regardless, the Royal Horticultural Society once published a list of 254 plants that David Douglas introduced to England. These include *Picea sitchensis* (Sitka spruce), *Pinus lambertiana* (sugar pine), *Pinus ponderosa* (Western yellow pine), *Pinus radiata* (Monterey pine), the California poppy, five species of monkey flower and 18 of lupine.

As for the Douglas fir, capable of growing to a height of 270 feet over a 500-year period, it has gained various common names such as Oregon pine, red pine, Puget Sound pine, Oregon spruce, Douglas spruce, red fir, yellow fir, Oregon fir and spruce fir. Its various scientific names include *Pinus Douglasii, Pseudotsuga Douglasii, Pseudotsuga Menziesii* (in honour of Archibald Menzies) and *Pseudotsuga taxifolia.*

JOHN SCOULER

Prior to Charles Darwin's visit to the Galápagos Islands in 1835, the first six scientists to visit the islands also proceeded to visit British Columbia. The sixth of these men, young John Scouler, was as much impressed by the Haida as the oddities of the Galápagos.

As part of Alessandro Malaspina's scientific expedition, botanists Antonio Piñeda and Luís Neel, along with naturalist Tadeo Haenke, first stopped at the Galápagos in 1780, then reached Nootka Sound.

Fifteen years later, in 1795, Archibald Menzies, botanist with Captain George Vancouver, visited a desolate area of the Galápagos, on the northwest side of Isabela Island but found little of interest.

The first scientists known to have gathered samples from the Galápagos were two young Scotsmen, David Douglas and Scouler. They arrived at James Island in the Galápagos on the Hudson's Bay Company brig *William and Ann* on January 9, 1825. Many of their samples were lost or destroyed, but Sir Joseph Hooker cited thirteen Galápagos plants gathered by Scouler and five from Douglas in a paper he published on Darwin in 1847. David Douglas and John Scouler are therefore credited with gathering the first botanical samples for scientific research from the Galápagos Islands.

Hired to serve as a medical officer on the *William and Ann,* Scouler (1804–1871) sailed from the Galápagos with his University of Glasgow classmate, Douglas, and made some of the first botanical and geographic observations of the Pacific Northwest: "When we consider the abundance of provisions this beautiful country affords," he wrote, visiting the Strait of Juan de Fuca, "we shall not be surprised at the great population it maintains; and, probably no Indians in North America have less difficulty in procuring their food than the tribes from the Gulf of Georgia to the Columbia River; the sea yields an abundant supply of fishes of the most delicious kinds, as various species of mullet, turbot, and cod; every rivulet teems with myriads of salmon; and the meadows and forests produce an endless variety of berries and esculent roots. The collection of the latter forms the occupation of the women and children, while the men are occupied in procuring the former, and both are carefully dried for winter stores."

Scouler visited the Queen Charlotte Islands in 1825 and noted, "Around Skittegass [Skidegate], the potato is now pretty extensively cultivated, and they brought us plenty to sell. One cannot but rejoice at this symptom of commencing civilization, which, if persevered in, will limit their wanderings, and give them better ideas of property, and teach them that more is to be gained by cultivating their fertile soil, than in following salmon up every creek, or spending days in the uncertain support of the chase."

Scouler's zeal for collecting almost got the better of him when he stole three skulls from a Haida burial place in 1825. Pursued back to the ship by furious Haida, he hastily retreated from the area.

Nonetheless, Scouler viewed the Haida as "far above the natives of the Columbia in the scale of intelligence." On his return journey, Scouler visited Nootka Sound and found that the sources for furs had been exhausted: "Nootka, which excited so much contention between the courts of Madrid and London, is now completely neglected by every civilised power, & the state of poverty in which they are at present affords little inducement to the visits of mercantile adventurers."

Prior to 1850, Scouler was one of the precious few physicians who visited the Pacific Northwest without dire consequences. The Astorian trader Alexander Ross later observed: "It had often been a subject of remark among Colombians how unfortunate a certain class of professional men had been in that quarter, physicians and surgeons."

The casualty rate for physicians prior to the long life of Dr. William Fraser Tolmie was such that the existence of a jinx was presumed. Here is a brief inventory of Scouler's medical peers:

- Welsh-born doctor David Samwell survived Captain James Cook's visit to Nootka Sound in 1778, but his fellow surgeon on the *Resolution*, William Anderson, died of tuberculosis in August of 1778 off the coast of Alaska.
- John MacKay, assistant surgeon for Captain Strange in 1786, barely survived his one year as a "guest" of Chief Maquinna and apparently died as an alcoholic in India, a shattered man.
- Alexander Purvis Cranstoun, surgeon for Captain Vancouver on the *Discovery*, was invalided home from Nootka Sound in 1792, replaced by Archibald Menzies, a botanist.
- According to Alexander Ross, a physician identified as Doctor White arrived in Astoria in 1811, but "became suddenly deranged, jumped overboard, and was drowned."
- Ross also recorded that a Doctor Crowley was sent away from Fort George (Astoria) to be tried for murder after he allegedly shot a man in cold blood; as well, a surgeon on the ship *Colonel Allan* shot himself to death in his cabin while anchored near the fort in 1816.
- The Hudson's Bay Company trader and surgeon Alexander McKenzie (not the explorer) was killed by Aboriginals at Hood Canal in 1828.
- Doctor Richard J. Hamlyn quarrelled with Chief Factor John McLoughlin at Fort Vancouver and left the fort in 1830.
- Unable to cope with an outbreak of malaria that killed thousands of Aboriginals, the Edinburgh-educated physician John Frederick Kennedy contracted the disease, threatened to quit, and was sent to Fort Simpson.
- Also trained in Edinburgh, the conceited twenty-two-year-old Meredith Gairdner sailed with twenty-year-old

William Fraser Tolmie on the *Ganymede* in 1832, reaching Fort Vancouver some seven-and-a-half months later, where he coped with more than 600 malarial patients in 1833, only to die of consumption (pulmonary tuberculosis) in Hawaii in 1837.

THOMAS DRUMMOND

Much to his astonishment, David Douglas crossed paths with yet another Scottish protégé of his Glasgow botany professor, Sir William Jackson Hooker, during his explorations in New Caledonia in July of 1827. This was Thomas Drummond, born in the rural parish of Inverarity, Forfar, in the County of Angus, Scotland, in 1793.

As the sons of the head gardener on the Fotheringham Estate, both Thomas Drummond and his older brother James studied horticulture and had distinguished careers. Prior to his arrival in Canada in 1825 as part of Rear-Admiral John Franklin's second Arctic expedition, Thomas Drummond published his first book on Scottish mosses, *Musci Scotici*, two of which were named for him: *Orthotrichum Drummondii* and *Equisetum Drummondii*.

While Franklin went on to suffer his ignominious fate in the Arctic Ocean, Drummond was dispatched to explore the Canadian Rockies, crossing into British Columbia via Athabasca Pass in 1826. When he was not avoiding bears and wolverines, he narrowly escaped plummeting from a ledge of rock while encountering a herd of mountain sheep. A yellow mountain flower named *Dryas Drummondii*, the Drummond Icefield and Mount Drummond commemorate his time in Canada. The "Great Scottish Muscologist" returned to Scotland where he published another book about mosses, containing information about his Canadian discoveries, and he served as the first Curator of the Belfast Botanic Garden (1828–1831). Eager for more adventure, Drummond travelled to Texas and sent 750 species of plants to Professor Hooker, as well as 150 specimens of birds—the first Texas collections distributed to scientists. He wintered on uninhabited Galveston Island, almost starving to death, then returned to New Orleans. Overcoming cholera and diarrhea, he proceeded to Mexico and returned again to New Orleans in December of 1834 with a fever. Still ill in February of 1835, he explored parts of Florida before dying in Havana, Cuba, in March.

[BY SEA]

JOHN JEWITT

"John . . . be my slave. You say no, dagger come!"
—CHIEF MAQUINNA TO JOHN JEWITT, 1803

"My heart leapt for joy at the thought of getting my liberty."
—JOHN JEWITT, 1805

By far the most famous first-hand, written account of early relations between Euro-Americans and Aboriginals in British Columbia is John Jewitt's memoir of his nearly three years in captivity on the west coast of Vancouver Island from 1803 to 1805. Jewitt, a blacksmith, was one of two survivors of a massacre in 1803. His Robinson Crusoe-like chronicle of "white slavery" has reputedly never been out of print since he self-published a 48-page version in 1807. By 1931, only seven copies of Jewitt's original edition were known to exist, worth more than $25,000 each. A later version that became popular was enhanced and edited by Richard Alsop.

Born on May 21, 1783, John Rodgers Jewitt was the son of Edward Jewitt, a blacksmith in Lincolnshire, England, who wanted his son to further his education and become a surgeon. When his father moved his business to the seaport of Hull, John Jewitt heard tales of the sea and signed on as the armourer on the *Boston*, an American sailing ship that left England and rounded Cape Horn for what was then called Vancouver's Island to participate in the emerging China-based trade for sea otter skins.

After a favourable voyage of six months' duration, the *Boston* anchored five miles north of Friendly Cove (Nootka Sound) on March 12, 1803. The following day, Maquinna, the "tyee" or chief of the nearby Yuquot settlement, led a flotilla of canoes to visit the *Boston*, greeting Captain John Salter in English. Maquinna undoubtedly had mixed feelings about Salter's arrival. While his tribe's relations with Spanish Captain Martínez had proved problematic, and Captain Tawington and his men had ransacked his village eighteen years before, Maquinna's people had nonetheless benefitted by establishing Friendly Cove as the hub of the sea otter fur trade on the West Coast.

It is not known for certain whether the chief that greeted Salter was the same leader named Maquinna who had met Captain James Cook in 1778 (or if he was a successor who had inherited the hereditary title), but it is certain Maquinna understood far more English than Salter realized. Salter's under-estimation of Maquinna's pride and intelligence would soon have lethal consequences.

At first, the two sides traded amicably, exchanging gifts. Salter gave Maquinna a double-barrelled fowling piece. The following day Maquinna reciprocated with

This famous charcoal sketch of "Macuina" was completed at Nootka Sound by Tomás de Suría in 1791. It is often used to represent Chief Maquinna, John Jewitt's captor, in 1803, but in 2005 Canadian government officials and Nuu-chah-nulth leaders formally agreed there were two Chief Maquinnas between 1774 and approximately 1820. Maquinna is an hereditary title.

a gift of 18 wild ducks. Trouble arose only when Maquinna had difficulty with the new gun he had received. When its lock jammed, Maquinna announced it was bad and needed repair. In Maquinna's presence, Salter spoke disparagingly about Maquinna, failing to appreciate that Maquinna fully understood the insult. The rifle was given to John Jewitt for repairs.

Jewitt later wrote, "Unfortunately he [Maquinna] understood but too well the meaning of the reproachful terms that the captain addressed to him. He said not a word in reply, but his countenance sufficiently expressed the rage he felt though he exerted himself to suppress it. I observed him, while the captain was speaking, repeatedly put his hand to his throat and rub it upon his bosom, which he afterwards told me was to keep down his heart, which was rising into his throat and choking him."

The insult was avenged on the following day. Maquinna revisited the *Boston* and invited half of Salter's men to go ashore to catch salmon. Upon Maquinna's signal, the Mowachaht then attacked and killed 25 crewmembers of the *Boston*, including Salter. They accidentally spared only Jewitt, who was injured and took refuge below deck, and John Thompson, a sailmaker, who hid in the hold during the attack and was found the following day.

Maquinna had observed Jewitt at his forge and recognized his value as a blacksmith. When Jewitt was revived, he had to promise to be a good slave and to make Maquinna weapons and tools. Jewitt successfully negotiated for the life of the other survivor, Thompson, who was twenty years his senior, by telling Maquinna that Thompson was his father. After Jewitt was asked to identify the severed heads of his former shipmates, the ship was ransacked and burned.

Thompson, from Philadelphia, remained bitter and violent, but Jewitt set about to endear himself to Maquinna's family and to learn the language. "I had determined from the first of my capture to adopt a conciliating conduct towards them," Jewitt recalled, "and conform myself, as far as was in my power, to their customs, and mode of thinking, trusting that the same divine goodness that had rescued me from death, would not always suffer me to languish in captivity among these heathens."

Jewitt, who turned twenty years old on May 21, 1803, managed to salvage a blank book from the *Boston*, and was encouraged by the illiterate Thompson to commence a journal. As he explained, "Thompson became very importunate for me to begin my journal, and as I had no ink, proposed to cut his finger to supply me with blood for the purpose whenever I should want it."

Jewitt began his journal on June 1 by boiling and filtering a blend of plant and berry juices with powdered coal. "I at length succeeded in obtaining a very tolerable ink, by boiling the juice of the blackberry with a mixture of finely powdered charcoal, and filtering it through a cloth," he wrote. "As for quills, I found no difficulty in procuring them whenever I wanted, from the crows and ravens with which the beach was almost always covered, attracted by the offal of whales, seals, etc., and which were so tame that I could easily kill them with stones, while a large clam-shell furnished me with an inkstand."

Although his writing was extensively doctored by an editor, Jewitt's reportage provided some of the first, extensive observations of how the Nuu-chah-nulth lived from day to day. He also provided detailed and mainly favourable impressions of his cap-

This imaginary portrait entitled "John Jewitt, Captive of Chief Maquina [sic] at Nootka, 1803" was completed by Charles William Jefferys in 1945, one of thousands of fanciful drawings of Canadian history by Jefferys.

tor, Maquinna, who became his friend. By establishing himself as an intermediary or "wholesaler" for the other tribes, sometimes playing the English off against the Spanish, Maquinna had become the most powerful chief in his area. Jewitt found him impressive. "He was dressed in a large mantle or cloak of the black sea-otter skin, which reached to his knees, and was fastened around his middle by a broad belt of the cloth of the country, wrought or painted with figures of several colours; this dress was by no means unbecoming, but, on the contrary, had an air of savage magnificence."

While Thompson remained estranged from his captors, Jewitt helped Maquinna improve his facility with English, he made knives and fish hooks for other chiefs, and he gave ornaments to their wives and children. In particular, Jewitt gained the favour of Maquinna's wife, and Maquinna's eleven-year-old boy also doted on him. In return, Jewitt was adopted into the tribe and taken by Maquinna to select a wife of his choosing.

After a feast of herring spawn and oil, Jewitt chose "a young girl of about seventeen, the daughter of Upquesta, chief." Her name was given by Jewitt as Eu-stoch-ee-exqua. After much speechifying and bargaining between Maquinna and Upquesta, Jewitt received his bride the following morning.

Another feast ensued at Maquinna's village where Jewitt was instructed that no sexual intercourse could occur for the next ten days. Jewitt, Eu-stoch-ee-exqua, Thompson and Maquinna's young son Sat-sat-sok-sis were thereafter accorded a separate apartment in part of Maquinna's house.

It is apparent from Jewitt's favourable description of Eu-stoch-ee-exqua that an affectionate relationship ensued. "I found my Indian princess both amiable and intelligent," he wrote. "She would indeed have been considered as very pretty in any country, and, excepting Maquinna's queen, was by far the handsomest of any of their women."

Although Jewitt likely had a child by Eu-stoch-ee-exqua, he refrained from describing this relationship, likely out of deference to his New England (post-Puritan) readership, and professed some reluctance to submit to the marriage.

Jewitt was accorded four slaves after he participated in a successful surprise attack on the village of Ayshart 50 miles to the south during which approximately six hundred warriors in forty canoes obliterated their opposition, taking many slaves and ruthlessly murdering the weak, elderly and wounded. Although Maquinna was considerate of Jewitt's health, he also advised him that he would be killed if he was ever caught trying to escape. According to Jewitt, Maquinna claimed he had killed six refugees from the American ship *Manchester*, ramming stones down their throats after they had tried to escape from his village.

Jewitt bided his time until July 19, 1805, when another trading brig, the *Lydia*, approached Friendly Cove. The captain of the *Lydia*, Captain Samuel Hill, had been alerted to the presence of the two English captives held by Maquinna by a friendly chief to the north.

Jewitt hastily wrote a note to Captain Hill and duped Maquinna into delivering it. His message begged Hill to invite Maquinna aboard, capture him, and demand the release of Thompson and himself. When other Nuu-chah-nulth advised Maquinna against boarding the ship, Maquinna asked Jewitt for advice and he naturally suggested it would be safe.

After the captain supplied Maquinna with an alcoholic drink, Maquinna was held at gunpoint. Following much agitation ashore, Jewitt and Thompson were successfully traded for Maquinna. The captain also persuaded the Mowachaht to return all items that had been taken from the *Boston* two years earlier. Oddly, Maquinna and Jewitt parted as friends, with Maquinna—according to Jewitt—inviting him to return.

Maquinna's motives for his retribution against the *Boston* and for keeping Jewitt at his side remain a matter for conjecture. The historian Robin A. Fisher and others have suggested the waning of the fur trade at Nootka Sound had damaged Maquinna's prestige among his people. According to Jewitt, Maquinna was sometimes criticized and threatened by his own people who resented the diminishment of trade with foreigners. Although Maquinna once held a potlatch at which he was able to distribute two hundred muskets and seven barrels of gunpowder, access to European commodities had greatly decreased. Chief Wickaninish's offer to purchase Jewitt from Maquinna was declined partially because Maquinna wanted Jewitt available as an intermediary if another trading ship arrived.

The *Lydia* left for China in August and did not reach its home port of Boston until the middle of 1807. *A Journal Kept At Nootka Sound* by John R. Jewitt was released that same year. Having accepted an Aboriginal wife at Nootka, Jewitt married Hester Jones on Christmas Day, 1809.

Jewitt's literary fame was not extensive until his narrative caught the attention of wealthy Hartford merchant Richard Alsop, known as one of the Connecticut Wits. Recognizing the commercial value of Jewitt's slim tale, Alsop in 1815 overcame Jewitt's "small capacity as an narrator" by conducting several interviews with Jewitt to embellish his rudimentary version. By using Daniel Defoe's *Robinson Crusoe* as his literary model, Alsop extensively rewrote Jewitt's original account and republished it at Middletown, Connecticut, as *A Narrative of the Adventures and Sufferings of John R. Jewitt*. . . . The ghost-written version refers to Jewitt as the lone survivor of the massacre of his crewmates when in fact Jewitt was one of two men spared.

As the "proprietor" of this work rather than its author, Jewitt applied for a copyright of the enhanced version, printed by Loomis & Richardson, on March 8, 1815. On that same day Jewitt copyrighted a song as its "proprietor," printed as a broadside, entitled *The Poor Armourer Boy, A Song*. He or Alsop had evidently mimicked a sea song of the parlour variety for his melodramatic text with rhyming couplets.

Jewitt set out in earnest to publicize the new Alsop version of his tale, peddling copies from town to town in a one-horse wagon. Alsop's expanded version provided "A list of words in the Nootkian Language, the most in use." At least 20 versions of this revised journal have appeared since 1815. An 1896 edition provided notes on Vancouver Island history and some added reminiscences by explorer Robert Brown.

Alsop began to regret his partnership with Jewitt after Jewitt set about selling his book and derivative broadside as far north as Maine and as far south as Maryland. With the assistance of successful playwright James Nelson Barker of Philadelphia, Jewitt appeared in a theatrical version of his ordeal that premiered on March 21, 1817. Entitled *Armourer's Escape: Or Three Years at Nootka*

John R. Jewitt and Mike Maquinna (now chief of the Mowachaht) met in 1987 at the Vancouver Museum as sixth-generation descendants of the white slave and his Aboriginal master. The dagger they display in this photo was made by Jewitt's ancestor for his captor approximately 183 years earlier.

Sound, this "Melo Drama, founded on the interesting narrative of Mr. John Jewitt," concluded with a rendition of *The Song of the Armourer Boy* by John Jewitt himself after he had performed an Indian war song in the language of the Nootkas.

No copy of this play has ever surfaced. There are no known reviews. The play ran for three successive nights, but evening revenues at the Philadelphia Theatre were less than encouraging. Jewitt continued to perform in his Nootka costume but his star flickered and his health waned. In an era when acting professionally was deemed less than respectable, his wife once wrote to him saying she would rather learn he was dead than hear he was "being at the theatre." The itinerant showman and book salesman eventually returned to his wife and children in Middletown. He died in obscurity in Hartford, Connecticut, on January 7, 1821.

The original Jewitt journal of 1807 was reprinted in 1931 by Charles E. Goodspeed & Company in Boston. The University of British Columbia has digitized Jewitt's 1807 *A Journal Kept at Nootka Sound* and the later *Narrative* version. The American Memory collection of the Library of Congress provides scanned pages from the original 1815 edition. Jewitt would doubtless be pleased to know a movie is forever in the works.

John Jewitt was not the first white man to reside in British Columbia for more than a year. That distinction belongs to an Irish-born, Bombay soldier who served as the assistant doctor on a fur trading ship that reached Nootka Sound in 1786. After falling ill, this man, named John MacKay, volunteered to remain as Chief Maquinna's guest at Yuquot and Tahsis from the summer of 1786 to the autumn of 1787.

JOHN D'WOLF

*"Capt. D'Wolf was one of the most compassionate
and benevolent of men."* —GEORGE H. VON LANGSDORFF

It is generally assumed that John Jacob Astor's creation of
Astoria at the mouth of the Columbia River provided the original spark for the fur trading industry of the Oregon Territory,
but, in fact, some little-known precursors built a short-lived settlement along the banks of the Columbia in 1810. One of the
main catalysts for this pioneering experiment was John D'Wolf
(1779–1872)—Herman Melville's uncle—who sailed along the
North Pacific coast in 1805 as captain of the American brig *Juno*.

A worldly adventurer who had gone to sea at age thirteen,
D'Wolf was a member of a prominent Rhode Island family that
prospered by owning merchant ships in the slave trade. After
eleven years at sea, D'Wolf, at age twenty-four, was hired by members of his family to navigate the newly purchased *Juno* to the
Northwest Coast to collect furs for China. It was a welcome promotion for D'Wolf, who was reportedly averse to the slave trade.

In April of 1805, laden with hardware, rum, tobacco, beads,
dried beef, firearms and cottons, his ship arrived on the north-
western tip of Vancouver Island at Newettee Harbour.

"Everything around us, the sea, the sky, and the precipitous
shore, covered with a forest of heavy timber, wore a most gloomy
aspect," he wrote. "We were visited daily by a great number of the
Indians, who generally brought with them a few sea-otter skins,
but not enough to make trade brisk. They were exceedingly sharp
in all their intercourse with us, being great beggars, withal. It
seemed impossible to satisfy them for their skins, and they were
ready to grasp at everything they saw. They were a very stout and

robust people, and in some things not destitute of skill. Their boats were hewn from a single log, and varied in size from sixteen feet in length and three in breadth, to thirty-five in length and six in breadth. Their paddles were made and ornamented with a great deal of neatness."

Proceeding north, D'Wolf reached New Archangel on the west coast of Baranov Island on August 17, 1805. In New Archangel (now called Sitka) he met Baron Nikolai Petrovich Rezanov, who was the Czar's representative on an attempt to circumnavigate the globe. D'Wolf befriended his physician, twenty-nine-year-old German naturalist George H. von Langsdorff, who had travelled through Polynesia on Krusenstern's voyage of exploration in 1804. (Langsdorff and D'Wolf would meet again in St. Petersburg in 1809.)

The journal of John D'Wolf, published in 1861, recalls how and why he sold his 206-ton ship to Rezanov, along with the remaining one-third of his outward cargo, saving the Russians from starvation, they having already eaten most of the supplies of their host, Russian Governor Baranov. At age sixty-five, wracked by arthritis, the emperor-like Baranov ladled vodka from a bucket that he always kept by his side.

To save the Russian colony from famine, Rezanov paid almost twice what the *Juno* and her entire cargo had cost its owners in Bristol. In addition, he provided D'Wolf with the Russian ship *Yermak* in exchange. Having already profited by selling one-third of his cargo to Baranov shortly after his arrival, D'Wolf was able to instruct his crewmen to sail to China without him in order to sell the one thousand pelts he had acquired in trade.

D'Wolf planned to sail to Siberia on the *Juno* with its new Russian owners, but Rezanov tarried, waiting for a second ship to be built. By winter's end, provisions were again running low, encouraging Rezanov to sail to California in the spring of 1806 in the hope of acquiring food from the Spanish.

During this bizarre escapade, Rezanov temporarily banished five of D'Wolf's American seamen on barren Alcatraz Island, and he decapitated some seabirds Langsdorff had collected as specimens, tossing their carcasses overboard. As well, the forty-year-old Baron managed to get himself betrothed to fifteen-year-old Maria de la Concepción Argüello, the youngest daughter of Don José "El Santo" Argüello, commandant of San Francisco.

Returning to New Archangel on June 21, Rezanov was triumphant. The trouble was that Rezanov could not marry without the Czar's permission, nor could his sweetheart marry him without the Pope's consent. A wedding date was set two years hence, for May 20, 1808.

Unable to abide further delays, D'Wolf took charge of the 25-ton brig *Russisloff*, and sailed with Langsdorff to the Russian coast, from where he would become become the first American to travel across Siberia from east to west, but it would take him 16 months after leaving Alaska to reach St. Petersburg.

Meanwhile, in a sudden haste to see the Czar, Rezanov crossed Siberia separately, travelling at a feverish pace, only to be thrown from his horse near Krasnoyarsk, just over the Urals, and die.

With Rezanov gone, Baranov was able to consider an idea supplied to him by D'Wolf, an idea that opened the way for the aforementioned American venture in Oregon in 1810, led by Captain Nathan Winshop.

In the early 1800s, Spain was prohibiting foreigners to trade with "their" Indians for sea otters along the California coast. In order to gain access to that potentially lucrative market, D'Wolf had suggested a plan to Baranov to circumvent Spanish restrictions—take Kodiak Indians from Alaska to conduct the offshore hunting.

Baranov was enthusiastic but his visiting superior Rezanov did not want to risk alienating the Spanish and therefore jeopardize the Russians' access to supplies. After D'Wolf left New Archangel, the idea lay fallow until the Winship family in Boston contracted with the Russians to employ Aleut hunters off the California coast in 1810.

Seeking a depot between the Russians in Alaska and the California sea otter grounds, Captain Winship decided upon the Columbia River because the Lewis and Clark expedition had wintered there in 1805–1806, allowing Winship to claim it was an American river, beyond Spanish jurisdiction.

In May of 1810, Winship sailed 40 miles up the Columbia River in the *Albatross*, with livestock and supplies. Here he attempted to build a fort, opposite present-day Oak Point, Washington, but Winship's crew were forced to forsake the enterprise by increasingly hostile Indians. Theirs was nonetheless the first attempt to make a permanent American fur trading depot on America's Pacific coast, albeit a failed one. Very soon thereafter, John Jacob Astor followed Winship's lead, establishing Astoria.

Some years later, at age thirty-five, John D'Wolf, married Mary Melville, and he subsequently had a profound influence on her young nephew, Herman Melville, who spent his summer vacations with D'Wolf's family at Bristol, Rhode Island.

The seafaring tales of "Nor'Wester John" stirred the boy's imagination, encouraging him eventually to seek his own adventures at sea, culminating in the novel *Moby Dick*. In homage, both Captain Langsdorff and Captain D'Wolf appear in Chapter 45 of the novel.

In *Moby Dick*, Melville describes a whale that John D'Wolf had encountered while on the *Russisloff* in the Sea of Okhotsk. "A whale bigger than the ship set up his back and lifted the ship three feet out of the water. The masts reeled and the sails fell all together, while we who were below sprang instantly upon the deck, concluding we had struck upon some rock; instead of which we saw the monster sailing off with the utmost gravity and solemnity, leaving the ship uninjured."

Continuing in the unusual semi-autobiographical style of *Moby Dick*, Herman Melville says, "Now the Capt. deWolf here alluded to as commanding the ship in question is a New Englander who, after a long life of unusual adventures as a sea captain, this day resides in the village of Dorchester near Boston. I have the honor of being his nephew. The ship was by no means a large one, being a Russian craft built on the Siberian coast and purchased by my uncle after bartering away the vessel in which he had sailed from home."

CAMILLE DE ROQUEFEUIL

Lieutenant Camille de Roquefeuil of France twice explored the coast of British Columbia during a voyage of 1816–1819, a circumnavigation of the globe intended to increase French prospects for commerce in the aftermath of Napoleon's overthrow. His unedited journal provides one of the most complete records of Aboriginal life in early nineteenth-century British Columbia. One of the two maps in his book is a detailed view of the world. The other shows the Pacific Coast from Alaska to California.

"Due to various circumstances and to certain timidity," according to the introduction to the French first edition, de Roquefeuil refrained from having his journal printed in 1820 when it was completed. He gave it to his family, allowing them to do with it as they pleased, whereupon one of his brothers shepherded the travelogue into print in 1823, eight years before he died. Although de Roquefeuil succeeded in making the third French circumnavigation of the world, under official government auspices, he was not promoted upon his return.

De Roquefeuil sailed from Bordeaux, in his ship the *Bordelaise*, in October of 1816 and arrived at Nootka, via Chile, in September of 1817. He carried 35 crewmen and three officers. Theirs was the first expedition to describe conditions at Nootka since the massacre of the *Boston*'s crew and the enslavement of John Jewitt. De Roquefeuil gave Maquinna a seven-gun salute.

The French obtained some furs at Barkley Sound, and de Roquefeuil described a village of "Nitinat" south of Nootka Sound. "We saw several men and a greater number of women, whose complexion differed from white only by a tinge of pale yellow. Some young people, of both sexes, had a colour, and many children would have been thought pretty in Europe. The greater number of the Indians have black hair, the remainder a light red, all wear the hair long, and the women comb it carefully, and divide it over the middle of the forehead. Both sexes dress the same as at Nootka, with this difference, that the women wear under their other garments a kind of apron of bark, not woven, but only fastened to a girdle. We saw many well-made women with good arms, but in general, very ugly hands. On the whole they are better looking than the women of Nootka, though there is something harsher in their countenances, chiefly owing to their narrow foreheads, which are wrinkled at an early age. We saw only three or four who in Europe would have any pretensions to beauty. One of them was the wife of Cia, who had received us hospitably; another, the wife of a great chief, was almost white; she had large black eyes, regular features, a fine countenance, and much propriety and dignity in her manners. The women and girls appeared as modest as those of Nootka, and still more reserved."

In 1817, the Frenchmen also visited a hill at present-day Masset in Haida Gwaii when it was designated as a fortress. De Roquefeuil wrote, "There is something picturesque in the whole appearance of this large village. It is particularly remarkable for the monstrous and colossal figures which decorate the houses of the principal inhabitants, the wide gaping mouths of which serve as a door. . . . Ascending the arm of the sea, there is, on the north side, above the largest village, a fort, the parapet of which is covered with beautiful turf, and surrounded by a palisade in good condition."

De Roquefeuil wintered in California and returned to the Pacific Northwest in 1818, jointly trading for furs with the Russians at Sitka. Their party was attacked by the Tlingits while they were anchored on the east side of Prince of Wales Island. Twenty of the hired Aleut men, on contract with the Russians, were killed, and the French explorer barely escaped with his life.

Camille de Roquefeuil visited Maquinna at Friendly Cove a second time, staying at Nootka for 19 days overall. Familiar with the unreliable reports of John Meares, who spread the word that

Maquinna was likely a cannibal, the Frenchman was taken aback when his ship's doctor found human bones that "led us to believe that they were the remains of a repast of cannibals." It was explained to him that the bones belonged to dead bodies unearthed by bears, but de Roquefeuil remained ill at ease visiting a ceremonial spot consecrated to festivities related to the whale fishery.

For early explorers, fear of cannibalism spread its reputation as much as any apparent evidence. "I know not whether it was the idea of an abominable repast suggested by the accounts of Meares, which had possessed my mind and cast a gloom over all this scene," he wrote. Born in 1781, de Roquefeuil died in 1831.

SAMUEL PATTERSON

Between 1802 and 1808, little-known American sailor Samuel Patterson, born in 1785, was a member of three expeditions to the Pacific Northwest, visiting Vancouver Island and Haida Gwaii, later known as the Queen Charlotte Islands. In 1805 he sailed aboard the American brig *Juno* when its captain and owner, John D'Wolf, Herman Melville's uncle, made his second fur trading voyage to the Pacific Northwest.

Patterson met the "white slave of the Nootka," John Jewitt, who was freed from captivity under Chief Maquinna in July of 1805. Ten years later, after John Jewitt successfully re-published an enhanced version of his journal as *A Narrative of the Adventures and Sufferings of John R. Jewitt*, Patterson decided he ought to take advantage of the genre and publish his own "Sufferings" with an imitative title. This *Narrative* was compiled and edited for Patterson by Ezekiel Terry, apparently because Patterson was so unhinged by his sufferings that he could not manage the task on his own.

Patterson's far-reaching memoir recalls visits to Guinea, Havana, Guadaloupe, California, the northwest coast of America, Australia, Canton and Fiji where he was shipwrecked in 1808 and remained for six months. It also recounts his voyages to Algiers in 1800–1802 aboard the frigate *George Washington*, and a slaving voyage in 1802. In 1807 Patterson was aboard the *O'Cain* that took some Russian fur hunters and 50 Aleuts and their canoes from Sitka to northern California where the Russians established Fort Ross for fur harvesting and agricultural reasons.

WILLIAM STURGIS

O ne of the earliest attempts to create a phonetic dictionary of Aboriginal languages for the Pacific Northwest was made by a young American sailor, William F. Sturgis, who first visited the West Coast in 1799, at age seventeen. From 1810 to 1850, much of the American fur trading along the Pacific Northwest coast was conducted under Sturgis' direction. In 1846, during a lecture in Boston, he declared that the only natural objects more attractive to him than sea otter pelts were "a beautiful woman and a lovely infant."

William F. Sturgis was born on February 25, 1782, in Barnstable, Massachusetts, where his father William E. Sturgis was a ship master. William F. Sturgis entered into the New England counting house of his uncle Russell Sturgis in 1796. A year-and-a-half later he became connected with James and Thomas Perkins who were engaged in the booming fur trade between the Pacific Northwest coast and China. Upon the death of his father in 1797, he went to sea to support the family. His employers at J. & T.H. Perkins were dispatching the *Eliza*, on which Sturgis acted as assistant trader. He was so good in this position that he was chosen chief mate of the *Ulysses*. He then served under Captain Charles

William Sturgis

Derby in the *Caroline* until Derby died and Sturgis took command. In 1804 the *Caroline* sailed from the Columbia River to Kaigahnee, just south of Prince of Wales Island in Alaska, amassing 2,500 sea otter skins that netted $73,034.

William Sturgis returned to Boston in 1810 and with John Bryant formed the house of Bryant & Sturgis, transacting business with the Pacific Coast and China. The firm of Bryant and Sturgis would continue for more than 50 years until Sturgis' death. He was known for his fair dealings with Aboriginals, as well as his proficiency at Latin. Sturgis once brought some 5,000 ermine skins from Leipzig and traded them for sea otter skins on a five (otter)-to-one (ermine) ratio, later turning a substantial profit in Canton.

In 1810 Captain Sturgis married Elizabeth M. Davis and sired one son and five daughters. He took great interest in public affairs, especially relating to the Pacific Northwest. For almost 30 years he was a member of the Massachusetts House or Senate. He was President of the Boston Marine Society and a member of the Massachusetts Historical Society. He died on October 21, 1863, at the age of eighty-one, leaving the Sturgis Library in Barnstable.

STEPHEN REYNOLDS

"Mutiny aborted! Normal hell restored!"
—THE JOURNAL OF STEPHEN REYNOLDS

American-born Stephen Reynolds, at age twenty-eight, embarked for the Pacific Northwest as a fo'c'sle hand on the 95-foot, 281-ton brig *New Hazard* in 1811, having left Boston equipped with pen and ink, evidently eager to record his impressions in a log. Although Reynolds was not exceptionally literate, he does record reading the 1754 novel by Samuel Richardson, *Sir Charles Grandison and the Honourable Miss Byron,* during his visit among the Haida in August of 1812. Reynolds' rare record of an ordinary seaman's perspective recounts two extensive visits to the Pacific Northwest, chiefly around the Queen Charlotte Islands, with brief sojourns in Hawaii and a voyage to the Orient. His name was recorded as Stephen Runnels on the crew list because it was only after the Revolutionary War that his father Enos Runnels changed the family surname to Reynolds.

Life aboard the *New Hazard* was particularly brutal. The oldest man aboard was aged thirty-three. Neophyte Captain David Nye, Jr., and his mate Samuel Gale, according to F.W. Howay, "were tyrants of a type rarely found in the American merchant service." There were 28 floggings and "rope's-endings" during the voyage.

After sailing north from Hawaii, the captain gave the cabin boy a "catting." Of 19 foremast hands, only eight escaped flogging. Reynolds himself was once flogged and put in irons after he and four others went ashore on June 11, 1811, without permission, near the northern tip of Vancouver Island.

On January 22, 1812, the Captain requested Reynolds to alert him if a rebellion was in the works. Eleven days later another crew member was put in irons and threatened with death for tossing his bread allowance overboard.

Reynolds explained, "Sebre Pratt, was dissatisfied with his allowance of bread. Mr. Hewes weighed it; said the allowance was full; upon which Sebre threw it overboard. He was shortly called aft; was ordered to be tied up. He cried out, 'Help! Help!' All hands went up to release him; the captain threatened to shoot them. Sebre was taken in the

Oil portrait of Stephen Reynolds in Honolulu, 1848, by J.M. Stanley

cabin; put in IRONS. Captain told them he had been told they were going to take the ship from him. I was charged with telling the news to captain because I was in cabin a few nights since after a shirt. ALL IS BUZZ!!!! Mutiny aborted! Normal hell restored!"

With the supply of sea otters severely depleted, and competition for them fierce, slave trading formed part of the expedition's commercial activities. On June 20, 1811, Reynolds recorded, "Sold all shrowton [oolachon oil] and two slaves: one slave five skins, one, three." Four more slaves were purchased by the ship at Cape Flattery on August 1. Following their captain's lead, sailors aboard the *New Hazard* later traded for slave women obtained from the Haida.

Due to the increasing competition for furs, the *New Hazard* spent an entire winter in the vicinity of the Queen Charlotte Islands. "Wednesday, 11 December. Setting coal-pit; sawing boards. Mr. Hewes ashore all afternoon. Two girls on board all night. Mr. Bruce sent me a fathom of India cotton last evening, for which I very much thank him. At eight got under weigh, towed out of the Key where we left some thin ice."

To trade for sea otter pelts, the ship carried "musquets, bread, molasses, sugar, India cottons, wearing apparel, hardware, gunpowder, paints, iron, rice, sheetings, shot, tobacco, woolens, woodenware."

In 1812 there were at least 13 ships on the coast, including the *New Hazard, Lydia, Packet, Albatross, Amethyst, Atahualpa, Beaver, Charon, Isabella, Katharine, Hamilton, O'Cain, Mercury, Pedler* and possibly *Sylph.* The *Lydia,* under Captain James Bennett, and the *New Hazard* sailed together for several months. Whereas most of the ships that visited the Pacific Northwest in the early 1800s were Boston-owned, the *New Hazard,* built in Newberry in 1810, as well as a ship named *Packet,* were both Salem-owned.

On July 10, 1812, near Masset, Reynolds reported their ship was approached by the "long-wished-for" *Packet* from Salem, under Captain Bacon, which had sailed from Boston in 1811 to relieve them. "Upon hearing this, the joy was so great that it almost made the dumb to speak," he writes.

The *New Hazard* proceeded to Hawaii for supplies and sandal-wood, crossed the Pacific to Canton in December of 1812, returned to Hawaii, sailed around South America and evaded a British naval barricade in order to reach the wharf at New Bedford on Christmas Day, 1813. The *New Hazard* sank after only eight years of service, during a voyage from Salem to Batavia in 1817.

Also in 1817, Reynolds sailed to the Pacific coast of South America on the *Ida*, then settled for the majority of his years in Hawaii where he married Susan Jackson in the 1820s and had five children. Reynolds maintained a diary of his life in Hawaii from 1822 to 1855.

Born on November 18, 1782, at Andover in Massachusetts, Reynolds died at age seventy-four at West Boxford, Massachusetts on July 17, 1857.

EDWARD BELCHER

The seven-year scientific voyage of the H.M.S. *Sulphur* to explore the Pacific Ocean and its shorelines began from Plymouth, England, in December of 1835 under the command of Captain Frederick William Beechey, accompanied by the *Starling*. After Beechey took ill at Valparaiso in Chile, Edward Belcher came aboard as the new captain of the *Sulphur* in February of 1837 at Panama. Belcher had previously sailed under Captain Beechey as a surveyor on the *Blossom*. He subsequently undertook surveys of harbours along the coast of California and northwest to Alaska, including Nootka Sound.

From San Blas, H.M.S. *Sulphur* sailed to the Sandwich Islands (Hawaii), Prince William Sound, the southern coast of Russian America (Alaska), New Archangel (Sitka), Nootka Sound, San Francisco and Central America. In 1839, the *Sulphur* and the *Star-*

ling made a second voyage to some of the same regions, stopping at Kodiak, Fort Vancouver, Fort Ross and Santa Barbara. Other locales visited under Belcher's command included the Sacramento River, the Marquesas, the Society Islands, the Tonga Islands, the New Hebrides, the Solomon Islands and New Guinea.

In 1843, Sir Edward Belcher (1799–1877) published his two-volume *Narrative of a Voyage Round the World, performed in Her Majesty's ship* Sulphur, *during the years 1836–1842, including details of the naval operations in China, from Dec. 1840 to Nov. 1841.* The fourth chapter provides his account of visiting Nootka Sound in 1837 and his meeting with "Chief Maquilla," sometimes described as the son-in-law to Maquinna. Belcher's two-volume book was reviewed by the *Edinburgh Review* in 1844. The surgeon on the *Sulphur*, Richard Brinsley Hinds, also published his zoological studies of the voyage, credited to Belcher, and collaborated on a botanical atlas with naturalist G. Bentham.

CHARLES WILKES

R enowned as a stern disciplinarian with an obsessive personality, Charles Wilkes became an influential character in the political history of the Pacific Northwest when he served as the young commander for the U.S. Surveying and Exploration Expedition of 1838–1842, leading a hydrographic survey of the Columbia River from its mouth to the Cascades, about 160 miles from the river mouth.

The Columbia River was integral to the overland fur trade on the Western Slope during the first half of the nineteenth century, but for many years nobody was certain who ought to control the route. The American sea captain Robert Gray, who named the Columbia River after his ship *Columbia Rediviva*, is usually cited as the Euro-American "discoverer" of the Columbia River in 1792, but the first European to record evidence of the river was the Spanish navigator Bruno de Hezeta in 1775.

Only five months after Gray had crossed the bar of the Columbia in 1792, Captain George Vancouver's second-in-command, Lieutenant William Broughton of the HMS *Chatham*, sent two survey boats upriver for one hundred miles, producing the first reliable map of the Columbia as far as the future site of Fort Vancouver.

After fur trader David

Charles Wilkes

Thompson became the first man to map the Columbia River for the North West Company and the British warship, *Racoon*, ceremoniously took charge of the river mouth in 1813, the American warship *Ontario* returned the favour in 1818. By the time British naval commander Edward Belcher led *Starling* and *Sulphur* upriver as far as Fort Vancouver in 1839, the issue as to whether Great Britain or the United States ought to pursue claims to the Columbia waterway was thoroughly perplexing.

Charles Wilkes first undertook a personal reconnaissance of the area north of the the Columbia in May of 1841 by travelling overland from Nisqually (Puget Sound), down the Cowlitz River to the Columbia, passing Mount St. Helens along the way, and reaching the river's mouth.

In July he returned to the river mouth in his flagship *Vincennes*. He then sent it southward to California and took charge of another vessel, the 224-ton brigantine *Porpoise*, better suited to exploring the river and crossing the bar. At Fort George he also bought a 250-ton merchant brig, the *Oregon*, to follow his survey boats upriver.

By August, Wilkes' expedition reached Fort Vancouver where he dined with Dr. John McLoughlin and George Simpson, Governor of the Hudson's Bay Company. Wilkes confided to Simpson that he planned to recommend to the U.S. government that it should claim all territory northward as far as 54° 40' north. This was alarming and important news to Simpson who promptly wrote to the British Foreign Office advising them of the need to retain control of all land north of the Columbia River.

Lieutenant William M. Walker completed another American naval survey upriver as far as the Cascades; Lieutenant Oliver Hazard Perry undertook similar work along the Willamette River. Concurrently Charles Wilkes visited 40 American settlers in the Willamette Valley and discussed with them the logistics of eventually establishing a civil government under the U.S. flag.

Although Wilkes eventually advised the American government that the Columbia River harbour was too dangerous for anchorages and safe passage, and the Puget Sound area of Seattle ought to be deemed more essential to U.S. interests, his invasive presence for most of 1841 in an area largely under the administration of the Hudson's Bay Company greatly undermined the confidence of the British.

In 1841 Wilkes published an important map of the Oregon Territory that included the British Columbia coastline. Describing the Pacific Northwest, he once wrote: "Not a shoal exists within the Straits of Juan de Fuca, Admiralty Inlet, Puget Sound, or Hood's Canal. . . . No country in the world . . . possesses waters equal to these."

Wilkes' survey work established many place names within Washington State (such as Elliott Bay, Maury Island, Hale Passage, Hammersley Inlet), and he named McNeill Island for Hudson's Bay Company sea captain William Henry McNeill.

Although he twice faced a court martial for his alleged overuse of the cat-o'-nine-tails (and was acquitted), Wilkes was awarded the Founders Medal by the Royal Geographical Society in 1847.

The capricious Wilkes had a varied and controversial naval career, rising from Superintendent of the Depot of Charts and Instruments at Washington, D.C., to the rank of Rear Admiral. He is credited with the discovery of Antarctica in December of 1839 (hence Wilkes Land in Antarctica) and his personality influenced Herman Melville's depiction of Ahab in *Moby Dick*. In fact, Melville included details of Wilkes' *Narrative of the United States Exploring Expedition* in the famous novel.

Born in New York City on April 3, 1798, Wilkes died on February 8, 1877, in Washington, D.C. His remains were re-interred in Arlington National Cemetery in 1920. Among his admirers was Charles Darwin.

EUGENE DUFLOT DE MOFRAS

One of the rarest books about the Pacific Coast of North America is *Exploration du Territoire de l'Orégon, des Californies et de la Mer Vermeille, Executée Pendant les Années 1840, 1841 et 1842* by the Frenchman sent to Mexico City in 1839 to ascertain the viability of commerce from California to Alaska.

Eugene Duflot de Mofras sailed to the Bering Strait and back, then provided a large map of the West Coast. He charted the major ports from San Blas to the Aleutians, including the mouth of the Columbia River and Nootka Sound.

A collection of Mofras' writings was edited by Marguerite Eyer Wilbur and published in 1937 as *Duflot De Mofras' Travels on the Pacific Coast*. The book contains descriptive accounts of the Oregon territory, Vancouver Island, the Fraser River and several HBC forts.

[NEW CALEDONIANS]

DANIEL HARMON

Nicknamed "the priest" by his fur trading companions, Daniel Harmon was an intensely moral and intelligent American whose enduring marriage to Elizabeth Laval, or Duval ("my cherished companion"), the Métis daughter of a French-Canadian voyageur and a "Snare" [Snake Indian] woman, exemplified his unusually loyal nature.

The fourth son of a tavern-keeper, Daniel Williams Harmon was born at Bennington, Vermont (then part of New York), on February 19, 1778.

Raised with minimal schooling, Harmon joined the North West Company at age twenty-two in Montreal in the spring of 1800. Initially Harmon's opinions of his fellow fur traders were unsympathetic.

Habitually reading the Bible, Harmon disapproved of drinking and card playing on the Sabbath. "It is a lamentable fact that most of those who are in this wild part of the World, lay aside most of Christian and Civilized regulations and behave but little better than the savages themselves," he commented.

For 16 years Harmon was employed by the North West Company on the Saskatchewan, in Athabasca and in New Caledonia. He spent five years at the Swan River Department of central Saskatchewan, stationed at Fort Alexandria (built in 1795 and different from Fort Alexandria in British Columbia), Bird Mountain and Lac la Piche.

In 1802, when he was still a bachelor, Harmon declined a marriage with the daughter of a Cree chief at Fort Alexandria. The following year, he assumed guardianship of a half-Ojibwa son of another company man.

Harmon eventually accepted fourteen-year-old "Elizabeth" (Lisette) as his country wife, or *femme du pays, à la façon du pays* (in the custom of the country) on October 10, 1805, at South Branch Fort, Saskatchewan. She would bear him fourteen children, bury all but two, and remain faithfully at Harmon's side until the end of his days.

Harmon recorded his thoughts prior to the union: "This day a Canadian's daughter (A girl of about fourteen years of age) was offered me, and after mature consideration concerning the step I ought to take I finally concluded it would be best to accept of her, as it is customary for all the Gentlemen who come in this Country to remain any length of time to have a fair Partner, with whom they can pass away their time at least more sociably if not agreeably than to live a lonely, solitary life, as they must do if single.

"In case we can live in harmony together, my intentions now are to keep her as long as I remain in this uncivilized part of the world, but when I return to my native land shall endeavour to place her into the hands of some good honest Man, with whom she can pass the remainder of her Days in this Country much more agreeably, than it would be possible for her to do, were she to be taken down into the civilized world, where she would be a stranger to the people, their manners, customs, Language.

"Her mother is of the Tribe of the Snare Indians, whose country lies about the Rocky Mountain. The Girl is said to be of a mild disposition, even tempered, which are qualities very necessary to make an agreeable Woman and an effectionate [sic] Partner."

Harmon's prediction that he would feel obliged to part with Lisette would prove incorrect. After two years in the Athabasca District, the Harmons were relocated to New Caledonia, arriving at Fort St. James on November 7, 1810, then reaching Fraser Lake on December 29, 1810.

From 1810 to 1819, they mainly lived at Fort St. James and Fort Fraser. Harmon was placed in charge of Fort St. James from 1811 to 1813. Later he briefly visited Nazko in 1815 and Fort Chippewyan in 1817.

In New Caledonia, the fur trading was complicated by the fact that the Carrier people of north-central B.C. spoke three separate dialects and were attuned to a fishing economy rather than trapping. As well, access to beaver lands and salmon fisheries were traditionally proprietory, a system that fur traders had difficulty comprehending.

Although bitterly cold winters, relations with Carrier Indians and obtaining food were challenging, isolation could prove equally daunting in the "Siberia of the fur trade," particularly if someone craved serious conversation about religion and literature.

In 1813, stationed at Stuart Lake in New Caledonia, Harmon wrote: "No other people, perhaps, who pursue business to obtain a livelihood, have so much leisure, as we do. Few of us are employed more, and many of us much less, than one fifth of our time, in transacting the business of the Company. The remaining four-fifths are at our own disposal.

"If we do not, with such an opportunity, improve our understandings, the fault must be our own; for there are few posts, which are not tolerably well supplied with books. These books are not, indeed, all of the best kind; but among them are many which are valuable. If I were deprived of these silent companions, many a gloomy hour would pass over me. Even with them, my spirit at times sinks, when I reflect on the great length of time which has elapsed, since I left the land of my nativity, and my relatives and friends, to dwell in this savage country."

Two years before the North West Company was subsumed by the HBC in 1821, Daniel Harmon decided to return to Vermont via Montreal. This decision was made partially in response to declining prospects for the western fur trade in general, but also in response to residual grief.

In 1811, Harmon had very reluctantly accepted an offer from Jules Quesnel to escort their four-year-old son George Harmon back to Montreal, then send him onto his relatives in Vermont to enable the boy to be educated. Daniel Harmon and Lisette were later devastated to learn their son had died of scarlet fever in

Vergennes, Vermont, on March 18, 1813. Harmon wrote: "Her [Lisette's] distress at receiving this intelligence was greater, if possible, than my own. I endeavoured, by some introductory remarks on the uncertainty of earthly things, to prepare her mind for the disclosure which I was about to make. Her fears were alarmed by these remarks, and she probably discovered in my countenance something to confirm them. When I informed her that our beloved son was dead, she looked at me with a wild stare of agony and immediately threw herself on the bed, where she continued in a state of delirium during the succeeding night."

"Without detracting in any way or measure from the merits of Mackenzie's work," writes Graham Ross in his study of Daniel Harmon, "it is fair and just to say Harmon's Voyages and Travels *is equally important in the literature." Harmon's privately printed 432-page memoir of New Caledonia, from an obscure printer in Andover, Massachusetts, was not reviewed or widely circulated. It was not reprinted until 1905. "Other than the portrait of him in the museum in Bennington," writes Ross, "there is no memorial to Daniel Williams Harmon anywhere."*

Unable to fully reconcile himself to the loss of his son, George, as well as the death of his own father in Vermont, Harmon decided it was time to forsake New Caledonia, but not his devoted wife.

Harmon wrote: "I design to make her regularly my wife by a formal marriage. Having lived with this woman as my wife and having children by her, I consider that I am under a moral obligation not to dissolve the connexion, if she is willing to continue it. The union which has been formed between us, in the providence of God, has not only been cemented by a long and mutual performance of kind offices, but also by a more sacred consideration. . . .

"We have wept together over the departure of several children, and especially over the death of our beloved son George. We have children still living who are equally dear to both of us. How could I spend my days in the civilized world and leave my beloved children in the wilderness? How could I tear them from a mother's love and leave her to mourn over their absence to the day of her death? How could I think of her in such circumstances without anguish?"

When the Harmons reached Fort William, with their two remaining daughters, Sally and Polly, the couple was formally married in a Christian ceremony at the North West Company headquarters on August 19, 1819. Five days later, Lisette gave birth to another son, John. Only two days after this birth, the fivesome departed for Montreal.

The Harmons completed their four-thousand-mile exodus from New Caledonia to Vergennes, Vermont, on September 11, 1819, crossing most of the continent in only eleven weeks. Five years later Daniel Harmon founded Harmonville (now called Coventry) in Vermont with his brothers Argalus and Calvin. There he managed a trading post and a sawmill on the Black River.

He also served as a church deacon, setting a penalty for drunkenness as the clearing of one stump. Later the *Vermont Historical Gazetter* would wryly comment, "This proved to be more effective at clearing land than at preventing drunkenness." It was soon determined thereafter that the price of pulling out one stump should fairly be one pint of rum.

Following the births of six more children in Vermont between 1821 and 1838, Daniel Harmon made one final journey with his family to Montreal in the spring of 1843. Their destination in the winter of 1843 was Sault-au-Récollet, Quebec, on Île de Montréal, ostensibly because their son-in-law, Calvin Ladd, married to Polly Harmon, had purchased land there in 1842.

Shortly after his arrival in Quebec, Daniel Harmon died at age sixty-five on April 23, 1843. Although his burial site is unknown, the Harmon family monument in Mount Royal Cemetery can be found near the grave of David Thompson. Lisette Harmon died at Sault-au-Récollet, Montreal, on February 14, 1862, aged seventy, and she was buried in Lot G-11 of Mount Royal Cemetery. The Harmons' youngest daughter Abby Maria committed suicide in Ottawa by drowning, and was buried in her mother's grave.

Whereas the first editor of Harmon's journal, Reverend Daniel Haskell, was critical of Harmon's prose, later historians have praised his writing as one of the most useful records of fur trading in Canada. Harmon was a fair-minded and lively journalist, observing customs and people with relatively little prejudice. In 1801, for example, he described an inter-racial wedding, one that undoubtedly had much in common with his own just four years later:

"Payet, one of my Interpreters, has taken one of the Native's Daughters for a Wife, and to her Parents he gave in Rum & dry Goods etc. to the value of two hundred Dollars, and all the cerimonies attending such circumstances are that when it becomes time to retire, the Husband or rather Bridegroom (for as yet they are not joined by any bonds) shews his Bride where his Bed is, and then they, of course both go to rest together, and so they continue to do as long as they can agree among themselves, but when either is displeased with their choice, he or she will seek another Partner . . . which is law here."

Harmon's journal included two appendices, allocated to "Indians East of the Rocky Mountains" and "Indians West of the Rocky Mountains." The latter appendix provides Harmon's Carrier language information derived from both the Stuart Lake and Nadleh dialects.

In 2006, with support from the Friends of Fort St. James Historic Site, Daniel Harmon's great-great-great-grandson, Graham Ross of Victoria, made arrangements with the daughter of W.K. Lamb to republish hardcover and softcover editions of Harmon's fur trade journal using the version edited by W.K. Lamb, adding an introduction by Jennifer Brown.

JOHN CLARKE

When the cutthroat competition between the Hudson's Bay Company and the North West Company was at its zenith, it was not uncommon for a man of action and daring, such as John Clarke, to work and fight for both sides, as well as to have affiliations with other companies.

Known to be haughty and arrogant, Clarke's tumultuous career has been described in a book by his daughter, Adele Clarke, called *Old Montreal*, and in the files of George Simpson. In addition, Washington Irving, in his book *Astoria*, described Clarke, who became the founder of Spokane, Washington, as "a tall, goodlooking man, and somewhat given to pomp and circumstance."

Upon visiting Fort Vancouver, the artist Paul Kane noted that the common Chinook greeting used for all white men along the Columbia River was Clak-hoh-ah-yah, an expression which he believed was derived from the Aboriginals hearing men at Astoria say, "Clarke, how are you?" It has been conjectured that the Chinook word *klahowya* could be a derivative expression.

Born in Montreal in 1781, Clarke was said to be a distant relative of John Jacob Astor via his mother, whose maiden name was Ann Waldorf. At age fifteen he entered into the service of the fur trade and became a clerk for the North West Company in 1804. He worked at Fort Vermilion on the Peace River during 1804 and 1805 and also along the Mackenzie River.

Clarke was placed in control of Fort St. John on the Peace River in 1809. This fort was moved several times after it began as Rocky Mountain Fort, established by Alexander Mackenzie in 1794, until its closure in 1823. It reopened in 1860 and became the basis for Fort St. John, the largest B.C. community north of

John Clarke

Prince George, located at Mile 47 of the Alaska Highway.

In 1810 Clarke left the North West Company and joined the Pacific Fur Company of John Jacob Astor, whereupon he was placed in charge of the second expedition to Astoria in 1811. After a 212-day voyage from New York with Ross Cox and George Erminger, Clarke arrived at Astoria on the Columbia River in May of 1812. It was soon decided that Clarke should travel inland and establish Spokane House on the Spokane River as a deliberate attempt to provide competition for James McMillan of the rival North West Company.

With the onset of the War of 1812, Clarke was summoned back to Astoria to witness its prudent surrender to the North West Company, his former employers.

Refusing to re-enter the service of the Nor'Westers, Clarke led an overland expedition consisting of 62 people back to the east in June of 1813. In 1814 he worked for Lord Selkirk and joined the Hudson's Bay Company.

From 1815 to 1819 he aggressively opposed the North West Company in the Peace River and Lake Athabasca regions. Most notably, in 1815, Clarke took one hundred men to Potato Island, within present-day Alberta, to build Fort Wedderburn for his new employers. The competition for furs was such that, when Clarke's construction crew was faced with starvation, the chief factor of the nearest North West Company fort, only a mile away, refused to provide any food. Clarke had to set off from Lake Athabasca with 50 men to reach Fort Vermilion.

Animosities continued. On October 7, 1816, Clarke was arrested and detained at Fort Chipewyan by the North West Company as a disturber of the peace. Established in 1788 by Alexander Mackenzie's cousin, Roderic Mackenzie, Fort Chipewyan was initially located on the south shore of Lake Athabasca. It was relocated to its present site on the northwest shore of Lake

Athabasca in 1798. Visited by David Thompson in 1804 and Simon Fraser in 1805, it claims to be Alberta's oldest, continuously inhabited European-established settlement.

In April 15, 1817, Clarke was re-arrested on the same charge and held at various locations until his release on December 12, 1817.

Vain and sometimes extravagant, Clarke was occasionally seen as a liability by his Hudson's Bay Company employers who had censured him in 1815 for not keeping a journal, but his vehement dislike for the North West Company was considered an asset.

Eventually Fort Wedderburn, built by Clarke, was abandoned in favour of Fort Chipewyan when the North West Company was absorbed into the Hudson's Bay Company on March 26, 1821. Despite his volatile behaviour and the objections of the North West Company, John Clarke was made a Chief Factor when the two companies united. At the time, the North West Company had 97 posts and the Hudson's Bay Company had 76.

John Clarke's third wife, Mary Ann Trutter-Tranclar

After a year's leave of absence, Clarke oversaw the Lower Red River district but his poor record led to his demotion to the Lesser Slave Lake district, then to the Swan Lake district. Clarke's performance was continuously unsatisfactory until his retirement in 1835.

At Spokane House, Clarke had "married" Josephte Kanhopitsa. In 1816, he had entered into a somewhat more formal arrangement with Sapphira Spence, the mixed blood daughter of Joseph Spence, but she died soon after their union. In 1830, Clarke married Mary Ann Trutter-Tranclar, of Neuchatel, Switzerland, and they had four sons and four daughters. Clarke remained in Montreal until his death in July 28, 1852.

ALEXANDER ROSS

Alexander Ross arrived in the Pacific Northwest aboard the ill-fated *Tonquin,* commanded by Captain Jonathan Thorne, in March of 1811. He provided one of the best descriptions of the treacherous waters at the mouth of the Columbia River, known then as the Columbia Bar, but later known as Peacock Bar, in commemoration of the United States Exploring Expedition sloop-of-war *Peacock* that was wrecked there in 1841:

"The mouth of [the] Columbia River is remarkable for its sand-bars and high surf at all seasons, but more particularly in the spring and fall, during the equinoctial gales: these sand-bars frequently shift, the channel of course shifting along with them, which renders the passage at all times extremely dangerous. The bar, or rather the chain of sand-banks, over which the huge waves and foaming breakers roll so awfully, is a league [three miles] broad, and extends in a white foaming sheet for many miles, both south and north of the mouth of the river, forming as it were an impracticable barrier to the entrance and threatening with instant destruction everything that comes near it."

Two years after Ross' arrival, the *Racoon* under Captain William Black became the first warship to cross the bar, but was severely damaged during its exit and forced to make repairs in San Francisco.

Having left Scotland in 1804, Alexander Ross tried his hand at teaching, but later became a clerk in John Jacob Astor's Pacific

Alexander Ross, 1855, and his third wife Isabella

Fur Company. Astor, influenced by his dinners at the Beaver Club in Montreal, hosted by Alexander Henry (the Elder), had founded the American Fur Company in 1808 and then the Pacific Fur Company in 1810 in response to trading opportunities he foresaw in the wake of the American expedition of Meriwether Lewis and William Clark in November of 1805. Astor's partners in this enterprise included John Clarke, Duncan McDougall, Alexander McKay, David Stuart, Robert Stuart, Donald McKenzie—all formerly affiliated with the Nor'Westers—as well as St. Louis trader Wilson Price Hunt, Gabriel Franchère and Jean Baptiste Perrault of Montreal.

Alexander Ross would be one of the most steadfast of the Astorians before it became part of the North West Company. He described how the the Astorians of the Pacific Fur Company struggled to establish Fort Astoria near the mouth of the Columbia River when he became one of the first year-round European residents on the Pacific Slope. With a Chinook dictionary and Ross's own speculations on the "Origin of the Oakinackens," Ross's fur trading memoir entitled *Adventures of the First Settlers on the Oregon or Columbia River* frankly recalls his career as the second European to reach Kamloops and the first European in the Similkameen Valley.

Alexander Ross reached Cumcloups ("the meeting of the waters") in 1812, after David Stuart of the Pacific Fur Company had seen the junction of the North and South Thompson Rivers in 1811. Ross took a wife from among the local Okanagan (or Okanogan) tribe and they had at least three children. She went with him to Manitoba when he retired to the Red River Settlement in 1825, and he later became sheriff of Assiniboia. He died in 1856. She died in Winnipeg in 1886.

JOHN TOD

Once described as a man "of excellent principle, but vulgar manners," John Tod was one of the first important fur traders in New Caledonia, an area that included Fort Alexandria, Fort St. James, Fort Fraser, Fort George, McLeod Lake, Fort Babine and Fort Connolly.

In order to control the influx of mostly American miners to the Cariboo gold fields, the Colonial Office in London annexed the New Caledonia Department within its new Crown Colony of British Columbia in 1858.

Twenty years later John Tod wrote the *History of New Caledonia and the Northwest Coast*, the obscure forerunner to A.G. Morice's better-known *The History of the Northern Interior of British Columbia, Formerly New Caledonia, 1660–1880*. Tod's writing can be quaintly unsophisticated. In a letter to James Hargrave in 1843, he wrote: "Unfortunate Fur Traders, how few of you are doomed to taste the sweets of civilized life."

The first-born in a family of nine children, John Tod was born near Loch Lomond, Scotland, in 1794. He grew up west of Glasgow on the banks of the Leven River and left school at sixteen to work in Glasgow in the textile industry. He lost his position at eighteen when he refused to accept a double workload without adequate compensation.

Unemployed and at odds with his parents, Tod signed a five-year contract to work as an apprentice clerk for the Hudson's Bay Company in 1811. With copies of Robbie Burns' poetry, Buchan's *Domestic Medicine* and the Bible, he sailed on the *Edward and Ann* to York Factory on Hudson Bay. He was sent as a greenhorn to Fort Severn, where he wintered. Enduring much privation, he learned "Swampy Cree" for two years, then was transferred to oversee Island Lake and York Factory in succession.

John Tod was present in the mess hall at York Factory in the summer of 1821 to witness the dinner hosted by thirty-four-year-old George Simpson to unite the apprehensive traders of the Nor'Westers with their new HBC partners after the formalized merger of those two companies on March 26, 1821.

Todd wrote: "Evidently uncertain how they would seat themselves at the table, I eyed them with close attention from a remote corner of the room, and to my mind the scene formed no bad representation of that incongruous animal seen by the King of Babylon in one of his dreams, one part iron, another of clay; though joined together [they] would not amalgamate, for the Nor'Westers in one compact body kept together and evidently had no inclination at first to mix with their old rivals in trade."

Governor Simpson sent John Tod to New Caledonia in 1823. Tod initially joined James Murray Yale for one year at Fort George (Prince George, B.C.) before his posting at Fort McLeod. In the winter of 1825 and the spring of 1826, Tod was joined by an up-and-coming HBC employee named James Douglas.

Isolated and lonely at Fort McLeod, unable to speak English to anyone, Tod read a great deal and appreciated the companionship of "the singing girl" who

John Tod

Mrs. John Tod

he avowed was "possessed of an excellent ear for music & never fails to accompany me on the Flute with her voice when I take up the instruments." This was the first of Tod's country wives.

John Tod wrote to Edward Ermatinger about her in 1829: "You ask what is become of the girl who used to sing at McLeods Lake. I have a good mind to answer You as Mr. Boulton, our old messmate, would do but I have not his taste for smut unless it is wraped [sic] up in clean linen— Why then in plain language she still continues the only companion of my solitude—without her, or some other substitute, life, in such a wretched place as this, would be altogether unsupportable."

After nine years in New Caledonia, John Tod resolved to quit the HBC and started back to Scotland, only to receive long-awaited news that he was promoted to the rank of officer in the company. Having received his commission in 1834, Tod was granted a one-year leave. Sailing from Hudson Bay on the *Prince Rupert*, he met a governess, Eliza Waugh, whom he soon married in England.

The couple did not live happily ever after. In 1835, the Tods went to Rupert's Land via New York, then waited in the Red River District for Tod's new posting at Island Lake where Eliza suffered a mental breakdown in 1837. He took her to live with relatives in Wales, then returned to work in New Caledonia and at Fort Vancouver, Fort Alexandria (1839–1842), Kamloops (1842–1849) and Fort Nisqually on Puget Sound.

Legend has it that while working at the Kamloops site—first seen by traders of the Pacific Fur Company, then developed by the North West Company, then controlled by the HBC—John Tod was deemed "impossible to kill" by the local Aboriginals.

In 1846, upon being notified by the fort's interpreter Lolo of a planned attack, Tod showed his mettle by riding forth on a white mare to meet a war party of more than one thousand Aboriginals on the banks of the Fraser River. Tod informed them that small-pox had broken out at Walla Walla, and he had come to vacci-nate them. "I commenced to cut & vaccinate," he recalled, "those who were more noted rascals than others I laid into with a venge-ance." The would-be attackers retreated with sore arms.

Tod found property in Victoria in 1850. The first governor of the Colony of Vancouver Island, Richard Blanshard, appointed John Tod to serve on the colony's new executive council in 1851. There were only two other members: James Cooper and James Douglas. Tod, in effect, became one of the four most powerful men on Vancouver Island.

With its loyalties to the Hudson's Bay Company rather than the Crown, the new council made life difficult for Blanshard, who suffered from "neuralgia" (he drank) and was undermined at every turn by Douglas. After Douglas replaced Blanshard in September of 1851, thereby securing colonial control for the Hud-son's Bay Company, John Tod officially retired from the HBC on June 1, 1852, but remained on council. To outnumber the inde-pendence of councillor James Cooper, Douglas added two HBC sympathizers, Roderick Finlayson and John Work, to support Tod's HBC bias. Tod served as a Justice of the Peace, resolving disputes for one pound per day, and helped pass the first liquor tax in B.C.

Retiring from the council in 1858, Tod lived in Oak Bay where he played the flute and fiddle, enjoyed nature and recalled an unconventional life. In his retirement, he also wrote a manu-script that described the history of New Caledonia, one of the earliest documents pertaining to the interior of B.C.

In his writing, Tod did not entirely approve of the Hudson's Bay Company practice of enacting the death penalty without a proper trial: "I knew that it was illegal, strictly, for I had seen at York Factory the British Parliament Act."

Tod had one son named James with his first country wife at

York Factory, Catherine Birstone, and at least one child with his second country wife at Fort McLeod. One child was born to Eliza (Waugh) Tod, then he had another seven children with Sophia Lolo whom he met at the Thompson's River Post (Kamloops). After receiving news of Eliza's death in 1857, Tod married Sophia in 1863.

John Tod's biased opinions of so-called half-breeds were summarized in a letter to Edward Ermatinger in 1843: "Well have you observed that all attempts to make gentlemen of them, have hitherto proved a failure. The fact is there is something radically wrong about them all as is evidently shown from mental science alone, I mean Phrenology, the truths of which I have lately convinced myself from extensive personal observation."

John Tod died on August 31, 1882. The Tod house in Oak Bay is a heritage site. Tod Mountain near Kamloops, and Tod Inlet northwest of Victoria, bear his name.

JOHN WORK

True to his name, John Work remained a stalwart employee of the Hudson's Bay Company until the day he died in December of 1861. Remarkable for his endurance, Work survived a near-fatal attack by a bull, recurring eye troubles, inflamed tonsils ("quinsy") and a near-fatal fall from a tree that tore open his stomach and spilled some of his intestines. Work put his guts back into place himself and eventually overcame the injury.

Work never quit—and kept 16 journals to prove it. The former trading post clerk remained on the Board of Management for the HBC's Western Department at Fort Victoria, co-signing an important letter, dated November 24, 1858, that first listed the HBC's land claims in British Columbia. "It is pitiful to see him still clinging to service," said his old friend and fellow Irishman

John Work was in charge of Fort Simpson from 1835 to 1851.

John Tod, "as if he would drag it along with him to the next world."

With the passage of *An Act to Provide for the Government of British Columbia by the Imperial Parliament in London* in August of 1858, the imperial government of Great Britain revoked the Hudson's Bay Company's exclusive right to trade with Indians, whereupon HBC officials—initially through Work and Chief Factor Dugald MacTavish—sought ownership of lands adjacent to their forts as compensation. Governor James Douglas was initially conciliatory, but he shifted his approach when a new British government was elected under Lord Palmerston in June of 1859.

Newly appointed Colonial Secretary W.A.G. Young was far less sympathetic to the HBC than his predecessor Sir. E.B. Lytton, so James Douglas obeyed the winds of political change. Although the HBC had requested 98,225 acres, it was granted only 2,247 acres. After the first formal conveyance had occurred in 1863, the HBC continued to lobby for small land grants for the remainder of the nineteenth century, but these were relatively minor.

John Work's life and death mirrored the rise and fall of the Hudson's Bay Company in British Columbia. Born as John Wark in Derry, Ireland, in 1791, he joined the Hudson's Bay Company in 1814 and reached the Pacific Northwest in 1822. He explored the lower Fraser River in 1824 as a clerk for James McMillan, keeping the expedition's journal, then oversaw construction of Fort Colville where he served as a clerk (1826–1830) and commanded some of the Snake River expeditions towards California.

Having managed the HBC's most northerly post in New Cal-

154

edonia, at Fort Simpson (1835–1846), Work became one of three men who took charge of the HBC's Columbia River operations after John McLoughlin resigned. Work later moved to a farm in Hillside, now part of Victoria, and served on the Legislative Council of Vancouver Island.

After various liaisons with Aboriginal women, Work settled upon a relationship with Josette Lagace in 1826 and became as devoted to her as he was to the Hudson's Bay Company. She was a Métis (French voyageur father, Spokane Indian mother) who provided him with ten of his children. When they were formally married by Reverend Robert Staines at Fort Victoria many years after they met, James Douglas served as a witness for the ceremony.

John Work bought 583 acres north of Fort Victoria in 1852 and eventually became the largest individual landowner on Vancouver Island. Josette Work outlived her husband by more than 15 years, impressing everyone who met her as the epitome of a Victorian matron, even resembling Queen Victoria in one of her portraits.

The daughters of John and Josette Work married well-to-do British-born colonials but their two sons, John Jr. and David, never married and died at ages thirty-two and forty-nine respectively.

Mrs. John Work looking like Queen Victoria. Before she died in 1896, Josette Work, a Métis, met historian Hubert H. Bancroft, who wrote admiringly, "the Indian wife, in body and mind, was strong and elastic as steel."

PETER SKENE OGDEN

"Humorous, honest, eccentric law-defying Peter Ogden, the terror of all Indians, and the delight of all gay fellows." —TRADER ROSS COX

A shrewd, violent and enduring trader, Peter Skene (Skeene) Ogden became one of the more influential figures in New Caledonia in the 1830s and 1840s, erecting Port Simpson on the Nass River. Ogden later provided some of the most authentic reflections of how men worked and lived in New Caledonia, prior to the 1850s. "Pity that the Slavery Emancipation Act does not extend its influence to these remote shores," he wrote, while stationed at Fort Simpson in 1838.

Baptized as Peter Skeene Ogden in Quebec City in 1790, Ogden was the son of Chief Justice Isaac Ogden, a United Empire Loyalist, and Sarah Hanson. Growing up in Montreal, he had two brothers who were lawyers. After a brief association with the American Fur Company in Montreal, Ogden joined the North West Company as an apprentice clerk in 1809 and gained a permanent position in 1811. During his seven years in Saskatchewan he gained his lifelong reputation for violence and "bully-boy" tactics.

At Île-à-la-Crosse, he and fellow trader Samuel Black had serious altercations with their Hudson's Bay Company rival Peter Fidler. Placed in charge of a trading post located south of Île-à-la-Crosse at Green Lake, Ogden allegedly murdered an Aboriginal who persisted in trading with the rival Hudson's Bay Company. A HBC agent named McVicar reported that Ogden's victim was "butchered in a most cruel manner."

In his own defence, Ogden once confided, "In place, where the custom of the country, or as laws say, the *Lex non scripta* is our only guide, we must sometimes perform the parts of judge, jury, sheriff, hangman, gallows, all."

At the behest of the Hudson's Bay Company, Ogden was eventually indicted for murder in Lower Canada in 1818. The Nor'Westers quickly transferred him to their Columbia River department, enabling him to avoid prosecution. Ogden left behind a Cree woman who had born him two children, but all of Ogden's surviving, mixed-blood offspring would later be included in his will.

Upon his arrival at Fort George, near present-day Astoria, Oregon, Ogden was sent inland to winter at Spokane House, near present-day Spokane, Washington, then north to Fort Thompson, present-day site of Kamloops.

At Spokane House, Ogden met and married his second country wife, Julia Rivet, the Nez Percé daughter of a Canadian voyageur, who would bear him seven more children and prove to be an indomitable force. Having obtained his bride with a payment of fifty horses, Ogden sent for his two half-Cree boys from his preceding relationship, and they were cared for by Julia. Theirs would be a remarkable 31-year marriage, often interrupted by lengthy separations during Ogden's six Snake River expeditions.

Having been made a partner or "bourgeois" of the North West Company in 1820, Ogden had a career setback with the merger of the Nor'Westers with the Hudson's Bay Company in March of 1821. Due to their records of violence, he and Samuel Black were initially not accepted within the expanded HBC. He was permitted to remain in command at Fort Thompson until he chose to return to England, via Lower Canada, in 1822, to plead his case successfully for reinstatement, along with Black.

George Simpson and the HBC concluded that their penchant for hostilities might be put to constructive use: Simpson also worried that Ogden and Black might succeed in forming a rival company. Better to have them inside the tent than out.

In total, John McLoughlin sent Ogden to lead six "expeditions" into the largely uncharted Snake River country in the east of Oregon and beyond, so-named due to its many deadly snakes.

In spite of Spanish claims to it, England and the United States had decided this zone was potentially there for the taking. Assuming this territory would ultimately fall to the Americans, the HBC appointed Ogden and John Work to create a "fur desert" amid less-than-hospitable Nez Percé, Flathead, Blood, Peigan and Blackfoot Indians.

Governor Simpson provided blunt instructions to disregard all customary concerns for conservation. "We have convincing proof," he said, "that the country is a rich preserve of Beaver and which for political reasons we should endeavour to destroy as fast as possible."

Ogden's initial Snake River contingent, accompanied by an enclave of Americans led by Jedediah Smith, included 58 men, 30 women, 35 children, 268 horses, 352 traps and 22 leather lodges. Julia, her newborn son and her two young stepsons were among those who passed the winter of 1824–1825 in the Snake Country at the behest of Governor Simpson, who resented the excess expense of wintering in a fort.

After a raid on their camp by rival American freemen (mainly French Canadians and Iroquois), Julia realized that her baby and its cradle board were on one of the stolen horses. She hastened to the enemy camp, mounted the horse, grabbed the lead of another HBC horse carrying HBC furs, and galloped back to safety, ignoring the raised muskets of her assailants.

When Ogden's six-year-old son Charles contracted a chest cold and fever, Julia Ogden prescribed a "goose" to heal his condition. A HBC hunter obligingly shot one for her, but the goose fell to the earth on the far side of an ice-strewn river and none of the men was willing to retrieve it. Julia promptly shed her garments, swam across the river, grabbed the dead bird, and swam back to cook the goose. After she rubbed goose grease on the boy's chest and fed him goose soup, he lived.

Wives and children were later prohibited from accompanying Snake River expeditions, most of which were required to live off the land, but Julia Ogden participated in Ogden's fourth brigade. Her on-the-trail pregnancy resulted in a birth during a bit-

Peter Skene Ogden's taste for violence has been considered heroic by some. "Of all the lusty band of 'mountain men' who roamed the forests and streams of the Far West," wrote A.B. Maloney in the California Historical Quarterly, *"in the early days of the nineteenth century, none trapped more beaver, laughed louder, played wilder practical jokes, fought harder, or left his name on more places he discovered and explored than did Peter Skene Ogden. Nor did any travel further afield or perform a deed of greater bravery than his rescue of the surviving victims of the Whitman massacre at Waiilatpu."*

terly cold winter. That child lived for only two weeks.

Over six years Ogden trapped extensively and confronted rival traders in areas that included Wyoming, Utah, Nevada, Oregon, Idaho and California. During his second expedition to the Utah territory in 1828–1829, Ogden saw Great Salt Lake, and in 1830 Ogden visited California—the Mexican region south of the 42nd parallel. The town of Ogden, Utah, bears his name, as does Peter Skene Ogden State Park in central Oregon and Ogden Street in Las Vegas, Nevada.

Ogden's ability to withstand extreme conditions won the praise of John McLoughlin, but freezing temperatures, fever and combative Indians had cost the lives of numerous companions.

"This is certainly a most horrid life," Ogden wrote. "In a word I may say without exaggeration Man in this Country is deprived of every comfort that can tend to make existence desirable." To make matters much worse, malaria spread through the ranks of the Columbia River traders, afflicting some fifty men at Fort Vancouver, and Ogden contracted the disease. His convalescence delayed his departure to the lawless hinterlands of New Caledonia where, as selected by McLoughlin, he would be required to create a new trading post on the Nass River.

Having been relegated to her mother's lodge at Fort Nez Percé with four children, Julia Ogden waited several years before she took the initiative to re-unite with her ailing husband at Fort Vancouver. Consequently, she and her children were aboard the *Cadboro* in April of 1831 when it sailed from Fort Vancouver under the command of Lieutenant Aemilius Simpson, a Royal Navy officer on half pay, who had been hired in 1826 to supervise the HBC's maritime operations.

Perhaps a word should be added about Aemilius Simpson, a distant relative and school associate of George Simpson, who hired him for his "high character and respectable abilities."

Having helped build Fort Langley, Lieutenant Simpson gained the distinction of sailing the first European vessel up the Fraser River on June 22, 1827. In the spring of 1831, the *Cadboro* sailed with two other ships, the *Dryad* and the *Vancouver*, and reached the Nass estuary after one month's voyage. After Aemilius Simpson hastily chose the upriver location for Fort Nass, he followed his instructions to sail further north into Russian waters and investigate reports of a large river. He located the mouth of the Stikine River, approximately 140 miles north of the Nass, and reported his findings to Ogden at the nearly completed Fort Nass, but he erroneously concluded the river to the north was the Babine.

At age thirty-eight, Lieutenant Simpson suddenly fell victim to inflammation of the liver and died at Fort Nass, having suffered severely for several days. Ogden changed the name of the new trading post to Fort Simpson in his honour.

To assist Ogden at Fort Simpson, Chief Factor McLoughlin sent him Donald Manson, the clerk on Samuel Black's Finlay River expedition, who undertook a detailed survey of the lower Nass River and determined that the Nass would not be suitable as a navigable route to the Interior. Manson's survey shifted the HBC's attention to discover the potential of the Stikine.

Sailing on the *Cadboro* in the spring of 1832, Ogden was met by Baron Ferdinand von Wrangel, the newly appointed governor of Russian America, in Sitka harbour, whereupon Ogden attempted to negotiate a new contract to provide the Russians with various supplies.

Wrangel shrewdly surmised the well-organized HBC traders were potentially more threatening to Russian commerce than the independent Yankee clippers, whose numbers had dropped on the Pacific Northwest coast from approximately 15 ships per year in the early 1800s to approximately five per year in the 1830s, so he was unwilling to provide Ogden and the HBC with reasonable terms. As a result, Ogden was unable to establish a second trading post north of Fort Simpson in 1834. Fort Simpson was therefore relocated further away from the hostile Russians, to the south.

Ogden was rewarded for his efforts with a new commission as Chief Factor for the Hudson's Bay Company in charge of New Caledonia. He took charge at Fort St. James on Stuart Lake in 1835, replacing Peter Warren Dease (1788–1863), a former Nor'Wester who had received the posting in 1821.

After approximately seven years, Ogden wrote his "Notes on Western Caledonia," essentially a memorandum of instructions and advice for his successor, Donald Manson, who took charge in June of 1844. "Having now been stationed seven years in this District, I cannot say much in favour of the Carriers, a brutish, ignorant superstitious beggarly sett of beings. . . ."

Ogden took a one-year furlough in England in 1844. Upon his return in 1845, he was appointed to a board of management for the Columbia district with McLoughlin and James Douglas.

Privately, Governor Simpson had once assessed Ogden as "one

of the most unprincipled Men in the Indian Country, who would soon get into habits of dissipation if he were not restrained by the fear of those operating against his interests, and if he does indulge in that way, madness, to which he has a predisposition, will follow as a matter of course."

But Ogden proved competent as an administrator and remained more or less married to Julia. Upon McLoughlin's retirement in 1846, Ogden co-managed the area with James Douglas and John Work. In 1847 he played a decisive role in the resolution of a hostage-taking after Cayuse Indians killed 14 people and took 47 prisoners near present-day Walla Walla, Washington, during the so-called Whitman Massacre. Ogden's reputation and his payment of $500 worth of goods liberated the white prisoners.

Ogden remained prominent in the fur trade until his death in Oregon City on September 27, 1854, leaving an estate worth $50,000. After he was buried in Oregon City's Mountain View Cemetery, Ogden's brother and sister began legal proceedings to disinherit Ogden's Julia and their children, despite Ogden's clear resolve in his will: ". . . should any relation of mine or any other individual attempt to dispute this my Last Will and Testament I . . . declare that I disinherit them as fully as the law authorizes me."

Unlike McLoughlin, Ogden had never solemnized his marriage to Julia with Christian paperwork. McLoughlin intervened in this dispute and provided a compromise solution. (Ogden's friend Samuel Black similarly refused to solemnize his marriage to Angelique Cameron, thereby enabling his white relatives to challenge the inheritances of their part-Aboriginal kin.)

It is generally assumed that Peter Skene Ogden was the uncredited author of *Traits of American-Indian Life and Character*, a collection of 16 accounts by "A fur trader." So much has been written about the pre-colonial history of Vancouver Island and so little, by comparison, exists as a literary record for New Caledonia, that Peter Skene Ogden's rough accounts still warrant scrutiny by historians.

SAMUEL BLACK

"This outlaw is so callous to every honorable or manly feeling that
it is not unreasonable to suspect him of the blackest acts."
—GEORGE SIMPSON

Samuel Black was an illegitimate child who was baptized in Scotland in May of 1770. Raised in County Aberdeen, he left Scotland at age twenty-two and joined the North West Company in 1804 where he soon gained a reputation for terrorizing members of the "Honorable Company" with his swashbuckling behaviour, sometimes in concert with his kindred spirit Peter Skene Ogden. Fiercely loyal to his employers who acknowledged he was "a desperate character," Black intimidated most of the Hudson's Bay Company traders except for George Simpson who, when entering Black's Lake Athabasca trading territory in 1820, declared, "I am however armed to the Teeth, will sell my Life in danger as dear as possible and never allow a North Wester [to] come within reach of my Rifle if Flint Steel & bullet can keep him off."

The personal animosity between Simpson and Black explains why Black, along with Peter Skene Ogden and Cuthbert Grant, did not initially receive positions when the Hudson's Bay Company amalgamated with the Nor'Westers in 1821, placing Simpson in charge of the Northern Department. At age fifty-one, Black was temporarily forced into retirement, upon which he received a ring from his comrades that was engraved, "To the most worthy of the Northwesters [sic]." But the shrewd Simpson was not one to allow personality conflicts to overrule his practical sense of business. He hired Ogden and Black as chief traders about a year later, and also hired Cuthbert Grant at a lower rank. At their meeting in July of 1823 at York Factory, Simpson described his former adversary Black as "a Donquixote [sic] in appearance, ghastly, raw-boned and lanthorn jawed, yet strong vigorous and active . . . the strangest man I ever knew. . . . A perfectly honest man and his generosity might be considered indicative of a warmth of heart if he was not to be known to be a cold blooded fellow who could be guilty of any cruelty and would be a perfect Tyrant if he had the power."

It would suit Simpson's purposes if Black served as a "perfect Tyrant" as far away as possible, so Black was placed in charge of the Finlay River expedition that was sent to explore the western side of the Rocky Mountains, north of Fort St. James, in 1824, in keeping with Simpson's plans to expand the fur trade of New Caledonia into the far northwest. Having long yearned to make his mark as an explorer along the lines of Alexander Mackenzie, Black was eager to accept Simpson's unrealistic guidelines for the expedition.

In addition to finding the source of the Finlay River, Black was instructed to find a parallel, Arctic-bound "sister" river west of the Mackenzie River to enhance the fur trade. To satisfy Simpson's hopes, Black would have to travel approximately 1,500 miles in mostly uncharted territory. Ironically, it would be Black's failure to follow his own unruly instincts, and his unusual adherence to Simpson's directions, that would prevent him from joining the ranks of his legendary predecessors Mackenzie, Simon Fraser and David Thompson.

In the spring of 1824, Black and his clerk Donald Manson set out from Rocky Mountain Portage on the Peace River accompanied by six voyageurs, a Métis interpreter named La Prise and the interpreter's wife. Two canoeists soon deserted the arduous upstream expedition at a place that is still called Deserters Canyon. This pair made it all the way to the Churchill River before they surrendered and were sentenced before the Council of the Northern Department at York Factory to "be immediately Handcuffed and in that situation that they be publickly exposed during one full day on the roof of the Factory, afterwards that they be imprisoned during one week, fed on bread and water, and in winter that one of each be sent to winter among the Europeans at Churchill & Severn Forts." It is possible the deserters Ossin and Bouche received relatively lenient sentences because Black was notorious for being unreasonable.

Despite the necessity of continually towing their canoes in near-freezing, waist-deep water, Black's contingent averaged about twelve miles per day up the unknown river. To secure his place in history, Black kept a journal of this adventure in which he wrote, "men complain of numbness in their Arms their hands & wrists & Galled by the Snow Water." Disdainful of the scarce Sekani Indians they met, whom he described as "phlegmatic sheepish looking Gentlemen," Black was also disappointed by the lack of game, the poor prospects for fur trading and the caution of his experienced Iroquois foreman, Joseph La Guarde. "The lofty brakers dancing majestically in the Sun beams before us have begun to dance in La Guarde's brain," he wrote. By late June they succeeded in reaching Thutade Lake, the source of the Finlay and Peace Rivers.

Obliged to continue "to the northwestward," in accordance with Simpson's instructions, Black, on July 8th, secured some unenthusiastic assistance from the Sekanis. As his men grudgingly carried packs weighing 120 pounds, Black and Donald Manson were obliged to carry packs weighing less than half as much. After one week heading north, Black met members of a Tahltan band he described as the Thloadennies. During a nine-day resting period, a joint council of the Sekanis, Thloadennies and HBC voyageurs was held at which Black advised them "to tell no lies, for the White People hated Liars." The Thloadennies truthfully alerted him to the fearsome presence of the so-called Trading Nahannis who controlled their access to a large, westward flowing river that Black understood was called the Schadzue. With a superior food supply and access to Russian trade goods from the Pacific Ocean, the Nahannis were so formidable that none of the Thloadennies would agree to accompany Black any further north.

Fearful of the Nahannis, the Métis interpreter's wife persuaded her husband to desert Black's expedition on July 27. Black pressed stubbornly onward until he had to admit he had succeeded only in reaching the Laird River network at a tributary he acerbically named Turnagain River. By the end of September, Black's hazardous five-month expedition was over. Had he been able to follow the Schadzue River to its mouth on the Pacific, he would likely have become famous as the European discoverer of the Stikine River in northern British Columbia, a navigable river that would have provided an important avenue for Hudson's Bay Company commerce. Instead, Black had been obliged to continue to trudge northwards in search of an Arctic-bound river that did not exist. George Simpson acknowledged that Black had undertaken a stalwart journey into "perhaps as rugged a country as ever was passed," but Simpson failed to understand the commercial potential of the Stikine (Schadzue) River.

Black remained an intemperate character in the fur trade, working in the Columbia River and Thompson River areas. At Fort Kamloops, where Black was Chief Trader, he once challenged the touring botanist David Douglas to a duel after the scientist had insulted the Hudson's Bay Company during his visit in 1833. "Offensive and defensive preparation seems to be the study of his life," wrote George Simpson in his Character Book, "having Dirks, Knives & loaded Pistols concealed about his person and in all directions about his Establishment even under the Table cloth at Meals and in his Bed."

Black's penchant for violence and his low opinion of Aboriginals proved to be his undoing. After Black refused to provide a gun to a Shuswap chief named Tranquille, and that chief died later the same year, his wife concluded Black was responsible for the death by supernatural means. A man named Kiskowskin, said to be a nephew of Tranquille, murdered Black in the winter of 1841 by shooting him in the back of the head.

In death, Black played almost as important a role as in life. When the Chief Trader at Fort Alexandria, John Tod, arrived in Fort Thompson, he found Black's frozen body lying where he had been killed. Tod learned the story of Black's death from the

Hudson's Bay Company interpreter, Jean Baptiste Lolo, where-upon a vindictive and hostile investigation was undertaken for the HBC by Donald McLean.

McLean's legacy to British Columbia would turn out to be its most notorious outlaw gang, the so-called Wild McLeans, really just a ragtag outfit of misfits consisting of his sons Allen, Archie and Charley, along with Alexander Hare. Having shot and killed a member of the B.C. Provincial Police named John Ussher in 1879, the desperadoes shot another man named Jim Kelly during their getaway. They were taken into custody less than a week later. When the gang was hanged together at New Westminster on January 31, 1881, after they had surrendered for trial on December 13 to end a siege at Douglas Lake, sixteen-year-old Archie McLean gained the dubious distinction of being the youngest murderer ever executed in B.C.

When Donald McLean's harsh methods proved fruitless, John Tod was obliged to return to Fort Thompson and resume the search. Tod withheld ammunition and other trade goods, thereby making the lives of the surrounding Indians more difficult, and he offered a reward for information. When the HBC received news of Kiskowskin's whereabouts, Tod's clerk Cameron was sent with a search party to a nearby village where one of Kiskowskin's children was taken hostage. This strategy failed to draw Kiskowskin out of hiding, so the child was returned and relations with the Aboriginals worsened.

At this point, John Tod hired a local Indian, Grand Gule, who eventually led Cameron and his men to the fugitive. It was customary for the HBC to execute promptly any Aboriginal who killed a white man, usually by hanging. Knowing his fate, Kiskowskin reportedly leapt from the canoe in which he was being held captive and drowned. The score was considered settled. Grand Gule later became a chief, and the ne'er-do-well Donald McLean took charge of Fort Kamloops in 1855. Refusing a transfer in 1860, he homesteaded south of Clinton and was killed by one of the fugitive Tsilqot'ins during the so-called Chilcotin War of 1864.

As for Samuel Black, his white relatives disputed the outcome of his will in which he allocated his resources to his mixed-blood wife and their children. As has been seen, similar court challenges and legal arguments were lodged by the white relatives of traders Peter Skene Ogden, Hugh Faries, John Stuart, Alexander Fraser and William Connolly, all of whom challenged the legitimacy of mixed-blood heirs. Complicating matters, newly arriving clergymen towards the second half of the nineteenth century were usually willing to lend their opinion that a country marriage or blanket marriage (*sous la couverte*) qualified only as a "casual" relationship. Yet these marriage were vital to the fur trade. In 1805, Alexander Henry (the Younger) conducted a census of the North West Company's fifteen departments in Indian country: approximately one thousand men had taken 368 wives and had 569 children with them.

JOHN MCLEAN

According to W.S. Stewart, John McLean's account of his journey across Canada to work for the Hudson's Bay Company in New Caledonia is "another of those invaluable *récits de voyage* that enable us to piece together the history of the Canadian Northwest in its earlier days." Arriving in New Caledonia in 1833, McLean was taken aback to find the route via the Peace River required a 13-mile portage "through swamps and morasses," and that "the ascending and descending steep hills" took him eight days to complete. "I consider the passage of this portage," he wrote, "the most laborious duty the Company's servants have to perform in any part of the territory; and, as the voyageurs say, 'He that passes it with his share of a canoe's cargo may call himself a man.'" While he was in New Caledonia for three-and-a-half years, McLean met and later described James Douglas, Peter Skene Ogden and Peter Warren Dease.

Born in Argyleshire, Scotland, McLean was employed by the Hudson's Bay Company until 1845, mainly in eastern Canada where he became the first white man to traverse the Labrador Peninsula, discovering the Grand Falls of the Northwest River. His *Notes of a Twenty-Five Year's* [sic] *Service in the Hudson's Bay Territory* is unusual for its overt criticism of the Hudson's Bay Company in terms of its treatment of Aboriginals. He spent much of his retirement and married years in Guelph, Ontario, but left his wife Elora, to make his way to Victoria, via San Franscisco, in 1883, in order to reside with his daughter, Mrs. O'Brian. He died on September 8, 1890, at age ninety, and was buried in the Presbyterian Plot of the Ross Bay Cemetery in Victoria.

ROBERT CAMPBELL

In the annals of the Hudson's Bay Company, boldness in the wilderness counted for less than accurate bookkeeping and corporate profits. A case in point is the remarkable but little-admired Yukon and New Caledonia explorer Robert Campbell.

As the son of a Perthshire sheep farmer in Scotland, Campbell was filled with enthusiasm for life in the new world by a return visit to Scotland in 1830 by his cousin, James McMillan, who had become a Chief Factor for the Hudson's Bay Company. "I heard for the first time of the Great North-West and the free and active life that awaited one there. . . ," Campbell wrote. "I became possessed with an irresistible longing to go to that land of romance and adventure." More precisely, Campbell dreamed of making his mark as a famous explorer, to be mentioned in history books alongside Alexander Mackenzie.

With McMillan's assistance, Campbell successfully applied for a HBC position as sub-manager for a new experimental farm proposed for the Red River settlement. At age twenty-two, he took his leave from the family farm in June of 1830 and sailed with McMillan, whose furlough had expired, Chief Trader Donald Ross, as well as several apprentice clerks and more than 30 labourers, from Stromness in Scotland for York Factory on Hudson Bay. Soon after his arrival, Campbell travelled to Kentucky where he purchased 1,475 sheep to stock the HBC's experimental farm, but diseases and various infections decimated the flock by the time Campbell reached Red River. Only 250 survived.

Robert Campbell

At Fort Garry for the winter, Campbell met another HBC veteran, Donald Finlayson, as well as George Simpson, who was also wintering at the fort. With plans for the farm abandoned, Simpson encouraged the strapping young Scot to apply for a transfer to the Mackenzie River District. "His last words to me," Campbell recorded, "were 'Now, Campbell, don't you get married, as we want you for active service.'" Rightly or wrongly, Simpson had identified the Mackenzie River District as a prime area for expansion. Campbell hoped his posting to Fort Liard in 1835 would be in keeping with his ambition to make his mark as an explorer.

Maintaining a correspondence with Simpson, Campbell volunteered to help establish a new post on Dease Lake, in what is now British Columbia, in 1837. He subsequently wintered at Fort Halkett and built a modest fort on the east shore of Dease Lake in July of 1838, five miles from its outlet. He then commenced to follow Simpson's instructions to explore further on the western side of the mountains, directing his attention "to pushing the trade across the Mountains and down the Pelly River."

Acompanied by "Hoole [Houle] and 2 fine young Indians Lapie and Kitza," Campbell abandoned their spruce canoes after 20 miles of paddling on Dease Lake and soon crossed the Stikine River on a so-called "Terror Bridge" built by Aboriginals. Campbell described it as "a rude ricketty [sic]structure of pine poles spliced together with withes and stretched high above a foaming torrent; the ends of the poles were loaded down with stones to prevent the bridge from collapsing. This primitive support looked so frail and unstable and the rushing waters below so formidable that it seemed well nigh impossible to cross it."

Campbell boldly or recklessly ignored the advice of local Indians and proceeded alone to meet Chief Shakes who owed much of his fearsome stature to his position as a middle-man with Russian traders at the mouth of the Stikine. Instead of being butchered, Campbell was led to the chief's tent where he was offered whiskey from the chief's cup. As Chief Shakes and his men freely imbibed, Campbell, a Presbyterian, went through the motions, and later recorded, "I was well armed, having pistols and dirk in my belt, and a double barrelled percussion gun, which was a great source of wonder to them as the only guns they were familiar with were single-barrelled flint locks."

Campbell's report of these events was probably self-congratulatory, but his poise under pressure seems genuine enough. "Shakes wanted me to fire so that he might see how the gun went off," he wrote. "Fearing this was only a ruse to render my gun harmless, I took the precaution to have ball, powder & cap in my hand ready to slip in immediately after firing a shot. With every report, the whole camp yelled, clapping their hands on their mouths at the same time, & the noise was frightful."

During this meeting Campbell gained more information about the Pelly and Stikine Rivers. He also learned that John McLoughlin and James Douglas were both known to the local Aboriginals who included a charismatic female leader described by Campbell as the "Chieftainess of the Nahanies." In his romanticized narrative, he describes how this impressive thirty-five-year-old protectoress enabled his men to make their return across the Terror Bridge unmolested.

Rather than explore the Stikine to its mouth at the Pacific,

Campbell returned to the new trading post at Dease Lake, having discovered that trading prospects were poor and game was not plentiful. Accordingly, he descended the Liard River in a birchbark canoe in order to gain additional trading supplies at Fort Simpson from Chief Trader Murdock McPherson, who soon proved himself to be the bane of Campbell's career. McPherson would give Campbell only enough supplies for his return trip to Dease Lake.

Surrounded by hostile "Russian Indians" at his Dease Lake post, Campbell wrote, "Our prospects were very gloomy. . . . Our efforts all winter to procure a bare living were never relaxed. We were scattered in twos and threes trying with nets & hooks for fish, & with traps, snares & guns for any living thing, bird or beast, that came in the way. Everything possible was used for food: 'tripe de roche,' skins, parchment, in fact anything. But much as we felt these privations, our greatest trouble was the passing & repassing of the Russian Indians, who kept us night and day in a state of alarm & uncertainty, particularly as it was impossible for us to be all together. . . . We were completely at their mercy. Most of us were so weak & emaciated that we could barely walk."

The starving fur traders received a temporary reprieve in February from the Chieftainess of the Nahanies who instructed her slaves to cook a sumptuous meal for Campbell and his men. About a month later, when more of her people returned to Dease Lake, unaccompanied by her, Campbell was dismayed to discover their attitudes towards him were as hostile as the "Russian Indians" led by Chief Shakes. One of Campbell's men died during the winter, and another two disappeared while trying to reach Fort Liard. Prior to leaving their wretched Dease Lake Post on May 8, 1839, Campbell and his men boiled the webbing of their snowshoes and the parchment from the windows for a final meal.

For surviving such terrible conditions, Campbell was promoted by Simpson to the rank of Clerk. After wintering at Fort Halkett in 1839–1840, Campbell was instructed by Simpson to explore extensively the Liard River, a major thoroughfare that gained its name from the voyageurs' term *Riviere au Liards* ("River of Poplars"). The Liard proved so exceedingly dangerous for travel that Campbell dubbed it the "River of Malediction."

Soon after, it was deemed no longer necessary for the HBC to push westward towards the Pacific because the HBC had signed a new agreement with the Russian American Company to facilitate development of coastal trade via the Pacific. Simpson therefore wrote: "I have turned my attention very particularly to the affairs of the McKenzies [sic] River generally, as there is a greater Field for the extension of trade there than in any other part of the Country."

In accordance with Simpson's fanciful expectations, Campbell once more doggedly set out to prove himself worthy of fame. Accompanied by his interpreter Francis Hoole and "my faithful Indians Lapie and Kitza," Campbell dutifully left Fort Halkett at the end of May, proceeded to Dease Lake, along the hazardous Liard River and reached "a beautiful sheet of water which, in honour of Lady Simpson, I called Frances Lake." He named a nearby landmark, Simpson's Tower, after his benefactor, and proceeded westward with a smaller party, on foot. He named Finlayson's Lake after Chief Factor Duncan Finlayson. Six days after leaving Simpson's Tower, he sighted the Pelly River, named for Sir John Henry Pelly, the HBC home governor, who remained in control of London business affairs from 1822 to 1852.

As much as Campbell tried to curry favour at every turn, carving the initials H.B.C. and the date in a tree trunk, and flying the HBC ensign, he ultimately fell afoul of his own reporting. Delighted to learn about the existence of the Pelly River, Simpson wrote, "you speak so favourably of the country in the neighborhood of Frances Lake, both as regards the means of living and the prospects of trade, that we have determined on extending our operations in that quarter."

Although Campbell and his exploration crew had not crossed paths with a single Aboriginal during their venture, he was instructed to establish a new post at Frances Lake. At the site of Simpson's Tower, first dubbed Glenlyon House, Campbell erected little-known Fort Frances in August of 1842. This was the first

HBC post built within the present-day boundaries of the Yukon.

Once more accompanied by "Houle and my 2 inseparables, Lapie and Kitza," Campbell further explored the Pelly River and spent several years in the Yukon, with limited success and much privation. Having undergone considerable hardship in northern British Columbia and the Yukon for ten years, Campbell wrote to George Simpson in the spring of 1847, saying: "here everything about my name is become stale and constant difficulty have all but overcome my ardour."

Discouraged, Campbell offered his resignation. George Simpson declined it, notifying Campbell's superior that his "exertions in the cause of Discovery" in the Yukon and northern New Caledonia were "beyond all praise." But after Campbell's 630-mile journey to Fort Simpson in the summer of 1847 to procure trade goods, he was once more stymied by the stinginess of Murdock McPherson, the Mackenzie District commander. "I have done all, but gone upon my knees to Mr. McPherson," he wrote to George Simpson. But no letter after the fact could provide him with adequate provisions for Pelly Banks, Frances Lake and a new post he hoped to erect on the Yukon River.

Cough-ridden and possibly asthmatic, Campbell nonetheless subjected himself to a daily regimen of outdoor baths. "As the season advanced," he wrote, "our cook would knock at my door to tell me the hole was made in the ice ready for me. I would then run down with a blanket round me, dip into the hole, out again, & back to the house, my hair frozen stiff before I got there."

Campbell commenced building Fort Selkirk at the forks of the Pelly and Lewes Rivers on June 1, 1848, gaining a reputation as a healer among the Indians soon thereafter by applying some medications to an Aboriginal man's leg. Much to Campbell's surprise, his patient recovered. A visit from the Chilkats of the Tlingit First Nation also buoyed Campbell's spirits as he imagined the potential for more trade along one of North America's largest rivers, but McPherson's reluctance once again to support adequately Campbell's initiative proved his undoing. Although Alexander Hunter Murray had established Fort Yukon at the forks of the Yukon and Porcupine Rivers in June of 1847, George Simpson did not realize the need to supply these new Yukon posts directly from York Factory, rather than from Murdoch McPherson's regional headquarters on the West Coast.

Ultimately, Campbell failed to achieve fame as the foremost explorer of the Yukon because Simpson firmly believed that exploration strictly for the sake of gaining geographical knowledge was an insufficient motive. When Campbell was mired at Frances Lake for several years, Simpson had advised him directly: "You seem to have been anxious to have proceeded down to the sea; that, however I think at present unnecessary, & would be impolitic, as it would bring us into competition with our Russian neighbours, with whom we are desirous of maintaining a good understanding." Campbell didn't receive his instructions from Simpson to "explore the Pelly downwards as far as I might deem advisable" until April of 1851. On this journey Campbell proved his conjectures were correct, that the Pelly and the Youcon Rivers were connected as one.

Campbell returned to Fort Selkirk in high spirits but his enthusiasm was not shared by Chief Trader James Anderson, newly appointed as director of the Mackenzie District in 1851. "I have a much higher opinion of Campbell's Zeal and Enterprise," wrote Anderson, "than of his judgement." Anderson decided the Frances Lake Fort established by Campbell was unnecessary and he was dismayed by Campbell's bookkeeping ("very chary of information") and his lack of profits. Campbell's reputation suffered an even more serious blow in 1852 when Chilkat Indians ransacked Fort Selkirk when Campbell was in charge. After 27 "demons" arrived on August 20, 1852, the fort's few occupants were overwhelmed the following day and expelled into the wilderness. "We were without a blanket amongst the party," Campbell commented, "and none of the men but myself had even a capot; nothing but their trousers, and in their shirt sleeves, with but two guns and a few shots of powder amongst us. The roaring and yelling of these painted fiends, smashing everything that came their way—and firing—beggars description."

Campbell and his men reached the camp of a friendly Wood Indian chief the next day, but by the time they returned to Fort Selkirk on the evening of August 23rd, the Chilkats "to our inexpressible vexation" had vanished. "Not a grain of powder or rag of clothing was left," Campbell wrote. "Cassettes, dressing cases, writing desks, kegs and musical instruments were smashed into a thousand atoms and the house and store strewed with the wreck, a sight to madden a saint."

When reports of this serious incident were prepared for HBC administrators Colville and Simpson, James Anderson privately advised, "It strikes me there was a want of due caution on our part." He criticized "poor Campbell" for his imprudent optimism in the face of poor results at both Frances Lake and Fort Selkirk. "It is my opinion that his sanguine disposition has caused him to estimate the prospects of Selkirk far too favorably—his views have been so long and intensely directed to one absorbing object that they have become distorted and he can no longer see things in their true colours."

To defend himself adequately, Campbell decided in November to trudge, dog sled and paddle three thousand miles across Canada from the Mackenzie River to Lachine, near Montreal, to speak with Simpson at his winter headquarters. He achieved his purpose at the end of March 1853, whereupon Simpson discounted Campbell's request for reprisals against the Chilkat perpetrators. Instead Simpson slyly reassured Campbell that nobody would assume any cowardice on his part and that he should take a well-earned furlough in Scotland, given his relative proximity to Europe.

Campbell passed a year in Scotland, during which time he became engaged to Miss Ellenora Stirling. He returned to Norway House in June of 1854, at which time Simpson reaffirmed his decision not to re-establish Fort Selkirk. Although Campbell would remain in the employ of the HBC for another 18 years, he would never achieve the renown he had craved. The four outposts he helped to generate—Dease Lake, Frances Lake, Pelly Banks and Fort Selkirk—were all abandoned. Only Fort Yukon, with which he had not been involved, would endure.

Campbell took charge of Fort Liard in 1854 and became Chief Trader for the Athabasca District in 1856, stationed at Fort Chipewyan. He married Ellenora Stirling at Norway House in 1859, became a Chief Factor in 1867, but was eventually dismissed because he disregarded company directives about trading routes for the transport of furs. He acquired a ranch in the wooded area of Riding Mountain, near Strathclair, Manitoba, in 1872, where he worked and edited his journals that were still unpublished when he died in 1894.

George Dawson named a minor tributory of the Pelly River after Robert Campbell in 1887, and the Yukon Territorial Council named a highway in his honour, but for the most part Robert Campbell's exploits are seldom cited. Although he named most of the principal rivers of the Yukon, leading pioneering efforts in northern British Columbia in the process, the opinions of faraway administrators obscured his considerable achievements. During Campbell's era, other significant Yukon explorers were Samuel Black, John McLeod and Murdoch McPherson.

Campbell recorded his adventures in journals that were published more than a century later as *Two Journals of Robert Campbell: 1808–1853* (1958). The first of these covers 1808–1851 and has been published from a copy of the original; the second covers the period 1850–1853 and was based on a rewritten account by Campbell after his original journal was destroyed by fire. Campbell's journals for his stints at Pelly Banks (1845–1847) and Fort Selkirk in the Yukon are available at the Public Archives of Canada.

"Company correspondence," according to historian Ken Coates, "suggests Campbell overestimated his importance, was at best a marginal trader and was not widely admired by his peers." But Clifford Wilson, a long-time editor of the Hudson's Bay Company's magazine *The Beaver*, who also served as the assistant director of the National Museum of Canada, has written a biography, *Campbell of the Yukon*, to suggest that Campbell's extensive explorations are worthy of respect and even admiration.

ALEXANDER HUNTER MURRAY

One of the most widely travelled fur traders on the North American continent, Scotsman Alexander Hunter Murray ventured as far south as the Red River in Texas, and southeast to Lake Pontchartrain near New Orleans, Louisiana, prior to becoming an employee of the American Fur Company in St. Louis, Missouri, in the mid-1840s.

Before Murray built and illicitly managed Fort Youcon, within Russian territory, just inside the Arctic Circle, for the Hudson's Bay Company, he had been appointed senior clerk under Chief Factor Murdoch McPherson in the Mackenzie River District. He arrived with his seventeen-year-old bride, Anne Campbell, daughter of Chief Trader Colin Campbell of Fort Chipewyan in the Athabasca District. The couple had married without a clergyman at Fort Simpson. This union was registered at St. John's Cathedral in Red River on August 24, 1846.

The couple first wintered together at Fort McPherson, then Murray left his bride for a time at Lapierre House on Bell River in order to establish Fort Youcon. To do so, Murray descended the Bell River to the Porcupine, then proceeded to its junction with the Yukon. Anne joined her husband at Fort Youcon where they stayed for three years, during which she gave birth to three daughters, and her husband attempted to compile a vocabulary of Indian dialects. He also kept busy trying to understand the geography of the area. "I have been able to form some idea of the courses of the Youcon and other rivers," he wrote, "of which hitherto very little was known."

Murray estimated there were approximately one thousand Aboriginal men and boys able to hunt in the area from the Pelly River to the Arctic. He also divided the Yukon Indians, or

"Kutchin," into eight tribes. He remained at Fort Youcon until 1851 when he was relieved of his duties due to ill health.

Murray served at several other posts prior to his promotion as Chief Trader at Pembina in 1856. After one year's furlough in Scotland in 1857, he took charge of Lower Fort Garry where he worked until he retired in 1867. He died at Bellevue on the Red River in 1874. Little is known about his early life. He was born at Kilmun, county of Argyll, Scotland, in 1818 or 1819.

The location of Fort Youcon (or Yukon) on the Porcupine River was kept secret for two decades. Although it was one of the most isolated HBC outposts, it was also one of the most consistently profitable. Other posts created by the HBC in the Yukon region included Peel's River, Lapierre's House (1846), Frances Lake, Pelly Banks and Fort Selkirk (1848). The HBC limited information about the Yukon River valley to discourage competition, delaying its distribution of charts and trading post locations. Although the Liard River explorations of John McLeod in 1831 were included on maps, the HBC suppressed information about the Porcupine, Pelly and Yukon River explorations of John Bell and Robert Campbell until 1853.

For the most part the Russians never intervened. Knowingly contravening their treaty with the Russians, the HBC did not withdraw from Fort Youcon until 1869, two years after the Americans purchased Alaska. This retreat up the Porcupine River only occurred when the Americans sent Captain Raymond of the U.S. Navy to ascertain Fort Youcon's location. The company moved its operations upriver to Rampart House until 1890 when another border survey revealed they were still trespassing on American territory.

A lively journal kept by A.H. Murray, with his sketches, was later edited by L.J. Burpee as *Journal of the Yukon, 1847–48.*

Alexander Hunter Murray

179

JOHN DUNN

In 1832, naval apprentice John Dunn arrived on the Pacific Coast aboard the *Ganymede* with fellow apprentice George B. Roberts. Although he was not a lively journal writer, he took a keen interest in the variety of commerce practised by the Hudson's Bay Company from the Columbia River to Fort Simpson, as documented by Richard Somerset Mackie in *Trading Beyond the Mountains*.

Dunn described Fort Vancouver as "the grand emporium of the Company's trade, west of the Rocky Mountains; as well as within the Oregon territory, as beyond it, from California to Kamschatka." He also provided the following description of how Aboriginal women prepared salmon for cooperage near Fort George.

"Mode of Curing Salmon. As soon as a cargo of Salmon is caught, the natives bring it to the trading post in their canoes. A number of Indian women are employed by the traders, seated on the beach, with knives, ready to cut up the fish. The salmon are counted from each Indian, for which a ticket is given for the quantity, large or small. After the whole of the salmon are landed, the Indians congregate round the trading shop for their payment, and receive ammunition, baize, tobacco, buttons, etc.

"The women employed by the trader commence cutting out the backbones, and cut off the heads of the salmon. They are then taken to the salter, and placed in a large hogshead, with a quantity of course salt. They remain there for several days, until they become quite firm. The pickle produced from these is boiled in a large copper kettle; and the blood, which floats by the boiling process to the top, is skimmed off, leaving the pickle perfectly clear.

"The salmon are then taken from the hogshead and packed in

tierces [casks], with a little more salt; the tierces are then headed up, and laid upon their bilge, or widest part, leaving the bung-hole open; the pickle is next poured in, until the tierce becomes full; a circle of clay, about four inches high, is then made round the bung-hole; into which the oil from the salmon rises. This oil is skimmed off; and, according as the salmon imbibes the pickle, more pickle is poured in, so as to keep the liquid sufficiently on the surface, and afford facility for skimming off the oil.

"After the oil ceases to rise to the circle around the bung-hole, the salmon is then supposed to be sufficiently prepared; the clay circle is cleared away and the hole is bunged up. Salmon, so cured, will keep good for three years."

John Dunn also described the lumber industry on the Columbia River where mostly Kanaka labourers were employed sawing up to 3,000 square feet of Douglas fir per day, "regularly shipped for the Sandwich Islands, and other foreign parts." Having visited the Queen Charlotte Islands in 1836, Dunn recorded, in 1839, that cultivation of pototoes, introduced to the Haida between 1800 and 1815, had resulted in substantial annual exports to Fort Simpson on the mainland. "I have known from five to eight hundred bushels traded in one season from these Indians at Fort Simpson," he wrote. In addition, Dunn observed the rearing of sheep for the wool trade by the Puget's Sound Agricultural Company and pronounced that, by 1844, the Hudson's Bay Company had established "a vast and complex machinery of internal and coasting commerce."

Twice stationed at Fort McLoughlin, he recorded that mostly Tsimshian were used as slaves by the northern tribes and the Bella Bella frequently served as middle men in the coastal slave trade. Although the HBC was not directly complicit, he noted, "These slaves, in barter, fetch a larger price to the northward than they do to the south; and are sold by the Nass tribe to the various inland tribes, for furs. These furs they again sell to the white traders for blankets, and other articles of use or luxury." Dunn concluded his journal, written in support of British claims to the Oregon Territory, by avowing the need for more missionaries."

ARCHIBALD MCDONALD

Few fur traders better symbolized the increased efficiency of the Hudson's Bay Company in British Columbia than Archibald McDonald. His unprecedented map of the B.C. interior in *Thompson River District Report, 1827* was beyond rudimentary. "McDonald unquestionably made use of information from other traders," wrote A.L. Farley in his *Historical Cartography of British Columbia.* "Unlike others, however, he was apparently interested in mapping and possessed no mean ability as a draughtsman."

With similar zeal, McDonald compiled the first census of the Fraser Canyon, by questioning Aboriginals he met in 1830. He also became the first person to export fish from British Columbia.

Placed in charge of Fort Langley, McDonald had written to HBC Governor George Simpson in 1831, reporting on his initial attempts to preserve salmon for shipping to foreign markets. Simpson was sufficiently impressed that he complied with McDonald's request for the services of "a good Cooper, that will know something of Fish curing."

The commercial fishing industry existed in British Columbia waters before McDonald's arrival, but he instigated the first commercial shipments abroad, a cargo of salted salmon sent to Hawaii. By 1838, James Douglas optimistically predicted Fort Langley would soon supply all the salted fish required along the Pacific Coast.

Archibald McDonald, one of the most successful frontiersmen of his era, was born in Scotland in 1790 as the thirteenth and youngest child of an Episcopalian Highlander. At age twenty-one he was hired as a clerk for the Earl of Selkirk and two years later he first arrived in Canada as the leader of Selkirk settlers to the Red River colony in 1813. Seven years later, after Lord Selkirk's death, he took employment as a clerk with the Hudson's Bay Company in the spring of 1820.

Just prior to the merger of the Hudson's Bay Company and the North West Company in 1821, McDonald had the good fortune to meet and befriend George Simpson during the latter's visit to the Athabasca Territory. Consequently, Simpson sent McDonald as an emissary and accountant to accompany Chief Factor John Dugald Cameron to his new posting at Fort George near the mouth of the Columbia River in 1821.

Upon his arrival on the West Coast, McDonald's main task was to prepare an inventory of the North West Company forts that the HBC had acquired in the Columbia District, such as Spokane House, Nez Percés (Walla Walla) and Okanagan (Thompson River).

In 1823, McDonald met Princess Sunday (Princess Raven, Kaole'xoa), the youngest daughter of the foremost Chinook chief Comcomly. She became his wife, but she died soon after giving birth to their only child, Ranald, early in 1824.

As an infant, Ranald was temporarily sent to Comcomly's lodge to be raised by his Chinook aunts. That same year McDonald fell in love with Jane Klyne—the daughter of the French-Canadian postmaster at Jasper House, Michel Klyne, and a Métis mother—and she became his second country wife when he took command of the Thompson River District (Kamloops and Okanagan) in February of 1826.

Happily relocated to Kamloops, McDonald renewed his acquaintance with the botanist David Douglas and raised a family that soon included Ranald, Jane's first-born son Angus, and Archibald Jr., born in 1828.

While on a furlough to London, McDonald's affiliation with David Douglas enabled him to introduce himself to Sir William Hooker, the famous horticulturalist who oversaw Kew Gardens. McDonald subsequently sent plant and animal specimens to the British Museum, Kew Gardens and to John Halkett, a HBC stock-

"[Archibald] McDonald and his kind were neither conquerors nor immigrants; they were the exiles who occupied the commercial garrisons. Garrisons, whether military or commercial, have been notorious for disregarding the sensitivities of those among whom they reside."—J.E. Foster, BC Studies

holder and naturalist.

Although he was staunchly pro-British, McDonald was ambivalent about the encroachments of Europeans. In 1840 he wrote to James Douglas expressing his concerns about land appropriations by the Puget's Sound Agricultural Society at Nisqually. He proposed a nature reserve, west of Puget Sound, to revive the beaver population ("the poor expiring Beaver race"), but his suggestion was not implemented.

Prior to the Oregon Treaty of 1846, the fur trading region had been jointly claimed by American and British interests, but afterwards new settlers began to dominate the Pacific Slope. McDonald wrote, "I am much bothered with a new race of men come on my hands. They are come across to settle. . . . But among their *besoins* [needs] not one has mentioned the words 'Beaver Trap.' What a change in the world."

McDonald also oversaw operations at Fort Colvile on the Columbia River, where he received his promotion to Chief Factor. Jean Murray Cole's book of McDonald's correspondence includes letters from the 1822–1828 period when McDonald was at Fort George and Kamloops, providing descriptions of family life with Jane Klyne, who had 13 of his 14 children. In 1834, McDonald formally married Jane at Red River.

"Rather than abandon her for a more suitable wife when his career warranted it," wrote J.E. Foster in *BC Studies*, "a practice not uncommon among his colleagues, McDonald saw to her education, apparently sufficient for their purposes and those of the children until they were old enough to be sent away to school. Jane Klyne McDonald appears to have made the transition from a daughter in a post master's family to the wife of a Chief Factor with no difficulty."

The largest section of Cole's collection of McDonald's letters covers 1834–1844, when he was in charge of Fort Colvile among the Spokane and Kettle Falls Indians. In 1844, the McDonalds lost three little boys to scarlet fever. Soon thereafter the McDonalds retired to Montreal, prior to moving to a property on the Ottawa River that he called Glencoe, near Carillon, in Lower Canada (Quebec), in 1847. There he lived as a gentleman farmer until his death on January 15, 1853. Jane McDonald died in 1879.

In August of 2002 approximately 50 people gathered at Fort Langley for a two-day "Outpost of Empire" symposium on the Northwest Coast fur trade. Earlier conferences had been held at Fort Vancouver in Washington State and at Sidney, B.C.

At the Fort Langley event, editor and biographer Jean Murray Cole signed copies of *This Blessed Wilderness: Archibald McDonald's Letters from the Columbia, 1822–44*, her collection of letters by her ancestor Archibald McDonald who had been placed in charge of Fort Langley from 1828 to 1833, taking over from James McMillan.

RANALD MACDONALD

The remarkable and sad tale of Ranald Macdonald's life as a *bois brulé*, or "half-breed," is one of the rare documented cases of the plight of a mixed blood offspring on the Western Slope in the early days.

Born in Fort George, Oregon, in 1824, Ranald Macdonald was the son of Scottish-born fur trader Archibald McDonald (who spelled his surname McDonald) and Kaole'xoa, the daughter of Tillamook Chief Comcomly, who died soon after her son was born. It has been suggested that Ranald Macdonald was unaware of his Aboriginal ancestry until his late teens or early twenties, but this seems unlikely given his father's chronic worries about his welfare, as stated in letters to his fur trade peers such as Edward Ermatinger. "All the wealth in Rupert's land will not make a half-breed either a good parson, a shining lawyer or an able physician, if left to his own discretion while young," Archibald McDonald wrote in 1836. Three years later, having sent his son to Ermatinger's care in the small Ontario town of St. Thomas, McDonald confessed, "I cannot divest myself of certain indescribable fears." McDonald's plan was to give his son some training as a gentleman in Ontario: "If he can only keep out of egregious acts of impropriety til we can once more have him back in the Indian country, I shall consider it a great point gained. . . . Here . . . he may just crawl through like the Black Bear does—lick his paws. We are all most unfortunate parents."

Ranald Macdonald gained an unlikely position as a bank clerk but felt estranged in Ontario, "while sitting, like a Simon Stylites, on my high stool in the Bank of Elgin, with little money or means." When a white girl rejected his advances in St. Thomas, Macdonald began to be worried by his mixed blood. He began to wonder

186

Ranald MacDonald in custody with Japanese scholars. Woodcut by William Klamm.

about three shipwrecked Japanese sailors that he had seen as a boy at Fort Vancouver in 1834. Allegedly believing that Japanese were "similar to the Indians and probably ignorant, so that an educated man might make himself something of a personage among them," he hatched a very unusual plan. Rejecting the prospect of alienation in either Ontario or Indian country, he opted for service as a sailor sometime in the early 1840s.

To make better sense of his own life, Ranald Macdonald reputedly theorized there was a racial link between North American Aboriginals and the Japanese. Consequently, after spending several years at sea, Macdonald secured a place as a deckhand on an American whaling ship that would be passing in the vicinity of Japan. During a period when foreigners were prohibited from entering that country, Macdonald arranged with his captain to be set adrift with a few books in a small boat in June of 1848. At age twenty-four, he marooned himself on Rishiri Island, near Hokkaido, and presented himself as shipwrecked. Seeing his books, the Japanese apparently assumed he was a scholar of some sort, and spared his life.

During Macdonald's ten-month stay in Japan, he was taken to Nagasaki where he taught English to 14 scholars prior to his deportation in 1849. It was Ranald Macdonald's tutelage that enabled the Japanese to understand Admiral Parry when he arrived in Japan several years later in 1854.

In Japanese documentation of his visit, there is no reference to Macdonald's mixed blood background. For one exotic period of his life, he was able to gain acceptance and respect. Upon leaving Japan on an American ship, with the help of a Dutch mediator in Nagasaki, Macdonald once more worked as a sailor, eventually living in northern Washington State and British Columbia. He spent nearly 30 years of his life within British Columbia, including time as a member of the Vancouver Island exploring expedition in 1864, but he was unable to prosper in his various small business enterprises. Married, but ever the loner, Ranald Macdonald was buried in an Indian cemetery near Curlew, Washington.

Ranald Macdonald woodcut by William Klamm

Ranald Macdonald has since been credited with writing an autobiography that was, in fact, a concoction of notes reshaped after his death. According to Juliet Pollard in *BC Studies*, Nos. 91–92, "Much of the manuscript was not written by Macdonald, but was the work of another fur trader son, Malcolm McLeod, an Ottawa lawyer, who, with Ranald's assistance, incorporated Ranald's narrative into various manuscripts of his own. In the course of this undertaking in the early 1890s, the elderly McLeod, who had never been to Japan and the aged Macdonald, who had lost his Japan notes, turned to other books, especially Richard Hildreth's *Japan As It Was and Is* (1855) for inspiration. At times the borrowing bordered on plagiarism."

In order to encourage positive views of Aboriginals, Macdonald's collaborator, Malcolm McLeod, inserted passages about Christian charity and brotherly love in his friend's memoirs, adding his own suppositions about racial links between Japanese and Aboriginals (which were later credited to Macdonald). Upon discovering Ranald Macdonald's handwritten version of one of his co-written manuscripts, William S. Lewis and Naojiro Murakami allegedly reinforced the notion that Macdonald was motivated by a desire to make racial links between the Japanese and Aboriginals, as outlined in a foreword to *McDonald of Oregon*, a biography by E.E. Dye in 1906. Dye chose to spell the surname as McDonald, in keeping with his father Archibald's surname. Lewis and Murakami switched the spelling to MacDonald for their purposes, but Ranald himself had preferred Macdonald.

[END OF AN ERA]

NARCISSA WHITMAN

*"The poor Indians are amazed at the overwhelming numbers
of Americans coming into the country. They seem not to know
what to make of it."* —NARCISSA WHITMAN

The letters of Narcissa Whitman constitute the earliest writings by any woman from the Pacific Northwest to appear as a book. But her notoriety has more to do with her death than her life.

Narcissa Whitman's stubborn desire to serve as a missionary near Fort Walla Walla, at Waiilatpu, six miles from the present site of Walla Walla, Washington, resulted in her murder at the hands of Cayuse and Umatilla Indians on November 29, 1847. Although Whitman was a victim of her own hubris and not a heroine, her life is sometimes lauded for her bold resolve to accompany her husband as one of the first two white women to pass through the Rocky Mountains in 1836.

Narcissa Whitman was born Narcissa Prentiss on March 14, 1808, the third of nine children, in Prattsburg, Steuben County, New York. She was the eldest daughter of a distiller, miller and carpenter whose ancestor Henry Prentice emigrated from England prior to 1640. At age eleven she joined the Congregational Church after her religious awakening during a revival meeting in 1819. Inspired by reading about the missionary life of Harriet Boardman in India, she decided at age sixteen to "consecrate [herself] without reserve to the Missionary work waiting the leadings of Providence." After Narcissa Prentiss providentially rejected the marriage proposal of Henry Harmon Spalding, a fellow student at Franklin Academy in Prattsburg, she taught kindergarten and school in both Prattsburg and Bath, New York. Upon her family's move to Amity, New York, she attended a lecture by Reverend Samuel Parker in 1834 about the need for missionaries on the west side of the continent. On her behalf, Parker wrote to the American Board of Commissioners for Foreign Missions but her gender and her status as a single woman prevented her from gaining a posting.

Only two months later, Narcissa Prentiss became engaged to Marcus Whitman, a physician who had also been recruited by Parker as a potential missionary. Possibly this arrangement had more to do with pragmatism than providence. Born in Rushville, New York, on September 4, 1802, only 25 miles from Prentiss' birthplace, Whitman had practised medicine for four years in Canada prior to his becoming an elder of the Presbyterian church. After their betrothal, Narcissa Prentiss successfully applied to the ABCFM in March of 1835, and Marcus Whitman scouted for potential mission sites. They were married on February 18, 1836. The next day they left New York, never to return.

In the spring of 1836, the newlyweds departed from Liberty, Missouri, in one of two covered wagons, escorted by trappers from the American Fur Company. In the other wagon was Narcissa's

Narcissa Whitman, one of the first two white women to cross the continent

former suitor, Henry Harmon Spalding, along with his own new wife, Eliza Hart Spalding. By July, Narcissa Whitman was pregnant. That same summer, their entourage, including prospective missionary William H. Gray, was escorted through the Rockies by Hudson's Bay Company trappers, placing Eliza Hart Spalding and Narcissa Whitman in the history books as the first white women to cross the continent overland. They reached Fort Walla Walla in September and proceeded to Fort

Vancouver where they were warmly received by John McLoughlin.

With McLoughlin's assistance, Marcus Whitman established a mission site at Waiilatpu, "the place of the rye grass," to offer his medical and religious service to the Cayuse Indians. Narcissa joined him there in December, resisting McLoughlin's invitation to spend her first winter in the relative comfort of Fort Vancouver. At the same time Eliza Hart Spalding joined her husband at Lapwai among the Nez Percé, in present-day Idaho, about 125 miles from Waiilatpu.

Paul Kane's portrait depicts To-ma-kus, one of the alleged murderers of the Whitmans.

At first the Whitmans were fuelled by optimism as other missions were created by incoming missionaries in 1838. But gradually they realized their conversion rate among the Cayuse was negligible.

On Narcissa's birthday, she gave birth to Alice Clarissa Whitman, reputedly the first child born of American parents west of the Rocky Mountains, but the joy of her life was short-lived.

About two years later, the beloved child drowned in the Walla Walla River on June 23, 1839. Narcissa Whitman's evangelical spirit temporarily drowned with the child. She became depressed, retreated to her room, increasingly wrote to her family, suffered near-blindness and a nervous breakdown. As an antidote, she adopted four children of deceased migrants, then added seven more migrating orphans from the Sager family in 1844. For the next three years she would raise these children as her own while managing the drudgery of pioneer chores.

Narcissa Whitman was approximately five feet, six inches tall

192

Narcissa Whitman's death was sensationalized and elevated to martyrdom by newspapers that failed to consider why the Whitman Massacre had occurred.

with beautiful light-blonde hair; she dressed severely, and she wore a sunbonnet outdoors. A fellow minister once described her as "very graceful in her deportment and general carriage, slightly sandy complexion, a brilliant, sparkling eye, perculiarly [sic] so when engaged in animated conversation." It has been suggested that her formal manner might have been interpreted by the Cayuse Indians as haughtiness.

As the Oregon Trail attracted more white settlers every year, the Cayuse become less conciliatory. Squabbles between Marcus Whitman and Henry Spalding hardly benefitted Narcissa Whitman's mental health either. This friction, possibly exacerbated by Henry Spalding's sexual jealousy and pique, led ABCFM authorities to threaten to close both missions. Marcus Whitman was obliged to travel back to ABCFM headquarters and gain re-approval, thereby abandoning his wife to greater loneliness in the interim. On his return journey to the west, he guided a wagon train of one thousand migrants up the Oregon Trail. As his stature among new settlers increased, his stature among the Cayuse decreased.

The so-called Whitman massacre, or Walla Walla massacre, occurred in response to a measles epidemic that swept through the Oregon territories in 1847, killing approximately half of the children among the Cayuse, who recognized that a much higher percentage of white children were able to overcome the disease. As the epidemic worsened, and more white settlers streamed into the area, the Cayuse and other tribes became increasingly distraught and belligerent. The Whitmans chose to ignore various warning signs and overt threats from the Cayuse. Marcus

Whitman's inability as a physician to counteract the measles was problematic enough, but their situation became dire with the malevolent rumour-mongering of a newly arrived settler, Joe Lewis, who apparently suggested to the Cayuse that Dr. Whitman was not really trying to save them at all, but poisoning them instead. It is possible rival Catholic clerics (Pierre Jean de Smet, John Baptist Brouillet and Joseph Cataldo) might have maliciously supported such rumours.

Other motivations for the vicious attack of November 29, 1847, include the recent killing of a Walla Walla chief's son and the plain fact that both Whitmans were increasingly active in providing services to incoming settlers.

Cayuse Chiefs Tiloukaikt and Tomahas, along with Kiamsupkin, Iaiachalakis and Klokomas, allegedly led the massacre in which Dr. Whitman's body was dismembered and Narcissa Whitman killed. Other murder victims included Andrew Rogers, Jacob Hoffman, L.W. Sanders, Mr. Marsh, John Sager, Nathan Kimball, Isaac Gilliland, James Young, Frank Sager, Crockett Blewley and Amos Sales. The attackers burned down the mission buildings and held approximately 50 women and children for ransom. Peter Skene Ogden retrieved the prisoners in exchange for 62 blankets, 63 cotton shirts, twelve Hudson's Bay rifles, 600 rounds of ammunition, seven pounds of tobacco and twelve flints. Deadly retaliations made by whites in 1848 on innocent Aboriginals led to the so-called Cayuse War. Possibly the Walla Walla killings were exploited as a convenient excuse to liberate more territories for the influx of settlers. Eventually Tiloukaikt and Tomahas, along with three other men, agreed to be taken to Oregon City for trial in order to save their tribe from annihilation. Newly appointed Territorial Marshall Joseph Meek found them all guilty. Just before Tiloukaikt, Tomahas, Kiamsupkin, Iaiachalakis and Klokomas were publicly hanged on June 3, 1850, Tiloukaikt reportedly said, "Did not your missionaries teach us that Christ died to save his people? So we die to save our people."

The severely weakened Cayuse were forced to amalgamate with the Nez Percé and Yakima, so the ultimate outcome of the

Seal of the Territory of Oregon with the motto—alis volat propriis—"I fly with my own wings"

Whitmans' missionary work was the disappearance of the Cayuse tribe. The lives of Narcissa Whitman and Marcus Whitman are commemorated by the Whitman Mission National Historic Site in eastern Washington.

Narcissa Whitman never ventured into British Columbia, but her brutal murder, presented as martyrdom, drew national attention in the United States. It hastened the impetus for the United States to improve its control of the Oregon Territory in keeping with the newly signed Oregon Treaty of 1846 that formalized the present-day border between Washington State and British Columbia.

Less than one year after the Whitman Massacre, the U.S. portion of the western region below the 49th parallel north was recognized by an Act of the U.S. Congress as Oregon Territory on August 14, 1848. It included Idaho, Oregon and Washington as well as parts of Montana and Wyoming, west of the Continental Divide. A section of that territory located north of the lower Columbia River, as well as north of the 46th parallel east of the Columbia River, was subsequently designated to constitute the Washington Territory in 1853.

———

There are no authenticated portraits of Narcissa Whitman but artist Paul Kane visited the Whitmans' mission at Waiilatpu, in July of 1847. He sketched a woman who is generally presumed to have been Narcissa Whitman. These sketches, now in the Royal Ontario Museum in Toronto, were used as the basis for idealized portraits of Marcus and Narcissa Whitman (as shown on the cover of this book, courtesy of National Park Service, U.S. Department of the Interior) made by artist Drury Haight.

This fur press, still operational at Fort St. John in 1915, typically compressed furs for transport into 80-pound bundles appropriate for pack-horses to carry long distances.

III
APPENDIX

FIFTY FORTS

The first fort built by Europeans within British Columbia territory nearly produced a war between Spain and England. The second resulted in the annihilation of a Nuu-chah-nulth village during an American attack. The third gave rise to Fort St. John, the oldest non-Aboriginal settlement in British Columbia.

Below are 50 forts and depots built west of present-day Alberta prior to 1850.

1789 – Fort San Miguel	1825 – Fort Colvile
1791 – Fort Defiance	1827 – Fort Langley
1794 – Fort St. John	1827 – Fort Connolly
1798 – Rocky Mountain Fort	1829 – Fort Chilcotin
1805 – Peace River Portage	1829 – Fort Halkett
1805 – Fort McLeod	1831 – Fort Simpson
1805 – Fort Nelson	1832 – Fort Umpqua
1805 – Fort Clatsop	1833 – Fort McLoughlin
1806 – Fort St. James	1833 – Fort Nisqually
1806 – Fort Fraser	1835 – Fort Essington
1807 – Fort George	1837 – Fort Cowlitz
1807 – Kootenae House	1838 – Dease Lake Post
1807 – Fort Raymond	1839 – Honolulu
1811 – (Fort) Astoria	1840 – Fort Taku
1811 – Fort Okanogan	1840 – Fort Stikine
1811 – Fort Champoeg	1841 – Yerba Buena
1812 – Fort Thompson	1843 – Fort Victoria
1812 – Fort Spokane	1846 – Fort Pelly Banks
1812 – Fort Ross	1847 – Fort Youcon
1813 – William Henry Fort	1847 – Fort Yale
1818 – Fort Walla Walla	1847 – Fort Waters
1820 – Fort de Pinette	1848 – Fort Gilliam
1821 – Fort Alexandria	1848 – Fort Hope
1822 – Fort Babine	1848 – Fort Selkirk
1825 – Fort Vancouver	1849 – Fort Rupert

The first European military installation in B.C. was built by the Spanish at Friendy Cove.

1789 – In the wake of Captain James Cook's visit to Nootka Sound in 1778, **Fort San Miguel** was established on the west coast of Vancouver Island at Friendly Cove (aka *Cala de Los Amigos*), in Nootka Sound (*Puerto de la Santa Cruz de Nuca*), by the mercurial Spanish commander Esteban José Martínez.

After he complied with the Viceroy of New Spain's directive to make "a large hut" and to "pretend that you are engaged in setting yourself in a formal establishment," Martínez notoriously failed to follow his instructions to assert Spanish sovereignty "with prudent firmness, but without being led into harsh expressions which may give serious offense and cause a rupture."

Instead, Martínez commenced hostilities in May of 1789 when he fired a shot across the bow of the *Washington*, an American vessel captained by Robert Gray. After Martínez had gained control of Nootka Sound in the *Princesa* (26 guns), accompanied by Don Gonzalo Lopez de Haro in the *San Carlos* (16 guns), he seized the furs and supplies of the *Iphigenia*, a pseudo-Portuguese vessel that sailed under a symbolic commander named Captain Viana. The real captain on board was William Douglas, an Englishman. After an impasse of several weeks, Martínez allowed the *Iphigenia* and its crew to put out to sea.

Emboldened, Martínez seized the *North West America*, built and owned by Englishman John Meares, and made arrangements for its crew to be transported to China by the American Robert Gray. In July, Martínez apprehended a second British ship, the *Argonaut*, retaining its Chinese labourers and forcing Captain James Colnett and his crew to sail to the naval port of San Blas on the western coast of present-day Mexico, where they were held as prisoners.

Meanwhile the British Parliament was obliged to respond to the outrage of John Meares, who demanded reparations and retribution for the loss of his ship. Neither London nor Madrid was keen on another war, so protracted diplomatic negotiations commenced. Much to his surprise, Martínez received new instructions, via the supply ship *Aranzazu*: demolish Fort San Miguel at Nootka Sound. Martínez obeyed and departed for San Blas in October of 1789.

But Viceroy Revilla Gigedo of New Spain soon reasserted Spain's military presence at Nootka Sound, partly to forestall any advances from Russian traders to the north. A flotilla under Lieutenant Francisco Eliza, assisted by Lieutenant Salvador Fidalgo and Ensign Manuel Quimper, arrived to rebuild Fort San Miguel in 1790. With Catalonian emigrants recruited for service by Don Pedro Alberni, who took command of the reconstructed fortifications, the Spanish added a church, barracks, supply buildings, a hospital and gardens.

In order to cool its simmering conflict with England—known as the Nootka Crisis, or the Nootka Controversy—Spain sent the gentlemanly Captain Bodega y Quadra to negotiate a truce with Captain George Vancouver at Nootka Sound in 1792. A compromise could not be immediately reached by the two captains, but hostilities abated. The Spanish eventually abandoned once again their fort in 1795 in accordance with the Nootka Convention, signed in January of 1794, in which Britain and Spain formally agreed not to maintain any permanent base at Nootka Sound.

By the end of the twentieth century, even the indigenous population had mostly departed. Ray and Terry Williams, self-appointed guardians of the territory on behalf of the Nuu-chah-nulth First

Nation, are at present the only people living at Friendly Cove.

1791 – American fur trader and explorer Robert Gray erected **Fort Defiance** as a wintering headquarters on the shore of Mcares Island, in Clayoquot Sound, on the western edge of Vancouver Island, in order to refit his ship, *Columbia*, and to build a second vessel, *Adventure*. Having had deadly relations with Aboriginals in other waters, including the murder of a black manservant, Gray opted to respond to fearful rumours of an imminent attack by commanding his fifth mate, John Boit, to attack and burn the neighboring Nuu-chah-nulth village of Opitsat in the spring of 1792.

As the reluctant young commander of this pre-emptive American strike, Boit wrote on March 27: "I am sorry to be under the nessecity [sic] of remarking that this day I was sent with three boats, all well mann'd and arm'd, to destroy the Village of Opitsatah [sic]. It is a Command I was no ways tenacious off, and am grieved to think Capt. Gray shou'd let his passions go so far. This Village was about half a mile in Diameter, and Contained upwards off 200 Houses, generally well built for Indians ev'ry door that you enter'd was in resemblance to an human and Beasts head, the passage being through the mouth, besides which there was much more rude carved work about the dwelling some of which was by no means inelegant. This fine Village, the Work of Ages, was in a short time totally destroy'd."

Fort Defiance was destroyed by the Nuu-chah-nulth soon after Gray and Boit departed in the *Columbia* and the *Adventure*. Gray became famous as the first American to circumnavigate the globe and the first sea captain to cross the treacherous bar of the Columbia River, a waterway that he named after his ship. Almost two centuries later, the NASA space program named its spaceship *Columbia* in honour of Gray's ship. Fort Defiance was the first of two American-built forts within the confines of present-day British Columbia, the other being at Kamloops.

1794 – **Fort St. John**, the first white settlement in present-day mainland British Columbia, was founded for the North West Company by Alexander Mackenzie, who first reached the Peace River site in 1793. (Oddly enough, the earliest evidence of an Aboriginal settlement site in the province has been discovered only seven miles northwest of modern Fort St. John, at the Charlie Lake Cave site, dating back almost eleven centuries.) In May of 1793, Mackenzie provided an enthusiastic description of a site in the Peace River region that afforded "an excellent situation for a fort or a factory, as there is plenty of wood, and every reason to believe that the country abounds in beaver. . . . The country is so crowded with animals as to have the appearance, in some places, of a stall-yard, from the state of the ground, and the quantity of dung, which is scattered over it." Mackenzie was impressed by the "vast herds" of buffalo that roamed the Peace River Valley, an area he described as a "magnificent theatre of nature."

The fur trading encampment originated by Mackenzie was moved six times before operations ceased in 1823. Re-opened in 1860, south of the present community, this trading post was relocated across the Peace River by Francis Work Beaton in 1872, then moved again to Fish Creek, northwest of the town, in 1925. By the time the trading post finally ceased business, the city of Fort St. John had arisen on the Alaska Highway in north-eastern B.C., about forty-five minutes drive north of Dawson Creek.

1798 – Boasting a fur press, a storehouse, a "big house" and a 55-foot flagpole, **Rocky Mountain Fort** was one of the offshoots of the original Fort St. John. Erected on the south bank of the Peace River, just above the mouth of the Pine River, also known as the Sinew River, it has been documented by an anonymous "Journal of Rocky Mountain Fort" possibly written by Simon Fraser or Alexander McLeod. This journal describes activities during 1799 and 1800, leading some historians to suggest the post was established even earlier than 1798. According to John Stuart, writing in 1823, ". . . we encamped on the site of the Old Beaver [Moberly] River, first established in 1794, and where ten years afterwards I wintered."

The fort's population reached at least 14 residents, including four women and five children, before it was likely abandoned around 1804. David Thompson recorded his visit to the site on

March 6, 1804. His reportage helped Simon Fraser University archaeologist Knut Fladmark uncover the site in 1975. Test exca-vations in 1976 confirmed the presence of at least three stone chimney mounds. The Hudson's Bay Company briefly built Fort d'Epinette as a rival operation near the same location in 1820.

1805 – Established by Simon Fraser and his men on the Peace River, just below the Peace River Canyon, approximately 75 kilo-metres upriver from Rocky Mountain Fort, and probably replac-ing it, **Peace River Portage House**, also referred to as Rocky Moun-tain Portage House, remained operational for NWC expeditions into New Caledonia until 1814. Re-opened briefly, it served as the embarkation point for the northward expedition of Samuel Black and Donald Manson in May of 1824. Re-opened again in the 1860s, the trading depot served as one of the forerunners of Hudson's Hope, now situated about 60 miles west of Fort St. John.

1805 – Recognized by the *Encyclopedia of British Columbia* as the longest continuously occupied European settlement in B.C., the town of McLeod Lake arose from **Fort McLeod**, a NWC trading post known as "Fort Misery." Fort McLeod (Trout Lake Post, McLeod's Lake Post) was founded by Simon Fraser on the "car-rying place" between the Peace and Fraser Rivers, on Trout Lake, in TseK'ene (Sekani or Sékanais) territory. Manned by James MacDougall, it was first called Trout Lake Post until it was re-named for Nor'Wester Archibald R. McLeod.

In 1828, George Simpson wrote in his private journal: "McLeods Lake is the most wretched place in the Indian Country; it pos-sesses few or no resources within itself, depending almost en-tirely on a few dried Salmon taken across from Stuarts Lake, and when the Fishery fails, or when any thing else occurs to prevent this supply being furnished, the situation of the Post is cheerless indeed." The trading post closed in 1952. Today McLeod Lake is a mainly Sekani community located north of Prince George, on the Hart Highway.

1805 – Named for Lord Horatio Nelson, hero of the Battle of Trafalgar, **Fort Nelson** was originally built in north-eastern B.C. by the North West Company about 80 miles south of Nelson Forks, the confluence of the Nelson and Liard Rivers. According to local historian Gerri Young, "Charts in existence mark a second Fort Nelson, further south on the Fort Nelson River, as being destroyed by fire in 1813. This fire occurred after a massacre of its inhabitants by Indians in 1813. About eight people, men women and children, were killed, and the post was abandoned until 1865."

Often described as British Columbia's third-oldest non-native settlement, Fort Nelson was relocated by the Hudson's Bay Company to the confluence of the Nelson and Muskwa Rivers in 1865, under the supervision of clerk W. Cornwallis King, until it was destroyed by a flood in 1890. The trading post was subsequently re-situated to higher ground upstream, across the river, to the east, in an area now known as "Old Fort Nelson." Situated on the Alaska Highway, the present town of Fort Nelson is located north of Dawson Creek.

1805 – With buckskin rotting on their backs, the beleaguered, 33-member Lewis and Clark Expedition finally arrived at the Pacific Ocean on a stormy November day, prompting Clark to write, "O! how horriable is the day." Sponsored by Thomas Jefferson, the cross-continental crew hastily established **Fort Clatsop** on the south side of the Columbia River. Their first views of the Pacific were from the north side of the Columbia, in what is now Washington State, but local Clatsop Indians advised them that elk were plentiful on the south side. Meriwether Lewis accordingly selected "the most eligible Situation for our purposes" across the river in what is now Oregon State.

Chief carpenter Patrick Glass, with one glass eye, supervised the building of a crude 50-feet by 50-feet stockade that included a private room for Shosone Sacagawea, her French-Canadian husband Toussaint Charbonneau and their newborn child, Jean Baptiste Charbonneau, nicknamed Pomp. One of three Expedition members to have his image recorded, Glass, born in Pennsylvania in 1771, later published the first account of the first American transcontinental crossing, in 1807, much to the consternation of Lewis.

204

Including a so-called parade ground approximately 48 feet by 20 feet, the second American log encampment on the Pacific Coast (after Fort Defiance) was declared complete on Christmas Eve. After a dismal winter, during which Clark recorded that Chinook women "are lude and Carry on Sport publickly," the fort was abandoned to "Coboway," chief of the Clatsop, as the Expedition departed for St. Louis in late March 1806. In 1847, Paul Kane sketched "the grave of Comcomly at Astoria, Chief of the Chinooks," who had met the Lewis and Clark expedition in 1805 and who had controlled at least 300 slaves.

In 1955, local citizens erected a replica of Fort Clatsop, based on journal entries and drawings, situated approximately five miles south of Astoria, Oregon. It is now operated as a tourist attraction and outdoor museum within Lewis and Clark National Park.

1806 – Fort St. James (Stuart's Lake Fort, Fort New Caledonia, Nakazeleh) became the most important fur trading centre in New Caledonia after it was established by Simon Fraser's canoe-maker, John Stuart, on what he describes as "the worst side of the Rocky Mountains," north of Vanderhoof, on the shore of

Fort St. James, the most northerly spot James Douglas reached in B.C.

205

Nakazeleh Lake (Stuart Lake), for the North West Company.

After Fort McLeod, Fort St. James is the second-oldest continually inhabited non-Aboriginal community in B.C. Here trader Daniel Harmon grew his own grains and vegetables as early as 1806. James Douglas arrived to work as an ambitious, young HBC trader in 1828. In 1883, newly arrived John McLean described the food at Stuart Lake as "scarcely fit for dogs."

Today, Fort St James National Historic Site is a restored Hudson's Bay Company post on the southern shores of Stuart Lake, modelled according to its appearance in 1896. The National Historic Site is situated 160 km. north-west of Prince George. (Follow Highway 16 west, turn north onto Highway 27 just beyond Vanderhoof, and proceed for approximately 45 minutes.)

1806 – Fort Fraser (Fraser Lake Post, Fraser's Lake, Natleh) was founded by Simon Fraser for the North West Company, west of Prince George, at the east end of Fraser Lake, about one mile from its outlet, in an area currently a part of Beaumont Provincial Park. Desperate for food supplies, Simon Fraser wintered here in 1806, whereupon John Stuart referred to the encampment as Fraser Lake Post.

When Fraser Lake Post was re-established in 1814, John Stuart advised Ross Cox: "The Carrier are naturally of an open and hospitable disposition; but very violent, and subject to sudden gusts of passion, in which much blood is often shed. However, those quarrels are soon made up, and as soon forgotten."

Fraser Lake Post wasn't referred to as a fort until 1824. As a hub for the Collins Overland Telegraph, it provided accommodation for surveyor and geographer George Mercer Dawson while he conducted his research for the Geological Survey of Canada 1876–77.

The last spike for the completion of the Grand Trunk Pacific Railway, the second transcontinental "belt of steel," was ceremoniously hammered into the ground at Fort Fraser in 1914. That year the Fort was closed and a Hudson's Bay Company trading post was relocated to the Nadleh Indian Reserve under the direction of William Bunting, the last HBC clerk for the area. That trading post site is still occupied by the Dakelh (Carrier).

1807 – First named for King George III, **Fort George**, forerunner to the city of Prince George, was founded by Simon Fraser as a temporary post to facilitate the building of rafts at the union of the Fraser and Nechako Rivers. Abandoned the following year, it was re-established in a roundabout way after Simon Fraser's trusty lieutenant, John Stuart, in 1820, first ordered George McDougall to build a trading post "at the Forks of Fraser's River, the natives of that place having been promised a Fort these several years past."

Instead of following Stuart's orders, McDougall inexplicably built west of the designated site, at a place known as Chala-oo-chick. When McDougall was ordered to leave his post in order to take command of Fort Alexandria in 1821, and his substitute, Thomas Hodgson, proved himself to be an unreliable drunkard, the youthful-looking James Murray Yale was sent by Stuart to serve as Hodgson's assistant. Chala-oo-chick was renamed Fort George shortly after Yale's arrival.

When John Stuart passed through Chala-oo-chick/Fort George in the spring of 1822 on his way to the Columbia District, he requested that Yale relocate the trading post to its original environs of 1807. Relatively inexperienced, Yale made little progress as a trader and initially failed to implement this move. It was not until late in 1822 that Yale succeeded in building a new store "at the Forks" that was 23 feet long by 17 feet wide, but by April of 1823, Yale himself had yet to move from Chala-oo-chick/Fort George, somewhere near the juncture of the Nechako and Chilako Rivers, to the juncture of the Nechako and Fraser Rivers.

The "new" Fort George was temporarily abandoned in August of 1823 after two HBC employees, Joseph Bagnoit and Belone Duplantes, were murdered in their beds by an Aboriginal and their bodies eaten by dogs. The Fort was ransacked, not to be re-established until 1829. Fort George closed its operations in 1915, at which time Prince George was incorporated, and named for the Duke of Kent (not King George).

1807 – After David Thompson, his wife Charlotte, their three

Kootanae House replica (on hill), built in 1922

children and a contingent of voyageurs passed through Howse
Pass in the Rocky Mountains, they erected **Kootenae House**
(Kootenai House, Kootenay House) near the site of present-day
Invermere, at the north end of Windermere Lake, as the first fur
trading outpost in the south-eastern B.C. interior.

"From the State of the Country & the Situation of my Affairs,"
he wrote, "I found myself necessitated to lay aside all thoughts of
Discovery for the present & bend my whole aim to an establishment for Trade etc.—and as our pressing necessities did not allow Time for Thought upon Thought, I set off to look out for a
place where we might build."

Famine, fatigue and the lack of a local guide prompted
Thompson to build his three-sided log stockade against a cliff
face. Thompson cut the windows and hung the door. The structure leaked badly because suitable clay could not found to seal
the roof. Given the scarcity of salmon or game, Thompson's men
boiled meat from a freshly killed wild horse "But about 2 Hours
after eating the Horse Meat," Thompson writes, "we were seized
with sickness of the Stomach, & however much we wished to keep
the Meat in our Bellies, were obliged to throw it up."

The site of Kootenae House was uncovered by a 2005 archaeological dig. The name Kootenay was derived from the local Ktunaxa or Kutenai tribe.

1807 – The first American trading post within the Rocky Mountains was established by Manuel Lisa, the field trader for Lisa, Mendard, and Morrison Fur Company, who built **Fort Raymond** (Fort Ramon, Manuel's Fort) near the juncture of the Bighorn and Yellowstone Rivers in November 1807. Lisa, Menard, and Morrison expanded to become the St. Louis Missouri Fur Company in 1809.

1811 – After cantankerous Captain Thorn of the *Tonquin* foolishly sacrificed the lives of eight men during his impatient efforts to cross the bar at the mouth of the Columbia River in early March, **Fort Astoria** was built near the mouth of the Columbia by employees of the Pacific Fur Trading Company, a subsidiary of John Jacob Astor's American Fur Company. Handicapped by illness and hunger, the landing party of 33 men, including 11 Sandwich Islanders, commenced construction in April under the direction of Duncan McDougall, labouring "with an axe in one hand and a gun in the other."

David Thompson arrived shortly after the foundations were in place, and received cordial treatment from the mainly Canadian-and-Scottish-born Pacific Fur traders, even though Thompson

Fort Astoria

was employed by the rival Nor'Westers. Not long after the Canadian in charge of Fort Astoria, Duncan McDougall, accepted the daughter of Chinook chief Concomly as his bride in 1813, thereby cementing trading relations with the most powerful Aboriginal leader, more Nor'Westers arrived overland, under the direction of John George McTavish, in an effort to persuade McDougall he ought to surrender Fort Astoria peacefully.

Eventually the Nor'Westers persuaded McDougall it would be prudent to sell the fort for approximately one-third of the value of its furs on hand rather than lose it militarily (the War of 1812 was underway) upon the anticipated arrival of a British warship, the *Isaac Todd*. When a different British warship, the 26-gun *Racoon*, arrived five weeks after the sale had been finalized, its belligerent Captain William Black insisted upon making a formal ceremony of taking possession, raising the British flag on December 13, 1813, and renaming the modest bastion Fort George. McDougall remained to work for the new owners.

The long-overdue *Isaac Todd* finally arrived in April of 1814. When Fort Vancouver was built upriver in 1825, the original Astoria stockade was gradually reduced to a small fishing depot serving Fort Vancouver. The site was re-occupied by American Overlanders in 1843.

1811– Fort Okanogan was the first permanent white settlement in the area now called Washington State as well as the first inland trading post connected to Astoria. It was built just south of the 49th parallel in the summer of 1811, on the east bank of the Okanogan River, near its juncture with the Columbia River, after David Stuart, Alexander Ross and seven other men were sent upriver from Astoria in the company of David Thompson. Thompson described Stuart as "one of those intrepid souls who are born without fear."

After their 600-mile journey, Stuart's small contingent began to build a small dwelling on September 1. Also known as Fort Okanaigan or Fort Oakinacken, the fort would generate more than 40 spellings of its name before and after it was absorbed by the Hudson's Bay Company in 1821. A new fort was built one

Fort Okanogan, from a painting by John Mix Stanley

mile away in 1830, but phased out in 1846. A flood destroyed most of the site in 1894, but some remains of the fort are still identifiable. North of the 49th parallel, the spelling "Okanagan" is generally preferred.

Stationed at "Fort Oakinagan" in 1814, Nor'Wester Joseph McGillivray wrote: "This is a horribly dull place. Here I have been, since you parted from us, perfectly solus. My men, half Canadians and half Sandwich Islanders. The library is wretched, and no chance of my own books till next year, when the Athabasca men cross the mountains. If you, or any of your friends at Spokan [sic] do not send me a few volumes, I shall absolutely die of ennui."

1811 – Fort Champoeg (or Champooick) arose near the present site of Donald, Oregon, as another offshoot of Astoria, built by the Pacific Fur Company. Originally known as Fort Wallace or Willamette Post, it was sold to the North West Company in 1813 and enlarged by the Hudson's Bay Company. Its name Champoeg recalls the original white settlers of the Oregon Territory who were mainly French Canadians, or "Illinois River Men," such as François Rivet, born in Montreal around 1757. It is conceivable that some of these Francophone drifters might have made an overland journey to the Pacific Ocean prior to Alexander Mackenzie but there is no proof.

"The roving condition of the French Canadian is well known," wrote Thompson in his *Travels*, "[and] by the time of the conquest of Canada they had spread themselves far westward, but the Illinois River was their favourite. . . . At first there were about 350 Men, but their precarious way of life . . . soon reduced them; and at the cession of the country by Spain they were only full 150 men; the United States insisted on their becoming Settlers on the lands or retiring elsewhere; they chose the latter; took up their Rifles, and with their few women crossed the Missouri River...continually advancing westward toward the Mountains where I first met with them."

Fort Champoeg closed around 1861, although Champoeg State Park contains a museum with some exhibits about the fort. The exact location of the fort is unknown.

1812 – Fort Thompson (Fort Kamloops) was the first and only fort built on mainland British Columbia territory by an American company. After David Stuart of the Pacific Fur Company arrived at the confluence of the North and South Thompson Rivers in 1811, he returned to establish Fort She-whap [Shuswap] in 1812. Its manager, Alexander Ross, praised Stuart's leadership among the Aboriginals: "His eye saw everything at a glance, and his mild and insinuating manners won their affections."

Not to be outdone, Nor'Westers arrived in the fall of 1812, led by Joseph Laroque, and erected Fort Cumcloups or Cume-loops (from *T'kumlups*, meaning "meeting of the rivers"). When the Pacific Fur Company was taken over by the NWC in 1813, the

Fort Kamloops, 1865, at the meeting of the rivers

operations of the forts founded by Stuart and Laroque were merged as Fort Thompson, variously known as Thompson's River Post, the Forks, the She Whaps and Kameloops House. The HBC took control in 1821, retaining its operation at varying locations.

According to John McLeod, who manned the fort from 1822 to 1826, Fort Kamloops was "a troublesome and most arduous, as well as perilous charge." Even with the knowledge that its beaver returns were poor and the Aboriginals were threatening, George Simpson retained Fort Kamloops as a link in the Fraser-Columbia Brigade system. George Simpson decided he must replace McLeod because he "at best is nearly useless but (dogged as he is with a deranged Wife who even in her madness governs him) is now entirely so."

Archibald McDonald took over at Fort Kamloops in 1826 after trader Samuel Black was shot and killed by an Aboriginal. In charge of up to six hundred horses for pack-trains, McDonald noted, "Dried Salmon is the Staff of life and fortunately seldom fails." For Christmas, in 1826, he and his two employees celebrated by having "a good fat Dog & then three dried salmon each." George Simpson described Fort Kamloops as "a very unprofitable Establishment" during his second western tour in 1828.

In 1842, the implacable John Tod arrived from Fort Alexandria and rebuilt on the west bank of the North Thompson. Farming at Fort Kamloops increased under Donald McLean and William Manson. The discovery of gold at nearby Tranquille Creek in 1858 brought more than two hundred Chinese miners. Kamloops began to change from a fur trading fort to a frontier village with the advent of the Overlanders in the early 1860s. The first white child in the vicinity was born to Mr. and Mrs. Augustus Schubert in October of 1862. The Hudson's Bay Company closed the fort in 1893, the year Kamloops was incorporated.

1812 – Fort Spokane was built by the Pacific Fur Company but fell under the management of the North West Company, along with Fort Okanogan, in 1813. Earlier, in 1810, the North West Company had established Spokane House, north of present-day Spokane. The fort remained open until 1823; Spokane House remained open until 1826 when George Simpson transferred operations to Fort Colvile. A different Fort Spokane, constructed for troops in 1880, became an Indian school in 1899.

1812 – Fort Ross, the wooden palisade later known as the Ross Settlement, formally opened at Bodega Bay on the California coast on August 13, 1812. It gained its name from an abbreviated version of the word "Rossiya," referring to Tsarist Russia. It was mainly used to grow food and as a depot to enable hired Aleutians to hunt for sea otters. Although there are few documented cases of Russian fur hunters, or "promysloviki," operating on the British Columbia coast, Russians did eventually venture as far south as California and as far east as the Hawaiian Islands.

A brief history: Emel'ian Basov became the first Russian to gather furs east of Siberia by wintering on Bering Island in 1742–1743. Mikhail Nevodchikov reached the westernmost Aleutian island of Attu on September 25, 1745. Gregor Shelikov built the first permanent Russian settlement within the boundaries of present-day Alaska at Kodiak Island in 1784.

Russian emblem of Fort Ross

Created in 1799, the Russian-American Company, a monopoly similar in its mandate to the Hudson's Bay Company, established its headquarters at New Archangel (Sitka, Alaska). By 1806, it had its own territorial flag. Having arrived in Alaska in 1791, Alexander Baranov became the equivalent of George Simpson in the Hudson's Bay Company, a virtual emperor of operations, who began sending experienced Aleutian seal hunters on American ships to acquire sea otters along the coast of California, using kayaks.

Given the difficulties of securing supplies from Russia and Siberia, Russians sometimes contracted American sea captains to undertake joint ventures. When the Russians in Alaska became desperate for food, direct contact with the Spanish in California was established in 1806 by Nikolai Rezanov, the "imperial inspector and plenipotentiary of the Russian-American Company." He bought an American vessel, the *Juno*, at an inflated price, and sailed into San Francisco harbour to plead for relief supplies.

After six weeks of diplomacy, Rezanov's proposal of marriage to the teenage daughter of the Spanish commander did the trick: Rezanov obtained provisions from the Spanish, and he was later able to convince Baranov that Russians ought to establish their own agricultural and hunting depot in northern California.

Ivan Alexander Kuskov sailed into Bodega Bay in the *Kodiak* on January 8, 1808, bringing back more than two thousand sea otter pelts after six months. The northernmost Spanish settlement on the West Coast was at San Francisco Bay, so a contingent of 25 Russians and 80 Alaskan Aboriginals was sent under Kuskov's command to establish Fort Ross, approximately 100 miles north of San Francisco, in March of 1812. Arriving on the *Chirikov*, Kuskov ostensibly gained permission from the Kashaya Pomo Indians to build Fort Ross in exchange for "three blankets, three pairs of breeches, two axes, three hoes, and some beads."

A chapel was added to the barracks in 1824. Kodiak islanders in their "bidarkas" (hunting kayaks) ranged from the coasts of Baja California to Oregon in search of sea otters. More than 60 buildings arose outside the gates of Fort Ross as agriculture gradually replaced the importance of hunting (as the sea otter diminished). The fortress was deemed redundant after the Russian-American Company signed an agreement with the Hudson's Bay Company in 1839 that allowed the HBC to have open access to the Alaska Panhandle for hunting. In return, the HBC agreed to supply Sitka with provisions from its farms in Washington and Oregon, particularly Fort Nisqually.

When the Russians were unable to sell their Ross Settlement to the Spanish, they reached a sales agreement with John Sutter of Sutter's Fort in the Sacramento Valley in 1841. The Russians evacuated and Sutter's assistant, John Bidwell, retrieved most of the valuable items at Fort Ross—ammunition, hardware and livestock—for use at Sutter's Fort. Much later, in 1873, George W. Call established his 15,000-acre Call Ranch at the site.

The California Historical Landmarks Committee purchased the remains of Fort Ross in 1903. The historical site was expanded to include more than 3,000 acres in 1992. Since then the California Department of Parks and Recreation has recreated the original fort for education and tourism purposes.

1813 – William Henry Fort was opened near the present-day site of Newberg, Oregon, by the North West Company, and possibly renamed Henry House in the following year.

1818 – Christened as Fort Nez Percé, the first of six **Fort Walla Wallas** was constructed by Donald Mackenzie of the North West Company near the confluence of the Columbia and Walla Walla Rivers. Two early versions were destroyed by fire. With a 20-foot high outer wall and four cannon, the third Fort Walla Walla became known as the "Gibraltar of the Columbia." With its reputation as one of the most impregnable forts west of the Rockies, the 100-foot-square fort increasingly served as a way station for Oregon Trail migrants. In 1845, Fort Walla Walla trader Archibald McKinlay noted, "Americans are getting as thick as Mosquettoes in this part of the world."

Fearful of Indian uprisings, the United States Army ordered the evacuation of Fort Walla Walla during the 1850s. A fourth fort was constructed 38 miles up the Walla Walla River; then another was constructed closer to the new settlement of Walla Walla. After it soon burned to the ground, a sixth fort was erected west of Walla Walla in 1858.

1820 – Fort de Pinette was established by James Murray Yale in the summer of 1820 on the south bank of the Peace River, just below the mouth of the Pine River, to provide HBC opposition to Fort St. John of the NWC. Also referred to as Fort St. George, this short-lived post was intended, in the words of George Simpson, "to facilitate our intercourse with the Free Iroquois and Natives of New Caledonia." It closed in favour of Fort St. John with the merger of the HBC and the "Master Pedlars" in 1821.

1821 – Fort Alexandria, the last trading post built by the North West Company in British Columbia, was originally located about 20 miles north of Soda Creek on the Fraser River. Fort Alexandria was relocated on the eastern bank of the river, below its junction with the Blackwater (West Road) River, by George McDougall when the NWC merged with the Hudson's Bay Company in 1821, the year usually cited for its foundation. It was moved again to a better fishing site on the west bank in 1836.

After Peter Skene Ogden built the first flour mill in B.C. at Fort Alexandria, he was replaced by John McGillivray as Chief Trader, who wrote: "Sir Alexander Mackenzie, in his voyage of discovery across the continent in 1793, came to the spot on which the fort is built, and was dissuaded by the Indians from following the course of the river to its mouth. . . . The principal rivers are Fraser's, Quesnel's, Rough Poplar, Chilcotin, and West Road. Of these Fraser's River only is navigable. It receives the waters of Quesnel's and West Poplar rivers, which issue from small lakes to the eastward."

Noted for its setting, Fort Alexandria became important as a way station for the care and breeding of 200 horses. Furs from New Caledonia were transferred from canoes to horses at Fort Alexandria for the long portage to the "Columbia commerces." After the Fraser Columbia Brigade System was discontinued in 1847, the post remained open until 1867.

1822 – Fort Babine (Fort Kilmaurs) was built by the Hudson's Bay Company near the north end of Babine Lake, the longest and largest natural lake in B.C., well-stocked with salmon. Fort Babine took its name from the French word for "large lip" in reference to labrets worn in the lower lip by the Dalkeh (Carrier) during the nineteenth century. It was originally named Fort Kilmaurs, after the parish in which its founder, William Brown, had been christened in Ayrshire, Scotland.

Willliam Brown was sent north from Fort George to establish the site. At that time the entire HBC personnel in New Caledonia consisted of only 36 "servants" and eight "gentlemen." The surplus salmon from Fort Babine's nets were sent to Fort St. James and Fort George. The presence of salmon alerted the Hudson's Bay Company to a connection to the ocean, prompting Brown and George Simpson to wonder if the north-flowing Babine River might connect with the imagined Cook's River (even though this has been shown not to exist by George Vancouver in 1794). An 1824 exploratory expedition led by Chief Trader Brown was aban-

doned and the connection with the Skeena River remained un-
discovered. Fort Babine closed temporarily in 1829 but was reopened and continued to operate until 1872. The settlement of
Old Fort marks its original location.

1824 – Fort Vancouver was erected about 100 miles from the
mouth of the Columbia River under the direction of John
McLoughlin. This site was chosen on the north side of the Columbia River, six miles from its juncture with the Willamette River,
on a prairie slope, about one mile away from the riverbank, as a
replacement for Fort George. Here the river depth was at least
14 feet during all seasons. Christened on March 19, 1825, Fort
Vancouver was moved closer to the river bank in 1829. Its 750-
foot-long stockade boasted a Governor's residence, a Bachelors'
Hall, the Columbia Library and a museum. A small town and a
1500-acre farm were outside its gates.

As the influx of American migrants along the Oregon Trail
commenced in earnest in 1843, effectively overwhelming a modest contingent of French Canadian farmers in the area,
McLoughlin repeatedly offered friendly assistance to the newcomers who were described by one historian as "this dreary broth-
erhood." Fort Vancouver continued to serve as the focal point
for the fur trade on the Western Slope until 1846 when the area

Fort Vancouver, 1845

218

officially became part of the United States. The HBC finally abandoned the site in 1860.

1825 – Fort Colvile was built by the Hudson's Bay Company
above the Kettle Falls Portage, on the Columbia River, at its junction with the Kettle River, after George Simpson decided to dis-
band Spokane House, located 60 miles to the east. In April,
George Simpson personally staked out the dimensions of Fort
Colvile, where he believed "an excellent farm can be made at this
place." He predicted sufficient grain and potatoes could be grown
to "feed all the Natives of the Columbia and sufficient number of
Cattle and Hogs to supply his Majesty's Navy with Beef and Pork."
Fort Colvile supplied food for New Caledonia and the Columbia
District, as well as seed-wheat for Fort Edmonton, and facilitated
the linkage of New Caledonia with the Columbia Department as
an integral part of the new Fur Brigade transportation system. It
was named for a member of the HBC's London committee,
Andrew Colvile, related to Lord Selkirk, whose wife was named
Wedderburn-Colvile. The first gold rush in Washington State
occurred at Fort Colvile in 1855. It remained operational until
1871. The site is now submerged under Lake Roosevelt. A different federal fort named Fort Colville was established upriver from
the HBC's Fort Colvile in 1859.

1827 – Just as Nootka Sound became the Mecca for fur trading in British Columbia during the late eighteenth century, **Fort
Langley** served as its equivalent in the early nineteenth century
as the first HBC-erected trading post above the 49th parallel.

Named for the HBC official Thomas Langley, Fort Langley was
erected after George Simpson made his first West Coast visit in
1824 and naively decided the Fraser River ought to be considered as a trading route to the interior. Not having seen the river,
and not having read Simon Fraser's account of the severe difficulties he faced while navigating the Fraser Canyon, Simpson
sent HBC trader James McMillan to explore the area around the
mouth of the Fraser River. McMillan and his 38 men left Fort
George in Oregon on November 24, 1824, to investigate possible
building locations. From Boundary Bay, at the 49th parallel,

McMillan's reconnaissance party paddled up the Nicomekl River, portaged to the Salmon River, and paddled to the Fraser River. They spent several days exploring the river banks.

After making his report, McMillan was instructed to return to the lower Fraser River in 1827 and begin construction of Fort Langley at the location now marked by Derby Reach Regional Park. The fort encouraged the relocation of Kwantlen people to a new village called Ts'elexwa:yel near the mouth of Kanaka Creek, in present-day Maple Ridge. Constructed partially to stop American expansion northwards, the facility soon attracted Aboriginal traders from the Fraser River area as well as villages in Nooksack, Skagit, Klallam, Songish, Sechelt, Saanich, Cowichan, Chemainus, Nanaimo and Squamish. Company farming was conducted at Langley Prairie.

To avoid flooding, the fort was relocated in 1839, two-and-a-half miles upstream at the mouth of the Salmon River, whereupon the Kwantlen shifted their village to Sqwalets on McMillan Island, directly across from the fort, and became known as the Langley tribe. The entire fortress, which consisted of four blockhouses and a stockade, burned to the ground in 1840, less than a year after it was built. James Murray Yale oversaw construction of a new compound 108 feet long and 82 feet wide. It was expanded to include housing for Kanaka labourers, an officers' residence or "Big House," a cookhouse, a cooper's shop, blacksmith shop, carpenter shop, warehouses and other residences.

Despite fires in 1848 and 1852, Fort Langley became the hub for thousands of gold prospectors who swarmed the bars of the Fraser River in 1858, erecting a shantytown outside its walls. Fearful that American gold seekers would enable the United States to annex the Fort Langley area, James Douglas, as Governor of Vancouver Island, initiated an act of the British Parliament to declare the mainland as a British Colony. Consequently, Douglas was sworn in as the first Governor of British Columbia in a ceremony conducted at the Big House of Fort Langley on November 19, 1858.

As the so-called birthplace of British Columbia, Fort Langley was slated to serve as the capital city of the new region until Colonel Richard Clement Moody of the Royal Engineers convinced government authorities to move the province's nominal headquarters to New Westminster. Fort Langley remained operational until 1895. Heritage Preservation and reconstruction of the site began in 1958 to coincide with the B.C. Centennial. The Fort Langley tourist site is now operated by Parks Canada. Incorporated in 1873, the Township of Langley shares the distinction of being one of the two oldest municipalities in B.C., along with Chilliwack.

1827 – Located north of Babine Lake, on Bear Lake, north of the 56th parallel, **Fort Connolly** (Connolly's Lake, Bear Lake) was built by James Douglas for the Hudson's Bay Company and named for Douglas' father-in-law, William Connolly, the Chief Factor for New Caledonia.

Marooned in the remote Omineca posting with his Aboriginal wife and their three children, with a fourth on the way, Thomas Dears wrote in 1830: "I am now in a most horrid melancholy place, the very bowels of elementary strife—not a living soul seen here but twice a year. I get seldom or any news, and have nothing before my sight but eternal snows. In addition to this, there is a tribe to the South of us who we considerably dread." By 1829, New Caledonia clerk A.C. Anderson estimated the Aboriginal population surrounding Fort Connolly was only 137, but the trading post did not close until the 1890s.

1829 – **Fort Chilcotin** (Chilcotin's Lake) was built by the Hudson's Bay Company at the junction of the Chilcotin and Chilko Rivers, near the south end of Chilcotin Lake. Its construction, slated for 1827, had to be postponed after HBC employees assisted enemies of the Chilcotins during a tribal war near Fort Alexandria. In 1829, New Caledonia clerk A.C. Anderson estimated the Aboriginal population surrounding Fort Chilcotin had dwindled to 600, including children.

Operating as an adjunct to Fort Alexandria, the fort prompted veteran trader John Tod, in 1830, to write, "Little is expected from it." He referred to the surrounding area as Chill Cotton

Country. Some Chilcotins threatened to attack the relatively unprotected fort in 1838. The fort closed in 1844.

1829 – Operated under the aegis of the Mackenzie District, **Fort Halkett** was built by the Hudson's Bay Company where the Trout River flows into the east branch of the Liard River (known today as the Fort Nelson River) in northern British Columbia. After John Hutchison left Fort Simpson with a construction party of four men on June 27, 1829, they passed the remains of Fort Nelson, built by the North West Company in 1805, and abandoned in 1812 due to an "Indian massacre." They erected Fort Halkett in spite of George Simpson's estimation of Hutchison as "weak, delicate and not adapted for severe or active service." The fort was named for HBC director John Halkett, who had served as the executor of Lord Selkirk's will and assisted George Simpson with the reorganization of the Hudson's Bay Company in 1822. Its location was moved west in 1832, eventually giving rise to Nelson, B.C. Fort Halkett closed in 1875.

1831 – After George Simpson described the north coast as "a grand mart for furs" in 1824, **Fort Simpson** (Fort Nass) was built by the HBC on the Nass River, between Portland Inlet and the Skeena River. On a warm day in August 1830, Captain Aemilius Simpson, on the brigantine *Cadboro*, selected an exposed point

about 14 miles upriver, not realizing this location would be prone to icy winds in the winter. In 1831, Peter Skene Ogden established Fort Nass but changed its name to Fort Simpson to honour Aemilius Simpson, who died shortly after its creation.

Although the fur trading was profitable and the Nisga'a were cooperative, the *Dryad* arrived in August of 1834 to relocate the fort's personnel to the Stikine River. Russians prevented the brig from entering its destination. After a tense, ten-day standoff with the

Renowned as a captain of the Beaver, William Henry McNeill twice succeeded John Work at Fort Simpson: from 1851 to 1859, and from 1861 to 1863.

Fort Simpson, circa 1830s

Chichagoff, Peter Skene Ogden, in a rare display of non-combativeness, elected to head south of Nass Straits and east of Dixon's Entrance, about 160 miles away, to the sheltered waters of McLoughlin's Harbour. There Captain Duncan, Dr. William Tolmie and Ogden built a stockade for the second Fort Simpson (McLoughlin's Harbour). The *Dryad* departed on July 15, 1834, to bring back timbers from the original fort. The remains of Lieutenant Aemilius Simpson were disinterred and brought to the new fort.

During its first five years of operation, Fort Simpson generated 15,000 beaver pelts and its fur trade profits eventually exceeded those of any other Pacific post on the B.C. coast. In the 1830s, John Dunn described the Aboriginals arriving in their 30-to-50-foot-long canoes: "They remain mustered here for some weeks, making the fort a complete fair. It requires strict and good management, at this time, by the companies of officers, to protect the fort. . . . Skins are given, as presents, to the officers; and in the course of a day or two, the trader returns the compliment, by making them presents of British manufactured clothing." The Hudson's Bay Company brigantine introduced smallpox at Fort Simpson in 1836, but trade continued. By 1840 there were nine tribes with their winter villages near the fort, four surrounding

Fort Simpson and five on nearby Village Island. At one point, the winter population of Coast Tsimshian, described by George Simpson as the HBC's "homeguard," eclipsed two thousand. Tlingit, Nisga'a and Haida also traded at the fort. In 1842, Edward Allan opened a school at Fort Simpson, the first within the present-day borders of British Columbia.

1833 – Fort McLoughlin was built on rocky Campbell Island, at Lama Passage in Fitzhugh Sound, some 200 miles south of Fort Simpson, by order of Duncan Finlayson, near the present location of Bella Bella. Initially known as Millbank Sound, in reference to its access channel, Fort McLoughlin was erected near a village of 500 Aboriginals that George Simpson referred to as "Ballabollas." The original factor at Fort McLoughlin, John Dunn, was instructed to lower the prices given to skins, and "do away, if possible, with the injurious and degrading article of spirits, as a medium of barter; as the American vessels had previously been here, and had given immense prices, and sold spirits."

By 1841, Simpson estimated more than 5,000 Aboriginals were trading at Fort McLoughlin. When Charles Ross took over the post from Donald Manson in 1842, he estimated that the "Billbillah" population had grown to 1,500, augmented by 650 "Bellwhoola." The fort closed in 1843 with the construction of Fort Victoria.

1833 – After two Hudson's Bay Company ships were destroyed "crossing the bar" of the Columbia River—the *William and Ann* in 1829 and the *Isabella* in 1830—**Fort Nisqually** was built by Archibald McDonald on Puget Sound in present-day Washington State as an alternate port to Fort Vancouver. Chief Trader Francis Heron took over from McDonald at Fort Nisqually, located near Sequalitchew Creek on the Nisqually Delta.

The importance of Fort Nisqually, the first permanent European settlement on Puget Sound, was enhanced in 1841 when Sir George Simpson was delayed three weeks in the *Cowlitz* while waiting to cross safely the bar of the Columbia River. This frustrating delay encouraged Simpson to decide Fort Vancouver could be expendable—and Fort Victoria could function as a maritime alternative, along with Fort Nisqually and Fort Langley.

Dr. William Fraser Tolmie took charge of Fort Nisqually in 1843, overseeing construction of a new and expanded fort in 1846. Although the Americans gained control of Fort Nisqually in 1859, the Hudson's Bay Company did not receive compensation from the U.S. government for its Puget's Sound Agricultural Company holdings until 1869.

1835 – The Hudson's Bay Company built **Fort Essington** near the mouth of the Skeena River, at its juncture with the Ecstall River, taking its name from Essington estuary. This estuary was named by Captain George Vancouver in 1793 in honour of the Royal Navy captain William Essington. Tsimshians knew the site as Spokeshute, meaning "fall camping place." An Irish business-man named Robert Cunningham later re-adapted the surname for the multicultural boomtown of Port Essington, boasting six canneries in the second half of the nineteenth century.

1837 – Chiefly an agricultural centre, **Fort Cowlitz** (Cowlitz Farm) was built by the Hudson's Bay Company adjoining Fort Nisqually. Here Father Francis Blanchet introduced his ingen-ious Catholic indoctrination tool, the Catholic Ladder or "sa-cha-lee-stick," in 1839, when the first mission was established beyond Fort Vancouver. This St. Francis Xavier Mission was managed by Blanchet's assistant, Modeste Demers.

1838 – Named for HBC Factor Peter Warren Dease, **Dease Lake Post** was founded on the east side of Dease Lake, at Sawmill Point, by Robert Campbell, who used it as a base to explore the Stikine River. The fort was soon abandoned but the town of Dease Lake arose near the site, at the south end of Dease Lake, the result of the Cassiar gold rush of 1872. It is located on the Stewart/Cassiar Highway, 480 miles from Fort Nelson and 370 miles north of Terrace. Jade deposits to the northeast of Dease Lake have led to the slogan, "Jade Capital of the World."

1839 – A HBC trading post at **Honolulu** was established under the operation of George Pelly, a cousin of Sir John Pelly, Gover-nor of the Hudson's Bay Company. In his travels on the *Cowlitz* in 1842, George Simpson visited the Sandwich Islands for one month and met the King of Hawaii at his Lahaina palace on Maui. The Honolulu post became important as a recruitment centre for Hawaiian labourers known as Kanakas—their word for person or human. The Kanakas soon provided almost half of the Hudson's Bay Company work force on the Pacific Coast, giving rise to Kanaka communities at Vancouver's Stanley Park and at Kalama, Washington.

King Kamehameha I of Honolulu, 1816, as drawn by Louis Corney

The Kanaka Bar Tunnel in the Fraser Canyon attests to the existence of Hawaiian workers who had settled earlier at Kanaka Creek, near Fort Langley. Newcastle Island off Nanaimo has a Kanaka Bay. The Empress Hotel in Victoria is situated on the ruins of a shantytown that was called Kanaka Row. A few Hawaiian families lived at the "Kanaka Ranch" at the foot of Denman Street in Vancouver, site of the Bayshore Inn. Sawmill workers in North Vancouver lived at Moodyville's Kanaka Row, the second-largest Hawaiian settlement in B.C. after Salt Spring Island, where there is a Kanaka Road.

Salt Spring Islander Tom Koppel has published *Kanaka: The Untold Story of Hawaiian Pioneers in British Columbia and the Pacific Northwest*, and one of B.C.'s most active historians, Jean Barman, has published *Maria of the Islands*, a family portrait of the half-Hawaiian matron Maria Mahoi, born outside of Victoria, around 1857, probably in Esquimalt. Susan Dobbie's *When Eagles Call* is an historical novel about the Kanaka at Fort Langley. Barman and Bruce Watson later published *Leaving Paradise: Indigenous Hawaiians in the Pacific Northwest, 1787–1898*, a comprehensive study that identifies and catalogues Kanakas as individuals.

1840 – Fort Taku (Taco, Tako or Fort Durham) was founded by James Douglas, 15 miles south of Taku Inlet, after Douglas had travelled with Captain McNeill on the *Beaver* some 35 miles upriver. Venison was plentiful and the "Chilcat" people were willing to trade. Douglas visited Chilkat chiefs at a village to the north and learned how the crew of an American trading vessel had recently killed 45 Aboriginals. By 1841, some twelve hundred deer skins from Fort Taku had been sold in London. Fort Taku closed in 1843 with the construction of Fort Victoria.

1840 – Fort Stikine was the new name given by James Douglas to the Russian post of Fort Wrangell, built by the Russians on the northern tip of Wrangell Island, about 155 south of Juneau, in 1834. Known to the Russians as Fort Dionysius, or Redoubt Saint Dionysius, Fort Stikine adjoined mud flats "which oppressed the atmosphere with a most nauseous perfume," according to Douglas. Its ownership was transferred in accordance with a ten-year lease negotiated between the HBC and the Russians in 1839. This agreement arose after England had formally protested the forced withdrawal of the HBC's Peter Skene Ogden when he had attempted to build a HBC fort on the banks of the Stikine River in 1834, in keeping with an 1825 agreement. Two smallpox epidemics in 1836 and 1840 reduced the Tlingit population. Fort Stikine was abandoned in 1849.

1841 – After the HBC decided not to purchase the remains of Fort Ross for $30,000, **Yerba Buena** was established on the present site of San Francisco as the first HBC trading post in California. James Douglas succeeded in gaining permission from the Americans and the Spanish for the venture when he arrived in Monterey, California, on January 1, 1841, with 36 men aboard the *Columbia*.

John McLoughlin, Douglas' superior, sent his son-in-law William Glen Rae to acquire waterfront property on Yerba Buena Cove for $4,600. When Douglas and McLoughlin visited the HBC's new California headquarters on the *Cowlitz* on December 30, 1841, McLoughlin brought his daughter, Eloise, who was Rae's wife.

As the tiny community grew to include at least 12 houses and 50 residents by 1844, Rae failed to ingratiate himself with the locals. A hard-drinking Scot, prone to depression, Rae allowed his anti-Americanism to become widely known as he meddled in

Roadside plaque at Yerba Buena

local politics. On January 19, 1845, he shot himself to death, in the presence of his wife, after she learned he had been unfaithful to her.

The British vice-consul at Monterery, James Alexander Forbes, took charge of HBC operations until Dugald McTavish arrived in March of 1846 to liquidate the HBC's Montgomery Street assets at Yerba Buena for $5,000. By this time, John McLoughlin had resigned and the impetus for the HBC to expand into California seemingly died with him. The HBC building became a hotel that burned down on June 14, 1850. Four years later, when civic workers were digging a sewer line on nearby Commercial Street, they discovered a coffin. Looking through the oval glass window of this coffin, a local man named Charles R. Bond recognized the remains of William Glen Rae, whose body was re-interred in the Yerba Buena cemetery—now the site of San Francisco's City Hall.

1843 – When he chose the site for **Fort Victoria** (Fort Camosun) near arable land and the "Port of Camosack," James Douglas described it in his letter to George Simpson as "a safe and acces-

Fort Victoria by Henry Ware, 1845

sible harbour, well situated for defence, with Water power for Grist and Saw Mills, abundance of Timber for home consumption and Exportation and the adjacent Country well adapted for tillage and pasture Farms on an extensive scale." Initially constructed by 50 men and three officers, the fort became the HBC headquarters west of the Rocky Mountains, essentially replacing Fort Vancouver on the Columbia River. After the Colony of Vancouver Island was established in London in 1849, the first Legislative Assembly met inside the fort. Its bastions were destroyed in 1861 and its fur storehouse became the Theatre Royal, destroyed in 1892. Its location, near the waterfront, is marked on Fort Street in present-day Victoria.

1846 – **Fort Pelly Banks** was built on the banks of the Pelly River in the Yukon by former Fort Halkett clerk Robert Campbell. Abandoned after a fire in 1850, the site later gave rise to a Taylor & Drury trading post, then a Kaska settlement. The Ross River Dena Council and Yukon Heritage Resources commenced heritage site investigations of the Pelly Banks area in 2003.

1847 – **Fort Youcon** (Fort Yukon) was built illegally by the Hudson's Bay Company within Russian territory, near the junction of the Yukon and Porcupine Rivers, above the Arctic Circle. Its location was kept secret for two decades. Initially managed from 1847 to 1851 by its founder, Alexander Hunter Murray, and his seventeen-year-old bride, Anne Campbell, daughter of Chief Trader Colin Campbell, Murray's fort consisted of three log buildings surrounded by a 100-square-foot stockade with a bastion at each corner. Although it was one of the most isolated HBC outposts, it became one of the most consistently profitable. Other Yukon posts created by the HBC included Peel's River, Lapierre's House, Frances Lake, Pelly Banks and Fort Selkirk.

1847 – Born to French parents in Montreal in 1817, John Ovid Allard built **Fort Yale** at the behest of James Murray Yale, chief HBC trader at Fort Langley, who sent him with 20 men to an area on the Fraser River known as "The Falls." Obeying instructions to build a store and a "stopping place" near the foot of the Fraser Canyon, Ovid Allard constructed the HBC fort that expanded to become the community of Yale. Allard is rarely cited for his role in helping to generate what was once the biggest town north of San Francisco and west of Chicago, swelling to accommodate thirty thousand people, after the gold rush of 1858.

As for John Ovid Allard, he also constructed Simon's House at Spuzzum where the Columbia Brigade was able to traverse the Fraser River on a ferry. When Henry Newsham Peers found a safer and easier route down the canyon, Allard was instructed to abandon Fort Yale in order to build Fort Hope near where the Coquihalla River flows into the Fraser. Sent for a time to Nanaimo to serve as a superintendent for its new coal mines, John Ovid

In 1870, Fort Yale and the tent city of Yale hosted a meeting of politicians, known as the Yale Convention, that enabled British Columbia formally to become a province within the new Confederation of Canada. This drawing was done fifteen years later.

Allard eventually died at Fort Langley, another fort he had helped to build.

1847 – Fort Waters was rebuilt from the remains of Waiilatpu Mission house by Oregon Volunteers after the so-called Whitman Massacre. Located near Walla Walla, Washington, it is now the Whitman Mission National Historic Site.

1848 – Fort Gilliam was also built by Oregon Volunteers, near the present site of North Bonneville, Washington. A minor and short-lived site, it was also known as Camp at the Cabins.

1848 – Fort Hope was built by John Ovid Allard after access to and from Fort Yale was deemed too hazardous. During a trip with his men in the Fraser Canyon, Allard's expedition lost 70 horses and 80 pieces of freight. "Five men quit and one committed suicide rather than make the return with trade goods," Allard wrote.

The site for Fort Hope was chosen by HBC surveyor Henry Newsham Peers, who married one of James Yale's daughters in 1849. He died in 1864. After Fort Hope initially served as a transportation link between Fort Victoria and Fort Kamloops, it grew into a major supply depot for gold seekers. The trading post at Hope closed in 1892.

1848 – Fort Selkirk (Yukon) was founded by Robert Campbell where the Pelly River meets the Yukon. In 1852, soon after Campbell had relocated his post to higher ground, it was destroyed by Chilkat Tlingit warriors who resented the Hudson's Bay Company's interruption of their trade with Athabaskan First Nations. Forced to flee for his life, Campbell gained the protection of Selkirk Chief, Hanan, whose descendants still carry Campbell's name, given to the Chief by Campbell in gratitude.

Although Campbell succeeded in travelling all the way to Minnesota, mostly on foot, he was unsuccessful in his efforts to persuade the HBC to mount a counter-attack against the Chilkats.

A trader named Arthur Harper opened a store in 1892, but the Hudson's Bay Company didn't return to the Fort Selkirk site until 1938. The HBC abandoned Fort Selkirk for a second time in 1951.

1849 – Fort Rupert was built by the HBC in an effort to exploit coal resources at the north end of Vancouver Island. These deposits had been noted by local Kwakwaka'wakw in 1835. Recognizing the "klake stone" that was burned in the forges at Fort McLoughlin, Aboriginals at the north end of Vancouver Island were able to provide coal to the steamship *Beaver* as early as 1836 when John Dunn and Duncan Finlayson visited Beaver Cove during the inaugural tour of the ship. John Dunn wrote: "The natives were anxious that we should employ them to work the coal; to this we consented, and agreed to give them a certain sum for every large box. The natives being so numerous, and labour so cheap, for us to attempt to work the coal would have been madness." Fort Rupert continued to supply furs and shingles for the HBC until its buildings were sold in 1883 to HBC factor Robert Hunt, who operated a store there. Fort Rupert was mostly destroyed by fire in 1889.

This photo of the Fort McLeod Trading Post was taken by Bruce Lamb about thirty years after it was closed. The log building, known as the WM Trading Post, can be viewed as the final vestige of the Hudson's Bay Company's extensive fur trading network that operated in British Columbia for almost a century-and-a-half. Managed by Justin McIntyre, this post included scales for purchasing placer gold. It derived its name from the nearby WM Ranch on the Fraser River end of the portage from Summit Lake.

HBC Fort Langley, 1858, by James Madison Alden, of the U.S. Boundary Commission

DEPOTS OF COMPRESSED POWER

"These little picketed enclosures appearing at intervals of two or three hundred miles, like secluded foxholes in boundless prairies—what are they?

"To the unenlightened vision of the thoughtless red man they are magazines of celestial comforts, arms which give the possessor superhuman power in war and in the chase; containing implements of iron and steel whose cunning causes even nature to blush; woven wool which wards off cold, disease and death; glittering trinkets whose wealth raises wrinkled imbecility above the attractions of youth and talents; and above all, tobacco and that blessed drink of heaven which, indeed, can minister to a mind deceased, which places the body for a time beyond the reach of pain.

"To their builders, and to the white race everywhere, these solitary and contracted pens have a far different signification. They are depots of compressed power, dominating the land and all that is therein; they are germs of the highest human type; which shall shortly spring up and overspread the wilderness, causing it to wither beneath its fatal shade."

—HUBERT HOWE BANCROFT, *HISTORY OF BRITISH COLUMBIA*, 1887

233

BIBLIOGRAPHY

Abbott, G.H. *Coquille Vocabulary, Manuscript No. 125.* Washington, D.C.: National Anthropological Archives, Smithsonian Institution, 1858.

Adam, Graeme Mercer. *The Canadian North West, Its History and Its Troubles from the Early Days of the Fur-Trade to the Era of the Railway and the Settler, with Incidents of Travel in the Region and the Narrative of Three Insurrections.* Toronto: Rose Publishing Company; Whitby, J.W. Robertson & Bros., 1885.

Adams, John. *Old Square-Toes and His Lady: The Life of James and Amelia Douglas.* Victoria: Horsdal & Schubart, 2001.

Akrigg, G.P.V. & Helen B. Akrigg. *British Columbia Chronicle, 1778–1846: Adventures by Sea and Land.* Vancouver: Discovery Press, 1975.

Alcorn, Rowena L. & Gordon Dee Alcorn. *Paul Kane: Frontier Artist and Indian Painter.* Wenatchee: Daily World Press, 1971.

Allen, Opal Sweazea. *Narcissa Whitman: An Historical Biography.* Portland, Oregon: Binfords & Mort, 1959.

Ashby, Daryl. *John Muir: West Coast Pioneer.* Vancouver: Ronsdale, 2005.

Ballantyne, R.M. *The Pioneers: A Tale of the Western Wilderness Illustrative of the Adventures and Discoveries of Sir Alexander Mackenzie.* London: James Nisbet, 1883.

Bancroft, Hubert Howe, Amos Bowman Nemos & Alfred Bates. *The History of the Pacific States, Vol. XXVII British Columbia 1792–1887.* The History Company, 1887.

Barker, Burt Brown, ed. *Letters of John McLoughlin, Written at Fort Vancouver 1829–1832.* Portland: Oregon Historical Society, Binfords and Mort, 1948.

Barker, Burt Brown. *The McLoughlin Empire and Its Rulers: Doctor John McLoughlin, Doctor David McLoughlin, Marie Louise (Sister St. Henry); an Account of Their Personal Lives, and of Their Parents, Relatives and Children; in Canada's Quebec Province, in Paris, France, and in the West of the Hudson's Bay Company.* Northwest Historical Series 5. Glendale, California: Arthur H. Clark, 1959.

Barratt, Glynn. *Russia in Pacific Waters, 1715–1825: A Survey of the Origins of Russia's Naval Presence in the North and South Pacific.* Vancouver: UBC Press, 1981.

———. *Russian Shadows on the British Pacific Northwest Coast of North America, 1810–1890: A Study of Rejection of Defence Responsibilities.* Vancouver: UBC Press, 1983.

Beattie, Judith Hudson & Helen M. Buss, eds. *Undelivered Letters to Hudson's Bay Company Men on the Northwest Coast of America, 1830–57.* Vancouver: UBC Press, 2003.

Belcher, Edward. *Narrative of a Voyage Round the World, Performed in Her Majesty's Ship Sulphur, During the Years 1836–1842, Including Details of the Naval Operations in China, from Dec. 1840 to Nov. 1841.* London: Henry Colburn, 1843.

———. *H.M.S. Sulphur on the Northwest and California Coasts, 1837 and 1839: The Accounts of Captain Edward Belcher and Midshipman Francis Guillemard Simpkinson.* Ed. Richard A. Pierce & John H. Winslow. San Francisco: Book Club of California, 1969. Simpkinson's manuscript journal is in the University Library of Cambridge University.

Belcher, Edward & Richard Brinsley Hinds (uncredited). *The Botany... [and] The Zoology of the Voyage of H.M.S. Sulphur.* 2 vols. London: Smith, Elder, 1843.

Belyk, Robert. *John Tod: Rebel in the Ranks.* Victoria: Horsdal & Schubart, 1995.

Bigsby, John Jeremiah. *The Shoe and Canoe; or Pictures of Travel in the Canadas. Illustrative of Their Scenery and of Colonial Life; with Facts and Opinions of Emigration, State Policy, and Other Points of Public Interest.* 2 Vols. London: Chapman and Hall, 1850.

Binns, Archie. *Peter Skene Ogden: Fur Trader.* Portland: Binfords and Mort, 1967.

Bischoff, William Norbert. *The Jesuits in Old Oregon, 1840–1940.* Caldwell, Idaho: Caxton Printers, 1945.

Bishop, R.P. *Mackenzie's Rock: With a Map Showing the Course Followed by the Explorer From Bella Coola, B.C., to the Rock, and Illustrated with Views Along the Route.* Ottawa: National Parks Historic Site Series, 1925.

Black, Samuel. *Black's Rocky Mountain Journal, 1824.* Ed. E.E. Rich. London: Hudson's Bay Records Society, 1955.

Black, Samuel, E. E. Rich & A. M. Johnson. *A Journal of a Voyage from Rocky Mountain Portage in Peace River to the Sources of Finlays Branch and North West Ward in Summer 1824.* Ed. E.E. Rich. London: Hudson's Bay Record Society, 1955.

Blanchet, Francis Norbert. *A Comprehensive, Explanatory, Correct Pronouncing Dictionary, and Jargon Vocabulary, to which is Added Numerous Conversations Enabling any Person to Speak Chinook Jargon.* Portland: S.J. M'Cormick, 1852. At least seven editions were released with various titles up to 1879. A copy of the fifth edition in the British Columbia Archives is entitled *Dictionary of the Chinook Jargon: to which is added numerous conversations, thereby enabling any person to speak Chinook correctly.* Portland: S. J. McCormick, 1879. Later editions were compiled by John Kaye Gill (1851–1929). An 18th edition was published in 1960.

———. *Historical Sketches of the Catholic Church in Oregon During the Past 40 years; 1838–1878.* Portland: Catholic Sentinel Society, 1878.

Blanchet, Francis Norbert & Modeste Demers. *Notices & Voyages of the Famed Quebec Mission to the Pacific Northwest. Being the Correspondence, Notices, etc. of Fathers Blanchet and Demers, Together with Those of Fathers Bolduc and Langlois. Containing Much Remarkable Information on the Areas and Inhabitants of the Columbia, Walamette, Cowlitz and Fraser Rivers, Nesqually Bay, Puget Sound, Whidby and Vancouver Islands while on Their Arduous Mission to the Engages of the Hudson Bay Company and the Pagan Natives 1838 to 1847. With Accounts of Several Voyages around Cape Horn to Valparaiso and to the Sandwich Islands, etc. Englished out of the French by Carl Landerholm.* Portland: Oregon Historical Society, 1955.

Blanchet, Francis Xavier. *Dix Ans Sur La Côte Du Pacifique.* Quebec: Imprimerie de Leger Brousseau, 1873.

Bowsfield, Hartwell, ed. *Fort Victoria Letters 1843–1851.* Winnipeg: Hudson's Bay Record Society, 1979.

Brackenridge, H.M. *Journal of a Voyage up the River Missouri.* Baltimore: Coale and Maxwell, 1815.

Brine, Ralph Hunter. *Canada's Forgotten Highway: A Wilderness Canoe Route from Sea to Sea.* Galiano Island: Whaler Bay Press, 1995.

Brown, Jennifer S.H. *Strangers in Blood: Fur Trade Company Families in Indian Country.* Vancouver: UBC Press, 1980.

Bryce, George. *Mackenzie, Selkirk, Simpson.* Toronto: Morang, 1905.

———. *The Remarkable History of the Hudson's Bay Company Including That of the French Traders of North-Western Canada and of the North-West, XY, and Astor Fur*

Helen and Philip Akrigg

Companies. Toronto: William Briggs, 1900.

Bond, Rowland. *The Original Northwester: David Thompson and the Native Tribes of North America*. Nine Mile Falls, Washington: Spokane House Enterprises, 1973.

Burpee, Lawrence Johnstone. *On the Old Athabaska Trail*. Toronto: Ryerson Press, 1926.

———. *The Search for a Western Sea: The Story of the Exploration of North-Western America*. Toronto: Musson Book Company, 1908; Toronto, New York, London: Macmillan, 1935.

Campbell, Marjorie Wilkins. *McGillivray: Lord of the Northwest*. Toronto: Clark, Irwin, 1962.

———. *The North West Company*. Toronto: Macmillan, 1957, 1973; Vancouver: Douglas & McIntyre, 1983.

———. *The Nor'westers: The Fight for the Fur Trade*. Toronto: Macmillan, 1954, 1958, 1974.

———. *The Savage River: Seventy-One Days with Simon Fraser*. Toronto: Macmillan, 1968; Calgary: Fifth House, 2003.

Campbell, Robert. *Two Journals of Robert Campbell (Chief Factor Hudson's Bay Company), 1808–1853: Early Journal, 1808 to 1851, Later Journal, Sept. 1850 to Feb. 1853*. Ed. John W. Todd. Seattle: Shorey Books, 1958.

Carpenter, Cecelia Svinth. *Fort Nisqually: A Documented History of Indian and British Interaction*. Tacoma: Tacoma Research Service, 1986.

Chance, David H. *Influences of the Hudson's Bay Company on the Native Cultures of the Colvile District*. Moscow, Idaho: University of Idaho, 1973.

———. *Sentinel of Silence a Brief History of Fort Spokane*. Seattle: Pacific Northwest National Parks Association, 1981.

Cherrington, John. *The Fraser Valley: A History*. Madeira Park: Harbour Publishing, 1992.

———. *Mission on the Fraser*. Vancouver: Mitchell Press, 1974.

Clarke, Adele. *Old Montreal: John Clarke, His Adventures, Friends and Family*. Montreal: Herald Publishing, 1906.

Clayton, Daniel W. *Islands of Truth: The Imperial Fashioning of Vancouver Island*. Vancouver: UBC Press, 2000.

Cline, Gloria Griffen. *Peter Skene Ogden and the Hudson's Bay Company*. Norman: University of Oklahoma Press, 1974.

Coates, Kenneth & John Findlay, eds. *Parallel Destinies: Canadian-American Relations West of the Rockies*. Seattle: University of Washington Press, 2002.

Coats, R.H. & R.E. Gosnell. *Sir James Douglas*. Toronto: Morang, 1908, 1910, 1912; London: Oxford University Press, 1926.

Cole, Jean Murray. *Exile in the Wilderness: The Biography of Chief Factor Archibald McDonald, 1790–1853*. Don Mills: Burns & MacEachern, 1979.

Corney, Peter. *Voyages in the Northern Pacific: Narrative of Several Trading Voyages from 1813 to 1818, between the Northwest Coast of America, the Hawaiian Islands and China, with a Description of the Russian Establishments on the Northwest Coast: Interesting Early Account of Kamehameha's Realm, Manners and Customs of the People, etc, and Sketch of a Cruise in the Service of the Independents of South America in 1819, with a Preface and Appendix of Valuable Confirmatory Letters Prepared by Prof. W. D. Alexander*. Honolulu: Thos. G. Thrum, 1896. Reprinted as *Early Voyages in the North Pacific* by Ye Galleon Press in 1965.

Coues, Elliott, ed. *New Light on the Early History of the Greater Northwest: The Manuscript Journals of Alexander Henry, Fur Trader of the Northwest Company, and of David Thompson, Official Geographer and Explorer of the Same Company, 1799–1814: Exploration and Adventure Among the Indians on the Red, Saskatchewan, Missouri, and Columbia Rivers. 3 vols*. New York: Francis P. Harper, 1897.

Cox, Ross. *Adventures on the Columbia River, Including the Narrative of a Residence of Six Years on the Western Side of the Rocky Mountains, Among Various Tribes of Indians Hitherto Unknown: Together with a Journey Across the American Continent*. London: Henry Colburn and Richard Bentley, 1831, 1832, 1832; New York: J&J Harper, 1832; San Francisco: California State Library, 1942; Portland: Binfords & Mort, 1957.

D'Wolf, John. *A Voyage to the North Pacific and a Journey Through Siberia.* Cambridge, Massachusetts: Welch, Bigelow, and Co., 1861; Fairfield, Washington: Ye Galleon Press, 1968.

Daniells, Roy. *Alexander Mackenzie and the North West.* London: Faber and Faber, 1969.

Daunton, Martin J. & Rick Halpern. *Empire and Others: British Encounters with Indigenous Peoples, 1600–1850.* Philadelphia: University of Pennsylvania Press, 1999.

Davidson, George Charles. *The North West Company.* Berkeley: University of California Press, 1918.

Davies, John. *Douglas of the Forests: The North American Journals of David Douglas.* Edinburgh: Paul Harris Publishing, 1979.

Davies, Raymond Arthur. *The Great Mackenzie in Word and Photograph.* Toronto: Ryerson Press, 1947.

De Volpi, Charles P., ed. *British Columbia, a Pictorial Record: Historical Prints and Illustrations of the Province of British Columbia, Canada, 1778–1891.* Don Mills: Longman, 1973.

Demers, Modeste & F.N. Blanchet. *Chinook Dictionary, Catechism, Prayers and Hymns. Composed in 1839 & 1839 by Rt. Rev. Modeste Demers. Revised, Corrected and Completed in 1867 by F.N. Blanchet, with Modifications and Additions by Rev. L.N. St. Onge.* Montreal, 1871.

Douglas, David. *Journal Kept by David Douglas During his Travels in North America, 1823–1827. Together with a Particular Description of Thirty-three Species of American Oaks and Eighteen Species of Pinus. With Appendices Containing a List of the Plants Introduced by Douglas and an Account of his Death in 1834.* London: W. Wesley, 1914.

———. *The Oregon Journals of David Douglas, of his Travels and Adventures Among the Traders and Indians in the Columbia, Willamette and Snake River Regions During the Years 1825, 1826 and 1827.* Ed. David Sievert Lavender. 2 vols. Ashland: Oregon Book Society, 1972.

Douglas, James. *James Douglas in California, 1841; Being the Journal of a Voyage from the Columbia to California.* Ed. Dorothy Blakey Smith. Vancouver: The Library's Press, 1965.

Drummond, Thomas. *Musci Americani; or, Specimens of Mosses Collected in British North America, and Chiefly among the Rocky Mountains, During the Second Land Arctic Expedition Under the Command of Captain Franklin, R.N.* Glasgow, 1928.

Drury, Clifford M. *More About the Whitmans: Four Hitherto Unpublished Letters of Marcus and Narcissa Whitman.* Tacoma: Washington State Historical Society, 1979.

Dryden, Cecil Pearl. *Up the Columbia for Furs.* Illus. E. Joseph Dreany. Caldwell, Idaho: Caxton Printers, 1949.

Dunn, John. *History of the Oregon Territory and British North American Fur Trade: With an Account of the Habits and Customs of the Principal Native Tribes on the Northern Continent.* London: Edwards and Hughes, 1844.

Dye, Eva Emery. *McDonald of Oregon: A Tale of Two Shores.* Chicago: A.C. McClurg & Co., 1906.

———. *McLoughlin and Old Oregon: A Chronicle.* Chicago: A.C. McClurg & Co., 1900; , 1901, 1902, 1910, 1913; Doubleday, 1926; Portland: Binfords & Mort, 1936; New York: Wilson-Erickson, 1936.

Eaton, Diane & Sheila Urbanek. *Paul Kane's Great Nor-West.* Vancouver: UBC Press, 1995.

Elliot, T.C., ed. "David Thompson and Beginning in Idaho." *Oregon Historical Quarterly* 21 (1920): 49–61.

———. *David Thompson's Journeys in the Pend Oreille Country.* Seattle: Washington University State Historical Society, 1932.

———. *David Thompson, Pathfinder, and the Columbia River.* Kettle Falls: Scimitar Press, 1911.

Fawcett, Brian. *The Secret Journal of Alexander Mackenzie.* Vancouver: Talonbooks, 1985.

———. *Virtual Clearcut: or, the Way Things Are in My Hometown.* Toronto: Thomas Allen Publishers, 2003.

Finlayson, Roderick. *Biography of Roderick Finlayson.* Victoria, 1891.

Fisher, Robin. *Contact and Conflict: Indian-European Relations in British Columbia, 1774–*

Robin Fisher

1890. Vancouver: UBC Press, 1977, 1992.

Fitzgerald, James Edward. *An Examination of the Charter and Proceedings of the Hudson's Bay Company, with Reference to the Grant of Vancouver's Island*. London: Trelawney Saunders, 1849. Reprinted from the Colonial Magazine, August, 1848.

————. *Vancouver's Island, the New Colony*. London: Simmonds, 1848.

————. *Vancouver's Island, the Hudson's Bay Company, and the Government*. London: Simmonds, 1848.

Flandrau, Grace. *Koo-koo-sint, the Star Man: A Chronicle of David Thompson*. St. Paul: Great Northern Railway, 1927.

Franchère, Gabriel. *A Voyage to the Northwest Coast of America*. Ed. Milo Milton Quaife. Chicago: Lakeside Press, 1954. Reprinted in New York by Citadel Press in 1968.

————. *Adventure at Astoria, 1810–1814*. Ed. and trans. Hoyt C. Franchère. American Exploration and Travel Series. Norman: University of Oklahoma Press, 1967.

————. *Journal of a Voyage on the North West Coast of North America During the Years 1811, 1812, 1813 and 1814*. Ed. W. Kaye Lamb. Toronto: Champlain Society, 1969.

————. *Journal of a Voyage up the River Missouri, performed in 1811, by H.M. Bràckenridge (&) Narrative of a Voyage to the Northwest Coast of America in the Years 1811, 1812, 1813, and 1814; or the First American Settlement on the Pacific*. Ed. Reuben Gold Thwaites. Cleveland: The Arthur H. Clark Company, 1904. A republication of Volume VI in the "Early Western Travels, 1748-1846" series.

————. *Narrative of a Voyage to the Northwest Coast of America in the Years 1811, 1812, 1813, and 1814; or, the First American Settlement on the Pacific*. Ed. Jedediah Vincent Huntington. New York: Redfield, 1854.

————. *Relation d'un Voyage à la Côte du Nord-Ouest de l'Amérique Septentrionale, dans les Années 1810, 11, 12, 13, et 14*. Ed. Michel Bibaud. Montreal: De L'Imprimerie de C.B. Pasteur, 1820.

Fraser, Simon. *The Letters and Journals of Simon Fraser, 1806–1808*. Ed.W. Kaye Lamb. Toronto: Macmillan, 1960.

Galbraith, J.S. *The Hudson's Bay Company as an Imperial Factor, 1821–1869*. Toronto: University of Toronto Press, 1957.

————. *The Little Emperor: Governor Simpson of the Hudson's Bay Company*. Toronto: Macmillan of Canada, 1976.

Gardner, Alison F. *James Douglas*. Don Mills: Fitzhenry & Whiteside, 1976.

Garst, Doris Shannon. *John Jewitt's Adventure*. Illus. Donald McKay. Boston: Houghton Mifflin, 1955.

Gates, Charles M., ed. *Five Fur Traders of the Northwest: Being the Narrative of Peter Pond and the Diaries of John Macdonell, Archibald N. McLeod, Hugh Faries, and Thomas Connor*. Saint Paul: Minnesota Historical Society, 1965.

Gibbon, John Murray. *The Romance of the Canadian Canoe*. Toronto: Ryerson Press, 1951.

Gibson, James R. *The Lifeline of the Oregon Country: The Fraser-Columbia Brigade System, 1811–47*. Vancouver: UBC Press, 1997.

————. *Otter Skins, Boston Ships, and China Goods: The Maritime Fur Trade of the Northwest Coast, 1785–1841*. Montreal: McGill-Queen's University Press, 1992.

Gilbert, E.W. *The Exploration of Western America 1800–1850; an Historical Geography*. Cambridge: Cambridge University Press, 1933; New York: Cooper Square Publishers, 1966.

Gough, Barry M. *Distant Dominion: Britain and the Northwest Coast of North America, 1579–1909*. Vancouver: UBC Press, 1980.

————. *First Across the Continent: Sir Alexander Mackenzie*. Toronto: McClelland & Stewart, 1997.

————. *The Northwest Coast: British Navigation, Trade and Discoveries to 1812*. Vancouver:

UBC Press, 1992.

————. *The Royal Navy and the Northwest Coast of North America, 1810–1914: A Study of British Maritime Ascendancy.* Vancouver: UBC Press, 1971.

————. *To the Pacific and Arctic with Beechey; the Journal of Lieutenant George Peard of H.M.S. Blossom, 1825–1828.* Cambridge: Cambridge University Press, 1973.

Gough, Barry M, ed. *The Hudson's Bay Company in British Columbia: Forts Langley, Kamloops, Victoria and Simpson.* Burnaby: History Dept., Simon Fraser University, 1983.

————, ed. *The Journal of Alexander Henry the Younger, 1799–1814.* Toronto: Champlain Society, 1988, 1992.

Grant, Walter C. *Descriptions of Vancouver Island by Its First Colonist.* London: Royal Geographical Society, 1857.

————. *Remarks on Vancouver Island, Principally Concerning Townsites and Native Population.* London: Royal Geographical Society, 1859.

Green, Lewis. *The Boundary Hunters: Surveying the 141ˢᵗ Meridian and the Alaska Panhandle.* Vancouver: UBC Press, 1982.

Greenbie, Sidney. *Frontiers and the Fur Trade.* New York: John Day Company, 1929.

Hafen, Le Roy R., ed. *The Mountain Men and the Fur Trade of the Far West: Biographical Sketches of the Participants by Scholars of the Subject and with Introductions by the Editor.* 10 vols. Glendale, California: Arthur H. Clark Co., 1965–1972. Includes material on John Work and Peter Skene Ogden.

Hafen, LeRoy R. & Ann W. Hafen, eds. *The Far West and Rockies Historical Series, 1820–1875.* 15 vols. Glendale, California: Arthur H. Clark Co., 1954–1961.

Haig-Brown, Roderick Langmere. *Fur and Gold.* Toronto: Longmans, 1962.

Hardwick, Francis C., ed. *The Helping Hand: How Indian Canadians Helped Alexander Mackenzie Reach the Pacific Ocean.* Center for Continuing Education: Indian Education Resources Center, University of British Columbia, 1972.

Hardwick, Francis Chester, Phillip Moir & Sister Mary Paul. *The Helping Hand: The Debt of Alexander Mackenzie and Simon Fraser to Indian Canadians.* Vancouver: Tantalus Research, 1973.

Hargrave, James. *The Hargrave Correspondence.* Ed. G.P. Glazebrook. Toronto: Champlain Society, 1938.

Harmon, Daniel Williams. *A Journal of Voyages and Travels in the Interior of North America.* New York: Barnes, 1903; New York: Allerton Book Company, 1922. Edited by Daniel Haskel in 1820.

————. *Sixteen Years in the Indian Country. The Journal of Daniel Williams Harmon 1800–1816.* Ed. W. Kaye Lamb. Toronto: Macmillan, 1957.

Harris, R.C. *Old Pack Trails in the Proposed Cascade Wilderness.* Summerland: Okanagan Similkameen Parks Society, 1978.

Harris, R.C., Harley Hatfield & Peter Tassie. *The Okanagan Brigade Trail in the South Okanagan, 1811 to 1849: Oroville, Washington, to Westside, British Columbia.* Vernon: Wayside Press, 1989.

Harvey, Athelstan George. *Douglas of the Fir: A Biography of David Douglas, Botanist.* Cambridge: Harvard University Press, 1947.

Hayes, Derek. *First Crossing: Alexander Mackenzie, His Expedition Across North American, and the Opening of the Continent.* Vancouver: Douglas & McIntyre, 2001.

Henry, Alexander (the Younger). *New Light on the Early History of the Greater Northwest: The Manuscript Journals of Alexander Henry and of David Thompson, 1799–1814.* Ed. Elliot Coues. 3 vols. New York: Francis P. Harper, 1897; Minneapolis: Ross & Haines, 1965.

Hing, Robert J. *Tracking Mackenzie to the Sea: Coast to Coast in Eighteen Splashdowns.* Manassas, Virginia: Anchor Watch Press, 1992.

Holman, Frederick V. *Dr. John McLoughlin: The Father of Oregon.* Cleveland: Arthur H. Clarke Co., 1907.

Howard, Helen Addison. *Northwest Trail Blazers.* Caldwell, Idaho: Caxton Printers, 1963.

Howay, F.W. *A List of Trading Vessels in the Maritime Fur Trade, 1820–1825.* 5 vols. Ottawa:

239

Royal Society of Canada, 1930–34. Transactions of the Royal Society of Canada, Third Series, Section II. Vol. XXVIII.

————. *British Columbia: The Making of a Province.* Toronto: Ryerson Press, 1928.

————. *Builders of the West: A Book of Heroes.* Toronto: Ryerson Press, 1929.

Howay, F.W. & E.O.S. Scholefield. *British Columbia from the Earliest Times to the Present.* Vancouver: S.J. Clarke Publishing, 1914.

Howay, F.W., W.N. Sage & H.F. Angus. *British Columbia and the United States: The North Pacific Slope from Fur Trade to Aviation.* Toronto: Ryerson Press, 1942.

Hussey, John A. *Champoeg: Place of Transition: A Disputed History.* Portland: Oregon Historical Society, 1967.

————. *The History of Fort Vancouver and Its Physical Structure.* Portland: Washington State Historical Society, 1957.

F. W. Howay

————. *Preliminary Survey of the History and Physical Structure of Fort Vancouver.* Washington: Dept. of the Interior, National Park Service, 1949.

Irving, Washington. *The Adventures of Captain Bonneville, U.S.A., in the Rocky Mountains and the Far West.* London: R. Bentley, 1837; London: George Routledge & Sons, 1850; New York: G.P. Putnam, 1851; Norman, Oklahoma: University of Oklahoma Press, 1961.

————. *Astoria, or, Anecdotes of an Enterprise Beyond the Rocky Mountains.* Ed. Richard Dilworth Rust. 2 vols. Philadelphia: Carey, Lea & Blanchard, 1936; Lincoln, Nebraska: Bison Books, University of Nebraska Press, 1982.

————. *Rocky Mountains, or, Scenes, Incidents, and Adventures in the West; Digested from the Journal of Captain B. L. E. Bonneville of the Army of the United States, and Illustrated from Various Other Sources.* Philadelphia: Carey, Lea, & Blanchard, 1837; Paris: Baudry's European Library, 1837.

Jewitt, John. *A Journal, Kept at Nootka Sound by John Rodgers Jewitt, One of the Surviving Crew of the Ship Boston, of Boston, John Salter, Commander, Who Was Massacred on the 22d of March, 1803; Interspersed with Some Account of the Natives, Their Manner and Customs.* Boston: Printed for the author, 1807.

————. *A Narrative of the Adventures and Sufferings of John R. Jewitt, Only Survivor of the Ship Boston, During a Captivity of Nearly Three Years Among the Savages of Nootka Sound, with an Account of The Manners, Mode of Living, and Religious Opinions Of The Natives; Embellished with a Plate Representing the Ship in Possession of the Savages.* Ed. Richard Alsop. London: Longman, Hurst, Rees, Orme & Brown, 1816.

————. *A Journal Kept at Nootka Sound.* Boston: Goodspeed Press, 1931. A reprint of Jewitt's original 1807 version.

————. *The Adventures and Sufferings of John R. Jewitt, Captive of Maquinna.* Illus. Hilary Stewart. Vancouver: Douglas & McIntyre, 1987, 1995. Notes by Robert Brown.

————. *The Adventures and Sufferings of John R. Jewitt, Captive among the Nootka, 1803–05.* Ed. Derek G. Smith & Richard Alsop. Toronto: McClelland & Stewart, 1974.

————. *The Captive of Nootka, or, the Adventures of John R. Jewett.* New York: J.P. Peaslee, 1835.

Johnson, Enid. *Great White Eagle, the Story of Dr. John McLoughlin.* New York: Julian Messner, 1954.

Johnson, Robert Cummings. *John McLoughlin: Patriarch of the Northwest.* Portland: Metropolitan Press, 1935. Reprinted as *John McLoughlin, Father of Oregon* by Binfords & Mort in 1958.

Johnson, Wellwood Robert. *Legend of Langley: An Account of the Early History of Fort Langley and an Intimate Story of the Lives of Some, but Not All, of the Early Pioneers of the District of Langley.* Langley: Langley Centennial Committee, 1958.

Johnston, Sir Harry Hamilton. *Pioneers in Canada.* London: Blackie & Son, 1911.

Josephy, Alvin M. *David Thompson, Mountain Men and the Fur Trade of the Far West.* Ed. Le Roy Reuben Hafen. Vol. 3. Glendale, California: Arthur H. Clark Company, 1966.

Jujut, Abbe. *Mission of Oregon: An Account of the Apostolical Labours of MGR. Demers, Bishop of Vancouver.* Paris: Imprimerie de Vrayet de Surcy, 1851.

Kane, Paul. *Paul Kane's Frontier, Including Wanderings of an Artist Among the Indians of North America.* Ed. J. Russell Harper. Toronto: University of Toronto Press, 1971.

———. *Paul Kane, the Columbia Wanderer, 1846–7: Sketches and Paintings of the Indians and his lecture, "The Chinooks."* Ed. Thomas Vaughan. Portland: Oregon Historical Society, 1971.

———. *Wanderings of an Artist Among the Indians of North America: From Canada to Vancouver's Island and Oregon through the Hudson's Bay Company's Territory and Back Again.* London: Longman, Brown, Green, Longmans & Roberts, 1859; Toronto: Radisson Society of Toronto, 1925; Edmonton: Hurtig, 1968, 1974; Texas: University of Texas Press, 1971.

Karamanski, Theodore J. *Fur Trade and Exploration: Opening the Far Northwest, 1821–1852.* Norman: University of Oklahoma Press, 1983.

Kruzenshtern, Ivan Fedorovich. *Atlas of the Voyage Round the World.* Amsterdam; N. Israel; New York: Da Capo Press, 1813.

———. *Voyage Round the World in the Years 1803, 1804, 1805 & 1806: By order of His Imperial Majesty Alexander the First, on Board the Ships Nadeshda and Neva, under the Command of Captain A.J. von Krusenstern of the Imperial Navy.* Ed. Richard Belgrave Hoppner. 2 vols. London: J. Murray, 1813.

Lambert, Richard S. *Trailmaker: The Story of Alexander Mackenzie.* Toronto: McClelland & Stewart, 1957.

Lamirande, Emilien. *L'Implantation de l'Église Catholique en Colombie-Britannique, 1838–1848.* Ottawa: Extrait de la Revue de l'Université d'Ottawa, 1958.

Langsdorff, George H. von. *Bemerkungen auf einer Reise um die Welt in den Jahren 1803 bis 1807.* Frankfurt: Friedrich Wilmans, 1812.

———. *Voyages and Travels in Various Parts of the World During the Years 1893–7.* 2 vols. London: H. Colburn, 1813–14. Amsterdam: N. Israel, 1968.

Librarian W. Kaye Lamb edited journals and letters by Alexander Mackenzie, Simon Fraser, Gabriel Franchère and Daniel Williams Harmon. Painting by Brenda Guiled.

Laut, Agnes C. *The Conquest of the Great Northwest. Being the Story of the Adventurers of England Known as the Hudson's Bay Company.* 2 vols. Toronto: Musson, 1908; New York: George H. Doran, 1918.

Laveille, E. *The Life of Father De Smet, S.J.: Apostle of the Rocky Mountains.* Trans. Marian Lindsay, translator.New York: P.J. Kenedy & Sons, 1915; Chicago, Illinois: Loyola University Press, 1981.

———. *Le P. de Smet, apôtre des peaux-rouges, 1801-1873.* Liége: Dessain, 1913.

Lent, D. Geneva. *West of the Mountains: James Sinclair and the Hudson's Bay Company.* Seattle: University of Washington Press, 1963.

Lisiansky, Urey. *A Voyage Round the World, in the Years 1803, 4, 5, & 6: Performed, by Order of His Imperial Majesty Alexander the First, Emperor of Russia, in the Ship Neva.* London: John Booth, 1814

Loring, Charles Greely. *Memoir of the Hon. William Sturgis.* Boston: John Wilson & Sons, 1864.

MacDonald, Ranald. *The Narrative of His Life, 1824–1894.* Ed. William S. Lewis & Naojiro Murakami. North Pacific Studies Series 16. Portland: Oregon Historical Society Press, 1990.

———. *Ranald MacDonald: The Narrative of His Early Life on the Columbia Under the Hudson's Bay Company's Regime; of His Experiences in the Pacific Whale Fishery; and of his Great Adventures to Japan; with a Sketch of his Later Life on the Western Frontier, 1824–1894.* Eds. W.S. Lewis and N. Murakami. Forward by Donald J. Sterling. Spokane: Eastern Washington State Historical Society, 1923. Includes a manuscript originally titled "Japan Story Of Adventure Of Ranald MacDonald, First Teacher Of English In Japan A. D. 1848-1849."

Mackenzie, Alexander. *Alexander Mackenzie's Voyage to the Pacific Ocean in 1793.* Chicago: The Lakeside Press, 1931.

———. *Exploring the Northwest Territory: Sir Alexander Mackenzie's Journal of a Voyage by Bark Canoe from Lake Athabasca to the Pacific Ocean in the Summer of 1789.* Ed. T. H. McDonald. Norman: University of Oklahoma Press, 1966.

———. *The Letters and Journals of Sir Alexander Mackenzie.* Ed. W. Kaye Lamb. Cambridge: Cambridge University Press, 1970.

———. *Voyages from Montreal, on the River St. Lawrence, through the Continent of North America, to the Frozen and Pacific Oceans, in the Years 1789 and 1793: With a Preliminary Account of the Rise, Progress and Present State of the Fur Trade of That Country.* London: R. Noble, 1801; Edmonton: M.G. Hurtig, 1971.

Mackie, Richard Somerset. *Trading Beyond the Mountains: The British Fur Trade on the Pacific, 1793–1843.* Vancouver: UBC Press, 1997.

MacLeòid, Fionnlagh. *Alasdair MacChoinnich ann an Canada* Steòrnabhagh: Acair, 1991.

Malloy, Mary. *"Boston Men" on the Northwest Coast: The American Fur Trade, 1788–1844.* Fairbanks: University of Alaska Press, 1998.

———. *Souvenirs of the Fur Trade: Northwest Coast Indian Art & Artifacts Collected by American Mariners, 1788–1844.* Fairbanks: University of Alaska Press, 1998; Cambridge: Peabody Museum Press, 2000.

Malloy, Mary, ed. *A Most Remarkable Enterprise: Maritime Commerce & Culture on the Northwest Coast.* By William Sturgis. Marstons Mills: Parnassus Imprints, 1997.

Manson, Ainslie. *A Dog Came, Too: A True Story.* Illus. Ann Blades. Toronto: Groundwood, 1993.

———. *Alexander Mackenzie.* Toronto: Grolier, 1988.

Margaret, Helene. *Father De Smet: Pioneer Priest of the Rockies.* New York: Farrar, 1940.

Masson, L.R. *Les Bourgeois de la Compagnie du Nord-Ouest: Récits de Voyages, Lettres et Rapports Inédits Relatifs Au Nord-Ouest Canadien. Publiés Avec Une Esquisse Historique et des Annotations.* 2 vols. Côté, Quebec: De L'Imprimerie Générale A. Côté et Cie., 1889–1890; New York: Antiquarian Press, 1960.

McDonald, Archibald. *Peace River: A Canoe Voyage from Hudson's Bay to the Pacific by the Late George Simpson in 1828; Journal of the Chief Factor, Archibald McDonald, Who Accompanied Him.* Ed. Malcolm McLeod. Ottawa: J. Durie, 1872; Toronto: Coles Canadian Collection,

1970; Edmonton: M.G. Hurtig, 1971.

———. *The Fort Langley Journals 1827–30*. Eds. Morag Maclachlan & Wayne P. Suttles. Vancouver: UBC Press, 1998.

———. *This Blessed Wilderness: Archibald McDonald's Letters from the Columbia, 1822–44*. Ed. Jean Murray Cole. Vancouver: UBC Press, 2001.

McDonald, Pat. *Where the River Brought Them: 200 Years at Rocky Mountain House and Area*. Rocky Mountain House: Town of Rocky Mountain House, Bicentennial History Book Committee, 2001.

McKelvie, B.C. *Fort Langley: Birthplace of British Columbia*. Victoria: Porcepic Books, 1991.

———. *Fort Langley: Outpost of Empire*. Vancouver: Vancouver Daily Province, 1947.

McKenzie, Cecil W. *Donald Mackenzie, "King of the Northwest": The Story of an International Hero of the Oregon Country and the Red River Settlement at Lower Fort Garry (Winnipeg)*. Los Angeles: Ivan Deach, Jr., 1937; Markham, Ontario: Stewart Publishing & Printing, 2001.

McLean, John. *Notes of a Twenty-Five Year's [sic] Service in the Hudson's Bay Territory*. Ed. W. Stewart Wallace. 2 vols. London: Richard Bentley, 1849; Toronto: Champlain Society, 1932.

McLeod, Malcolm. *Peace River: A Canoe Voyage from Hudson's Bay to Pacific, by the Late Sir George Simpson (Governor Hon. Hudson's Bay Company) in 1828: Journal of the Late Chief Factor, Archibald McDonald (Hon. Hudson's Bay Company), Who Accompanied Him*. Ottawa: J. Durie & Son, 1872.

McLoughlin, John. *The Financial Papers of Dr. John McLoughlin: Being the Record of His Estate and of His Proprietory Accounts with the North West Company (1811–1821) and the Hudson's Bay Company (1821–1868)*. Ed. Burt Brown Barker. Portland: Oregon Historical Society, 1949.

McLoughlin, John. *John McLoughlin's Business Correspondence, 1847–48*. Ed. William R. Sampson. Seattle: University of Washington Press, 1973.

———. *The Letters of John McLoughlin from Fort Vancouver to the Governor and Committee*. Ed. E.E. Rich. 3 vols. Toronto: The Champlain Society, 1941–1944.

———. *Letters of Dr. John McLoughlin Written at Fort Vancouver, 1829–1832*. Ed. Burt Brown Barker. Portland: Binfords and Mort, 1948.

Mead, Robert Douglas. *Ultimate North: Canoeing Mackenzie's Great River*. Garden City, New York: Doubleday, 1976.

Meilleur, Helen. *A Pour of Rain: Stories From a West Coast Fort*. Victoria: Sono Nis, 1980.

Mitchell, Anne Lindsay & Syd House. *David Douglas: Explorer and Botanist*. London: Aurum Press, 1999.

Montgomery, Richard G. *The White-Headed Eagle, John McLoughlin, Builder of an Empire*. New York: Macmillan, 1934.

Morton, Arthur Silver. *A History of the Canadian West to 1870–71; Being a history of Rupert's Land (the Hudson's Bay Company Territory) and of the North-West Territory (including the Pacific Slope)*. London: Thomas Nelson & Sons, 1939.

———. *David Thompson*. Toronto: Ryerson Press, 1930.

———. *The North West Company*. Toronto: Ryerson Press, 1930.

———. *Sir George Simpson, Overseas Governor of the Hudson's Bay Company: A Pen Picture of a Man of Action*. Toronto: J.M. Dent, 1944.

Morwood, William. *Traveler in a Vanished Landscape: The Life and Times of David Douglas*. New York: Clarkson N. Potter; London: Gentry Books, 1973.

Murray, Alexander Hunter. *Journal of the Yukon, 1847–48*. Ed. L.J. Burpee. Ottawa: Government Printing Bureau, 1910.

Nelson, Denys. *Fort Langley, 1827–1927: A Century of Settlement in the Valley of the Lower Fraser River*. Vancouver: Evans & Hastings, 1927.

Nisbet, Jack. *The Mapmaker's Eye: David Thompson on the Columbia Plateau*. Pullman: Washington State University Press, 2005.

———. *Sources of the River: Tracking David Thompson Across Western North America*. Seattle: Sasquatch Books, 1994.

————. *Visible Bones: Journeys Across Time in the Columbia River Country.* Seattle: Sasquatch Books, 2003.

O'Meara, Walter. *Daughters of the Country: The Women of the Fur Traders and Mountain Men.* New York: Harcourt, Brace and World, 1968.

Ogden, Peter Skene. *Fort Simpson Journal.* Vol. 1, 1834–1837. Winnipeg: Hudson's Bay Company Archives B: 20 L: A :3, Public Archives of Manitoba, N.D.

————. "Journal of Expedition to Utah, 1825." Ed. David E. Miller. *Utah Historical Quarterly* 20 (1952): 159–206.

————. "Peter Skene Ogden's Notes on Western Caledonia." Ed. W.N. Sage. *British Columbia Historical Quarterly* 1 (1937): 45–56.

————. *Peter Skene Ogden's Snake Country Journals, 1824–1825 and 1825–1826.* Ed. Edwin E. Rich. London: Hudson's Bay Record Society, 1950.

————. *Peter Skene Ogden's Snake Country Journals, 1827–1828 and 1828–1829.* Ed. Glyndwr Williams. London: Hudson's Bay Record Society,1971.

————. *Traits of American-Indian Life and Character by a Fur Trader.* London: Smith, Elder, 1853; San Francisco: The Grabhorn Press, 1933.

Patterson, Samuel. *Narrative of the Adventures and Sufferings of Samuel Patterson Who Made Three Voyages to the North West Coast of America, and Who Sailed to the Sandwich Islands, and to Many Other Parts of This World Before Being Shipwrecked on the Feegee Islands.* Palmer, Massachusetts: the press in Palmer, 1817; Providence, Rhode Island: 1825; Ye Galleon Press, 1967.

Pethick, Derek. *James Douglas: Servant of Two Empires.* Vancouver: Mitchell Press, 1969.

————. *S.S. Beaver: The Ship That Saved the West.* Vancouver: Mitchell Press, 1970.

————. *Victoria: The Fort.* Vancouver: Mitchell Press, 1968.

Rakestraw, Donald A. *For Honour or Destiny: The Anglo-American Crisis over the Oregon Territory.* New York: Peter Lang, 1995.

Ray, Arthur J. *Indians in the Fur Trade: Their Role as Trappers, Hunters, and Middlemen in the Lands Southwest of Hudson Bay, 1660–1870.* Buffalo: University of Toronto Press, 1974, 1998.

Reynolds, Stephen. *The Voyage of the New Hazard to the Northwest Coast, Hawaii and China, 1810–1813.* Ed. F.W. Howay. Salem: Peabody Museum, 1938; Fairfield, Washington: Ye Galleon Press, 1970.

Rezanov, Nikolai Petrovich. *Rezanov Reconnoiters California, 1806: A New Translation of Rezanov's Letter, Parts of Lieutenant Khvostov's Log of the Ship Juno, and Dr. Georg von Langsdorff Observations.* Ed. Richard A. Pierce. San Francisco: The Book Club of California, 1972.

————. *The Rezanov Voyage to Nueva California in 1806, the Report of Count Nikolai Petrovich Rezanov of His Voyage to That Provincia of Nueva España from New Archangel.* Trans. Thomas C. Russell. San Francisco: The Private Press of Thomas C. Russell, 1926; Fairfield, Washington: Ye Galleon Press, 1988.

————. *The Romance of Nikolai Rezanov and Concepción Argüello: A Literary Legend and Its Effect on California His-*

A fanciful depiction of forty-year-old Baron Nikolai Rezanov with fifteen-year-old Maria de la Concepción Argüeüllo, daughter of the Spanish commander of San Francisco, in 1806, by Victor Arnautoff, as displayed at the Post Interfaith Chapel in San Francisco. See p. 124.

tory. Alaska History 48. Ed. Richard A. Pierce. Kingston; Alaska: Limestone Press, 1998.

Rich, E.E. *The Fur Trade in the Northwest to 1857.* Canadian Centenary Series 11. Toronto: McClelland & Stewart, 1967.

Rocheleau, J.E. *The Hills and Scenery Were the Principal Object: The Search for a Trade House.* Thompson Falls: Clark's Fork Forge, 2001.

Roe, Jo Ann. *The Columbia River: A Historical Travel Guide.* Golden, Colorado: Fulcrum Publishing, 1992.

————. *Ranald Macdonald: Pacific Rim Adventurer.* Pullman: Washington State University Press, 1997.

Roquefeuil, Camille de. *Journal d'un Voyage Autour du Monde, Pendent Les Années 1816, 1817, Et 1819.* 2 vols. Paris: Ponthieu, et al, 1823.

————. *A Voyage Round the World, between the Years 1816–1819.* London: Sir Phillips & Co., 1823.

Ross, Alexander. *Adventures of the First Settlers on the Oregon or Columbia River; Being a Narrative of the Expedition Fitted Out by John Jacob Astor to Establish the "Pacific Fur Company"; with an Account of Some of the Indian Tribes on the Coast of the Pacific.* London: Smith, Elder & Co., 1849; Chicago: R.R. Donnelley, 1923; Lincoln, Nebraska: University of Nebraska Press, 1986; Oregon: Oregon State University Press, 2000.

————. *The Fur Hunters of the Far West: A Narrative of Adventures in the Oregon and Rocky Mountains.* London: Smith, Elder & Co., 1855; Chicago: R.R. Donnelly & Sons, 1924; Norman: University of Oklahoma Press, 1956.

————. *Letters of a Pioneer, Alexander Ross.* Ed. George Bryce. Winnipeg: Manitoba Free Press Print, 1903.

————. *Red River Settlement: Its Rise, Process and Present State. With Some Account of the Native Races and Its General History, to the Present Day.* London: Smith, Elder & Co., 1856.

Rudland, Lenore. *Fort Fraser: Where the Hell's That?* Sechelt: Eric & Lenore Rudland, 1988.

Russell, Carl P. *Guns on the Early Frontiers: A History of Firearms from Colonial Times through the Years of the Western Fur Trade.* Berkeley: University of California Press, 1957, 1962; Lincoln: University of Nebraska Press, 1980; New York: Barnes & Noble, 1996; New York: Dover Publications, 2005.

Sage, W.N. *Sir James Douglas.* Toronto: Ryerson Press, 1930.

Saum, Lewis O. *The Fur Trader and the Indian.* Seattle: University of Washington Press, 1965.

Shardlow, Tom. *David Thompson, a Trail by Stars.* Montreal: XYZ Publishing, 2006.

Shore, Maxine & M.M. Oblinger. *Knight of the Wilderness: The Story of Alexander Mackenzie.* New York: Dodd, Mead & Company; Toronto: McClelland & Stewart, 1943.

Simpson, George, Sir. «The Character Book of George Simpson, 1832.» *Hudson's Bay Miscellany, 1670–1870.* Ed. Glyndwr Williams.Winnipeg: Hudson's Bay Record Society, 1975.

————. *Fur Trade and Empire: George Simpson's Journal; Remarks Connected with the Fur Trade in the Course of a Voyage from York Factory to Fort George and Back to York Factory, 1824–25; Together with Accompanying Documents.* Ed. Frederick Merk. Cambridge: Harvard University Press 1931, 1968.

————. *Journal of Occurrences in the Athabasca Department, 1820 and 1821, and Report.* Ed. E.E. Rich. London: Champlain Society for Hudson's Bay Record Society, 1938.

————. *London Correspondence Inward from Sir George Simpson, 1841–42.* Ed. Glyndwr Williams. Introduction by John S. Galbraith. London: Hudson's Bay Record Society, 1973.

————. *Narrative of a Journey Round the World, During the Years 1841 and 1842.* London: Henry Colburn, 1847.

————. *Narrative of a Voyage to California Ports in 1841–42, Together with Voyages to Sitka, the Sandwich Islands & Okhotsk, to Which Are Added Sketches of Journeys Across America, Asia & Europe.* Fairfield: Ye Galleon Press, 1988.

————. *Part of Dispatch from George Simpson, Esqr., Governor of Rupert's Land, to the Governor and Committee of the Hudson's Bay Company, London, March 1, 1829; Continued and Com-*

pleted March 24, and June 5, 1829. Ed. E.E. Rich. London: Champlain Society for Hudson's Bay Record Society, 1947.

Skinner, Constance Lindsay. *Adventurers of Oregon: A Chronicle of the Fur Trade.* New Haven: Yale University Press; Toronto: Glasgow, Brook & Co., 1920.

Smet, Pierre-Jean de. *Letters and Sketches, with a Narrative of a Year's Residence Among the Indian Tribes of the Rocky Mountains.* Philadelphia: M. Fithian, 1843; United Kingdom: Kessinger Publishing, LLC, 2005.

———. *New Indian Sketches.* New York; Boston; Montreal: D. & J. Sadlier, 1863, 1865; New York: 1886; New York: P.J. Kenedy, Excelsior Catholic Publishing House, 1895; Seattle: Shorey Book Store, 1971; Fairfield, Washington: Ye Galleon Press, 1985, 1999.

———. *Origin, Progress and Prospects of the Catholic Mission to the Rocky Mountains.* Philadelphia: M. Fithian, 1843; Fairfield, Washington: Ye Galleon Press, 1967, 1972, 1986.

———. *Oregon Missions and Travels over the Rocky Mountains, in 1845–46.* New York: Edward Dunigan, 1847; Fairfield, Washington: Ye Galleon Press, 1978.

———. *Western Missions and Missionaries: A Series of Letters.* New York: P. J. Kenedy, 1859; 1881; New York: James B Kirker, Late Edward Dunigan and Brother, 1863; Shannon, Ireland: Irish University Press, 1972.

———. *Life, Letters and Travels of Father Pierre-Jean de Smet Among the North American Indians.* 4 vols. New York: Francis P. Harper, 1905.

Smith, Dorothy Blakey. *James Douglas: Father of British Columbia.* Toronto: Oxford University Press, 1971.

Smith, Helen Krebs. *Sitkum Siwash: An Historical Drama about Dr. John McLoughlin of the Hudson's Bay Company and His Family at Fort Vancouver, 1839–1851, with Historical Notes and Critical References.* Lake Oswego: Smith, Smith, and Smith Pub. Co. 1976.

Smith, James K. *Alexander Mackenzie, Explorer: The Hero Who Failed.* Toronto: McGraw-Hill Ryerson, 1973.

Smith, Robin Percival. *Captain McNeill and His Wife the Nishga Chief.* Surrey: Hancock House, 2001.

Spargo, John. *Two Bennington-Born Explorers and Makers of Modern Canada.* Bradford: Green Mountain Press, 1950.

Sperlin, O.B., ed. "The Indian of the Northwest as Revealed by the Earliest Journals." *Quarterly of the Oregon Historical Society* 17 (1916): 1–43.

Stanton, William. *The Great United States Exploring Expedition of 1838–1842.* Berkeley: University of California Press, 1975.

Strong, Thomas Nelson. *Cathlamet on the Columbia: Recollections of the Indian People and Short Stories of Early Pioneer Days in the Valley of the Lower Columbia River.* Portland: Binfords & Mort, 1906.

Stuart-Stubbs, Basil. *Maps Relating to Alexander Mackenzie: A Keepsake for the Bibliographical Society of Canada (Société bibliographique du Canada).* Vancouver: University of British Columbia Library, 1968.

Sturgis, William. *The Journal of William Sturgis.* Ed. S.W. Jackman. Victoria: Sono Nis, 1978.

Szasz, Ferenc Morton. *Scots in the North American West, 1790–1917.* Norman: University of Oklahoma Press, 2000.

Thom, Adam. *The Claims to the Oregon Territory Considered.* London: Smith, Elder and Co, 1844.

Thompson, David. *Columbia Journals.* Ed. Barbara Belyea. Montreal: McGill-Queen's University Press, 1994.

———. *David Thompson's Journals Relating to Montana and Adjacent Regions, 1808–1812.* Ed. M. Catherine White. Missoula: Montana State University Press, 1950. Transcribed from a photostatic copy of the original manuscripts and edited with an introduction by M. Catherine White.

———. *David Thompson's Narrative, 1784–1812.* Ed. Richard Glover and J.B. Tyrrell. Toronto: Champlain Society, 1962.

————. *David Thompson's Narrative of his Explorations in Western America, 1784–1812*. Ed. Joseph Burr Tyrrell. Toronto: Champlain Society, 1916.

————. *New Light on the Early History of the Greater Northwest: The Manuscript Journals of Alexander Henry, Fur Trader of the Northwest Company, and of David Thompson, Official Geographer and Explorer of the Same Company, 1799–1814: Explorations and Adventure Among the Indians on the Red, Saskatchewan, Missouri and Columbia Rivers*. Ed. Elliot Coues. 3 vols. New York: Francis P. Harper, 1897; Minneapolis: Ross & Haines, 1965.

————. *Travels in Western North America, 1784–1812*. Ed. Victor G. Hopwood. Toronto: Macmillan, 1971.

Tichenor, Harold. *The Blanket: An Illustrated History of the Hudson's Bay Point Blanket*. Toronto: Quantum, 2002.

————. *The Collector's Guide to Point Blankets of the Hudson's Bay Company and Other Companies Trading in North America*. Bowen Island: Cinetel Film Productions, 2002.

Tod, John. *History of New Caledonia and the Northwest Coast*. 1878. Original copy in Bancroft Library, Berkeley, California.

Tolmie, William Fraser & George M. Dawson. *Comparative Vocabularies of the Indian Tribes of British Columbia: With a Map Illustrating Distribution*. Montreal: Dawson Brothers, 1884.

Tolmie, William Fraser. *Physician and Fur Trader: The Journals of William Fraser Tolmie*. Vancouver: Mitchell Press, 1963.

Tyler, David B. *The Wilkes' Expedition: The First United States Exploring Expedition, 1838–1842*. Philadelphia: The American Philosophical Society, 1968.

Van Kirk, Sylvia. *Many Tender Ties: Women in Fur-Trade Society, 1670–1870*. Norman: University of Oklahoma Press, 1980.

Vandiveer, Clarence A. *The Fur-Trade and Early Western Exploration*. Cleveland: Arthur H. Clark, 1929.

Vincent, William David. *The Astorians*. Pullman: State College of Washington, 1928.

————. *The Hudson's Bay Company*. Pullman: State College of Washington, 1927.

————. *The Northwest Company*. Pullman: State College of Washington, 1927.

————. *Northwest History*. Pullman: State College of Washington, 1930.

Wade, Mark S. *Mackenzie of Canada: The Life and Adventures of Alexander Mackenzie, Discoverer*. Edinburgh: Blackwood, 1927.

Wallace, W. Stewart, ed. *Documents Relating to the Northwest Company*. Toronto: Champlain Society, 1934.

————. *The Pedlars from Quebec, and Other Papers on the Nor'Westers*. Toronto: Ryerson Press, 1954.

Warre, Henry James. *Overland to Oregon in 1845; Impressions of a Journey Across North America*. Ottawa: Public Archives of Canada, 1976.

————. *Sketches in North America and the Oregon Territory*. London: Dickinson, 1848; Barre, Massachusetts: Imprint Society, 1970.

Whitman, Narcissa. *A Journey Across the Plains in 1836*. Portland: Oregon Pioneer Association, 1891, 1893.

————. *My Journal, 1936*. Ed. Lawrence L. Dodd. Fairfield, Washington: Ye Galleon Press, 1982, 1984, 1994, 2000.

————. *The Letters of Narcissa Whitman, 1836–1847*. Fairfield, Washington: Ye Galleon Press, 1986, 1997.

Whitman, Narcissa, Eliza Spalding & Clifford Merrill Drury. *Where Wagons Could Go: Narcissa Whitman and Eliza Spalding*. Nebraska: University of Nebraska Press, 1997.

Wilkes, Charles. *Narrative of the United States Exploring Expedition: During the Years 1838, 1839, 1840, 1841, 1842*. Philadelphia: Lea and Blanchard, 1845. Abridged edition published in 1851 by G. Putnam in New York.

————. *Theory of the Winds*. New York: G.P. Putnam & Co., 1856.

————. *Western America, Including California and Oregon, With Maps of Those Regions, and of "the Sacramento Valley."* Philadelphia: Lea and Blanchard, 1849.

Wilson, Clifford. *Campbell of the Yukon*. Toronto: Macmillan, 1970.

Woodworth, John & Hälle Flygare. *In the Steps of Alexander Mackenzie: Trail Guide*. Kelowna: J. Woodworth, 1987.

Woollacott, Arthur P. *Mackenzie and His Voyages, By Canoe to the Arctic and the Pacific, 1789–1793*. London, Toronto: J.M. Dent & Sons, 1927.

Work, John. *Fur Brigade to the Bonaventura: John Work's California Expedition 1832–1833 for the Hudson's Bay Company*. Ed. Alice Bay Maloney. San Francisco: California Historical Society, 1945.

———. *The Journal of John Work, a Chief-Trader of the Hudson's Bay Company, During His Expedition from Vancouver to the Flatheads and Blackfeet of the Pacific Northwest*. Cleveland: The Arthur H. Clark Co., 1923.

———. *The Journal of John Work, January to October, 1835*. Introduction and notes by Henry Drummond Dee. Victoria: C.F. Banfield, 1945.

———. *The Snake Country Expedition of 1830–1831: John Work's Field Journal*. American Exploration and Travel Series 59. Norman: University of Oklahoma Press, 1971.

Wright, Allen A. *Prelude to Bonanza: The Discovery and Exploration of the Yukon*. Sidney: Gray's Publishing, 1976.

Wrong, Hume. *Sir Alexander Mackenzie, Explorer and Fur-Trader*. Toronto: Macmillan, 1927.

Xydes, Georgia. *Alexander Mackenzie and the Explorers of Canada*. New York: Chelsea House, 1992.

THE PARTING OF THE BRIGADES, 1826

This painting by Walter J. Phillips depicts events described in the journal of a member of an overland brigade bound for Fort Vancouver as it parted company with a smaller expedition that was bound for New Caledonia in October of 1826. The diarist Aemilius Simpson, a neophyte on the Western Slope, proceeded down the Columbia River with James MacMillan, James Birnie, George Barnston, Thomas Drummond, Thomas Sinclair and 25 others. The westbound brigade, led by Joseph MacGillivray and James MacDougall, incorporated knowledge gleaned from James MacMillan's explorations with his guide Tête Jaune in 1825. They reached Fort St. James on November 3, 1826, validating a new route into New Caledonia (central British Columbia). HBC Governor George Simpson was soon able to implement a new "brigade system" for transport, amalgamating the Columbia (Oregon) Territory with New Caledonia—and making the fur trade west of the Rockies into a profitable enterprise. By 1828, New Caledonians were sending their spring shipments to Fort Okanagan, to be carried eastward by the Columbia Brigade via the Athabasca Pass. This image of the "parting of the brigades" at the Miette River was featured on the Hudson's Bay Company calendar of 1938.

David Thompson's overland route to the Pacific Ocean via the Columbia River was indisputably regarded as the primary artery for development after Archibald McDonald risked his life shooting Fraser River rapids near Yale in October of 1828. This incident was immortalized by the above painting by A. Sherriff Scott for the 1944 Hudson's Bay Company calendar. "I should consider the passage down to be certain Death, in nine attempts out of ten," wrote McDonald's employer George Simpson [depicted above, clutching his top hat]. "I shall therefore no longer talk of it as a navigable stream."

ABOUT THE AUTHOR

Alan Twigg has written and published *BC BookWorld*, a cultural newspaper, since 1987. In addition to his 13 books, he has produced six films about authors and a music CD with David Lester for poet Bud Osborn. He has conceived and coordinated numerous literary prizes, and created and compiled a public service reference site, hosted by Simon Fraser University, to offer free information on more than 8,000 British Columbia authors. In 2000, he received the first annual Gray Campbell Award for outstanding contributions to the writing and publishing community of British Columbia. Visit www.alantwigg.com

ALSO AVAILABLE

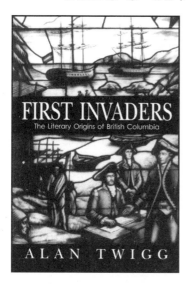

First Invaders recalls the drama and confusion arising from initial contacts, between 1774 and 1800, among Europeans, Americans and the First Nations on Canada's West Coast. It is the first volume in a series about the written history of British Columbia. *"I got lost and found in it," says author Edith Iglauer.*

Aboriginality is the first overview of all literary works pertaining to 170 Aboriginal authors and illustrators of British Columbia, including references to 300 titles and many original photos. *"Twigg's new book alters the face of Canadian literature," says historian Wendy Wickwire. "It is a must-read."*

$21.95 CDN; $18.95 USA;
ISBN: 1-55380-018-4

$24.95 CDN; $21.95 USA;
ISBN: 1-55380-030-3

RONSDALE

Published by Ronsdale • www.ronsdalepress.com